THE LURE OF THE MILLENNIUM

Detail from *The Vision of Saint John,* by El Greco (1541–1614)

THE LURE OF THE MILLENNIUM

The Year 2000 and Beyond

Raymond F. Bulman

ORBIS BOOKS
Maryknoll, New York 10545

The Catholic Foreign Mission Society of America (Maryknoll) recruits and trains people for overseas missionary service. Through Orbis Books, Maryknoll aims to foster the international dialogue that is essential to mission. The books published, however, reflect the opinions of their authors and are not meant to represent the official position of the society. To obtain more information about Maryknoll and Orbis Books, visit our website at www.maryknoll.org.

Copyright © 1999 by Raymond F. Bulman

Published by Orbis Books, Maryknoll, New York, U.S.A.

All rights reserved. No part of this publication may be reproduced or transmitted in any form or by any means, electronic or mechanical, including photocopying, recording, or any information storage or retrieval system, without prior permission in writing from Orbis Books, P.O. Box 308, Maryknoll NY 10545-0308, U.S.A.

Manufactured in the United States of America

Library of Congress Cataloging-in-Publication Data
Bulman, Raymond F., 1933-
 The lure of the millennium : the year 2000 and beyond / Raymond F. Bulman.
   p. cm.
 Includes bibliographical references and index.
 ISBN 1-57075-253-2 (pbk.)
 1. Millennialism. 2. Forecasting. I. Title.
BT891.B85 1999
236'.9–dc21   99-18537

*To my wife, Carole,
and my son, Raymond K.,
for the "gift of community"*

Contents

Preface · xi

Acknowledgments · xv

1. Crossing the Millennial Divide · 1

   Plans, Preparations, and Predictions / 2
   Millennial Movements around the Year 1000 / 7
   What Can We Learn from the Year 1000? / 15

2. Food Scarcity and Technical Abundance · 18

   Food for the World / 19
   The Technological Revolution / 22

3. Disharmony with Nature and Neighbor · 32

   Economy and Ecology: The Delicate Balance / 32
   Violence, Disease, and Other Forms of Destabilization / 37
   A Rallying Point for the Third Millennium? / 44

4. The Millennial Religious Response · 47

   Reactions from the Fanatical Fringe / 47
   Doomsday Preachers / 51
   Grassroots Believers: Evangelicals and Catholics / 57
   Mainline Millennialism and the Renewal of Faith / 62

5. On Reading the Book of Revelation · 67

   A Question of Artistic Style / 68
   The Core Message of the Book of Revelation / 70
   A Book of Violence and Revenge? / 72
   A Book of Prophecy / 74
   Mystical Numbers and "Clanging Symbols" / 77

6. The Reign of a Thousand Years — 82

The Meaning of the Millennium / 83
Harmony as a Sign of the Kingdom / 85
Raptures and End-Time Predictions / 88
Millennial Expectation in the Early Church / 92
Building the New Jerusalem / 94

7. America's Millennial Vision — 97

A Chosen Nation / 97
The Gathering of the Saints / 99
The Civil War as Apocalyptic Event / 102
Millennialism in Support of the American Dream / 104

8. A Story of Hope and Shattered Dreams — 112

The Rappites of New Harmony, Indiana / 112
The Great Disappointment and the Rise of Adventism / 117
Watching from the Tower of Zion / 122

9. A Story of Apocalyptic Violence — 127

Apocalyptic Violence in the Past / 128
The Jonestown Tragedy / 131
From Ruby Ridge to Mt. Carmel / 134
Mt. Carmel, David Koresh, and the Fifth Seal / 136

10. God's Soldiers of the End-Time — 143

The Militias and the Coming Armageddon / 145
Ideology and Strategies / 149
The Opening Shots: Oklahoma City and Justus Township / 153
Responding to the Militias / 156

11. On Reading the Signs of the Times — 158

Announcing a Turning Point in History / 159
Varieties of Literal Interpretation / 160
The Millennium as Symbol / 165
Breaking the Deadlock: The Age of the Spirit / 169
The Millennium as Turning Point / 172

12. The World at the Crossroads — 177

The End of the World-System? / 177
Historical Turnings and Epochal Transition / 186
At the Crossroads / 192

Conclusion: The Year 2000 and Beyond   195
   Millennial Vibrations / 196
   New Beginning and New Creation / 198
   The Demand for a Global Ethic / 199
   The Idea of Global Harmony / 202
   The Path to Global Harmony / 205
   Millennial Celebration / 211

Notes   215

Glossary of Special Terms   228

Index   231

Preface

This is a book about millennialism,* the biblically based belief in the return of Christ to establish a thousand-year reign of peace and harmony on earth. In practice, millennialism has had a very checkered history from the beginnings of Christianity to the present, inspiring illusion, destruction, and violence at least as often as it has encouraged high ideals and heroic human behavior. One task of this book is to give a brief overview of that history in the hope of pointing out both the excesses as well as the splendors of this ancient religious doctrine.

What history makes clear is that believers have often abused millennial faith by predicting dates for the end of the world and the glorious return of Christ. Such predictions run counter to Jesus' own admonitions, and have often set the stage for disillusionment, confusion, and, at times, even violent behavior. It is understandable, then, that many Christians today hesitate to speculate very much about the meaning of the millennium. On the other hand, it would be a major mistake to leave the concern for this genuinely biblical belief to the Jim Joneses and the David Koreshes of this world.

This is also a book about the human future at the outset of the third Christian millennium. The initial decision to begin research on this book was certainly inspired by a growing awareness of the imminent approach of the year 2000, but the principal focus of the book looks far beyond immediate preparations for that landmark date. While the book could possibly serve as a spiritual initiation to the new millennium, at least for those who read the book early enough, the real intent of the work is to draw upon the lessons of history to help provide a religious and moral basis

---

*The word "millennium" comes from the Latin words *mille* (thousand) and *annus* (year) and has been used from the first Christian centuries to denote the thousand-year reign of Christ described in Rev. 20:1–10.

for confronting the ethical challenges we all face as human beings once the new millennium has actually begun. In other words, long after the celebrations of New Year's Eve 1999 have become memories and the apocalyptic fervor of the end-time preachers of this decade has cooled down, the issues addressed in this book should remain vital concerns for all those interested in creating a more humanly fulfilling global society.

The conflict, disorder, violence, imbalances, scarcity, inequalities, and uncertainty that make up so much of our present human experience do not bode well for the human future. Furthermore, through the centuries, millennialism, at its worst, has only aggravated and multiplied disharmony of all sorts. At its best, however (i.e., when true to its own biblical roots), millennial belief has been able to hold up to human beings an image of universal harmony and cooperation, touching every aspect of life on this planet. With an eye to the past as well as to the present, the book will attempt to draw from the very best of the millennialist heritage in order to provide both perspective and inspiration for facing the challenges of the coming century. Hopefully, the more destructive examples from history will serve as warnings against the temptation to certain kinds of fanatical and overzealous missteps.

History also shows that the lure of millennialism has regularly captivated significant numbers of religious enthusiasts during the course of the two thousand years of Christianity. According to many historians, this fascination was particularly powerful during the period immediately preceding the year 1000, that is, at the start of the second millennium. French historian Henri Focillon, in his classic work, *The Year 1000*, describes this period as a time of terror and consternation at the prospect of the imminent destruction of the world. Today, at the dawn of the third Christian millennium, we once again hear a growing cacophony of prophetic utterances ranging from pronouncements of apocalyptic destruction to promises of millennial harmony and renewal. A certain apocalyptic anticipation already permeates the cultural atmosphere, and there can be no doubt that our times are experiencing an ever-heightening sense of millennial fervor in the waning years of the twentieth century.

What is surprising in all this is the frequency with which secular voices join those of their religious counterparts in projecting visions and predictions for the world's future. Strangely enough, secular prognostications about the coming millennium can be just as dire and foreboding as the frightening forecasts of any fire-and-brimstone prophecy preacher. A good number of both secular and religious seers seem thoroughly obsessed with omens of coming nuclear destruction, population explosion, ecological disaster, and economic collapse. Yet true to apocalyptic style, these same secular seers often detect inklings of a new and fairer age beyond their images of coming ruin and desolation. The more optimistic of these secular voices even portray the turn of the century as primarily an opportunity to heal wounds and help to build a more just and peaceful society.

Less surprising, of course, is the wide array of religious voices proclaiming the spiritual significance of the new millennium. Many of these voices are those of doomsday prophets, announcing the end of the world by the year 2000 or shortly thereafter. Such predictions come from all segments of the religious spectrum, not only from a variety of Christian leaders, but even from a number of Buddhists, Muslims, and Jews. Evangelical electronic ministries, in particular, have been working feverishly, producing videos and promoting pamphlets and books which are to prepare us for the "Last Days." Similarly, many of the Catholic devout are appealing to worldwide apparitions of Mary, bearing messages of imminent catastrophe to be followed by an era of God-given peace.

Christians of less fundamentalist leanings are more inclined to see the turn of the millennium as a time of celebration and spiritual renewal on the two thousandth birthday of the Christian movement. Pope John Paul II has been preparing his followers through a series of religious observances leading up to the year 2000 and by writing an apostolic letter about the meaning of the coming millennial jubilee. Mainstream Protestants as well as Catholics have initiated biblical lecture series, millennial conferences, and a variety of ecumenical services to help provide their membership with a proper theological and spiritual preparation for this major anniversary in the history of the Christian church. Even outside the whole ambit of religious believers, the approach of the year 2000 is setting off a wide variety of quasi-messianic expectations and utopian hopes.

All concerned human beings today have a tremendous responsibility for the coming generations of humanity, for they will have an enormous stake in the choices we make at the outset of the twenty-first century. Christians in particular, in celebrating the second millennial anniversary of their faith, are called upon to make these choices in light of their belief in the ideals symbolized in the image of the millennial reign of Christ. For this reason, the final chapters of the book will propose an authentic reappropriation of the millennial doctrine that hopefully can inspire and motivate today's Christians with the same zeal and enthusiasm that impelled their earliest predecessors.

Since millennialism is at its core a Christian belief, with ancient Jewish roots, this book will no doubt have a special meaning for those who share the biblical faith. On the other hand, the year 2000 also represents a secular landmark which challenges both people of faith and those of humanistic conviction to take stock of their contribution to the direction of history. For this reason the book is addressed not only to Christians, Jews, Muslims, and other religious people, but to all women and men of goodwill who feel a responsibility for the human future.

Acknowledgments

The author wishes to acknowledge the permission of the following institutions and individuals for pictures and illustrations contained in this book:

The Metropolitan Museum of Art, Rogers Fund, 1956, photograph © 1979, for a detail from *The Vision of St. John* by El Greco (Domenikos Theotokopoulos, 1541–1614). Stacey Rosenstock Impact Visuals, 24 West 25th Street, New York, for *New Year's Eve in Times Square, New York City.* Maryknoll Photo Archives, Maryknoll, N.Y., for photo of Bangladeshi mother and child. The Drawings and Archives Department of the Avery Architectural and Fine Arts Library, 1172 Amsterdam Ave., Columbia University, New York, N.Y. 10027, for the photo of a painting of the main entrance of the monastic church at Cluny.

Impact Visuals, for the photo by Kit Miller, copyright 1989, of Kayapo Indians of Brazil using video cameras. Impact Visuals also for the photo by Sean Sprague, copyright 1992, of a young woman and a child in a recently destroyed rain forest in Brazil. The Associated Press for a photo by Khalil Senosi, copyright 1998, of the bombing of the U.S. embassy in Nairobi, Kenya. Jack Van Impe Ministries for the photo of the Reverend Van Impe. MaxKol Communications, 109 Executive Drive, Suite D, Sterling, Va., for the photo of the cross at Mt. Krizevac, overlooking Medjugorje, which appears in *The Thunder of Justice,* by Ted and Maureen Flynn (Sterling, Va.: MaxKol Communications, 1992).

Bible Believers, Route 3, Box 92, Sherman, Tex., for the postcard of the rapture. The Drawings and Archives Department of the Avery Architectural and Fine Arts Library, Columbia University, for a black and white photograph of a classic portrait of Joseph Smith, and the Burke Library of Union Theological Seminary, New York, for the photograph of a page from an early edition of Joachim of Fiore's *Exposition of the Apocalypse.*

The author also wishes to express his gratitude and appreciation to the following persons and institutions:

To Mrs. Jane B. Owen of the Robert Lee Blaffer Trust for her generous support and unflagging enthusiasm for the book from its inception.

To the University Seminars at Columbia University for their assistance in preparation of the manuscript for publication and for providing opportunities in the University Seminar on Studies in Religion for airing some of the ideas presented in the book. To St. John's University for granting me additional research time and multifaceted faculty support.

To research assistants Roseanna Ciavarella, Luz Ramirez, Maria Cantasano, and Gheorghita Zugravu for their dedicated and competent efforts. To Kareen Williams for her help with proofreading the manuscript as well as with research. To Fran Fico for both her computer skills and geniality in preparing the manuscript.

In a special way to Brother Robert McCauley, F.M.S., Louis Di Lauro, and Professor William Keogan for their generous contributions of time and expertise in providing a wealth of information for the project.

Finally, to my wife, Carole, for her infinite patience, sage advice, and loyal support throughout the long process of writing this book.

– 1 –

Crossing the Millennial Divide

History knows any number of epochal moments when armies, nations, peoples, indeed, when whole civilizations cross over a major divide, which issues in a whole new arrangement of worldview, values, social and political structures, as well as new institutions.[1] The simplest paradigm for such moments is still Caesar's famous crossing of the Rubicon, accompanied by the unforgettable proclamation: "The die is cast." The special feature of crossing a historical divide is that once having crossed there is no way to return. The fall of the Roman Empire, the coronation of Charlemagne, the Renaissance, the Protestant Reformation, the discovery of the New World, the American, French, and Industrial Revolutions, the outbreak of World War I, the explosion of the atomic bomb, and the recent collapse of the Soviet Empire are but a few of these major milestones which constitute a transition so great that the new directions they set became irreversible.

Such epochal moments of history are ordinarily the result of extraordinary turns in human events, but at times their significance seems to be equally determined by the arrival of specific calendar landmarks, such as the turn of decades or of centuries, as when we speak of the 1960s or of the beginning of the twentieth century. Only two times, however, since the rise of the Christian movement (on which the Western calendar is based) has the world been faced with the prospect of crossing a millennial divide. Recent historical research has made it clear that all of Europe was very conscious of the first crossing in the year 1000, and all indications are that most of the world will either celebrate or observe in some significant way the transition to the year 2000. Even though a millennial divide is based on the fictive device we call a calendar, its emotional impact cannot be ignored, for rare indeed are the moments when we can celebrate on one occasion the start of a new year, a new decade, a new century, and a new millennium.

For the mathematical purist, the third millennium actually begins on January 1, 2001, since the Gregorian calendar moves from 1 B.C.E. to 1 C.E. without the intervention of a year 0. As a result, since the calendar intends to reflect the years since the birth of Christ, two thousand years from the year 1 is 2001 C.E., not 2000 C.E. What also adds to the arbitrariness of the millennial calendar date is an error made by a sixth-century monk (named Dennis the Little) who had been commissioned by the pope to draw up a standard liturgical calendar. Lacking the tools of modern historiography, his calculations about the birth of Jesus were off by several years, so that historians today would locate the birth of Christ around the year 6 B.C.E. rather than at Dennis's 1 C.E. Accordingly, the millennial date 2000 is something of a conventional mark on the calendar, a point not missed by the skeptical Stephen Jay Gould in his recent work, *Questioning the Millennium*.[2]

Questions of accuracy apart, there is no doubt that the appearance of three 0s on the calendar exercises an uncanny fascination over the human imagination. On the eve of the year 2000, people of many religions and cultures will be celebrating and dancing in the streets, even if the date holds for them no special religious significance and even if ordinarily they follow a very different calendar.

Plans, Preparations, and Predictions

Though some historians have tried to deny it, crossing the first millennial divide in the year 1000 was an epochal event approached with suitable awe, anxiety, as well as hope, at least by the more religiously focused population of medieval Europe. But if the first millennial crossing was so momentous, how much the more spectacular and world shaking shall be this second crossing of the millennial divide? As in the year 1000, we once again celebrate "the ritual death and rebirth of history as one thousand-year epoch yields to another,"[3] but this time we will make this momentous transition in an age of mass media and global com-

Celebrating the new year in Times Square. As New York City has become one of the world's major media capitals, its images of how the advent of years is greeted have become globally influential.

munications. From a look at the preparations well underway for a decade, it has also become apparent that those who, in the name of historical precision, choose to put off the observance of the millennium until the year 2001 may well find that they have missed the party.

Despite the intrinsically religious significance of the millennial date, society is far more secular than it was at the crossing of the first millennial divide. As religious media critic Phyllis Zagano has recently observed, even though midnight of December 31, 1999, will mark "the beginning of the third millennium of Christ's Incarnation,... it is entirely possible that most of the world will be watching the ball drop in Times Square."[4] Certainly a large amount of the travel plans, hotel bookings, and other preparations for New Year's Eve 1999 have to do with very secular celebrations and festivities to ring in the new millennium.

Much of the millennium hype, no doubt, results from the efforts of opportunistic entrepreneurs who see the potential of making enormous financial profit from the need of many to participate in this rare celebration of a millennial landmark —

whether they be motivated by a sense of being a part of history, or simply from the urge not to miss out on what might well turn out to be the "biggest bash" in history. New watches, billed as "The Third Millennium Challenge," which have been preprogrammed to count off to the year 2000 are already on the market. A new skin care product called Millenium is already available, and a new Manhattan hotel has been given the same name (misspelled with one *n* in both cases). Chrysler has produced a car called the Millennia (actually the plural of "millennium"), and Fidelity Investments has come out with a mutual fund called the New Millennium.

At the same time, the media are also attempting to capitalize on the more fearsome side of the powerful millennium theme, with a number of sci-fi Hollywood films such as *Impact* and *Armageddon* and massively promoted TV series such as Chris Carter's Friday night drama called *Millennium*. The series, starring Lance Henriksen, effectively creates an atmosphere of apocalyptic foreboding, filled with the sense of an unnamed and otherworldly terror. Not to be outdone by pop culture, John Updike has published a new novel called *Toward the End of Time*,[5] in which he attempts to provide the reader with a look into the new millennium. All this is but the tip of the millennial marketing iceberg. The biggest planning and economic opportunities seem to lie in the area of the travel and hotel industries.

The Japanese, who adopted the Western calendar only 125 years ago, are not going to miss out on the millennial bonanza. Nippon Travel Agency recently announced a twenty-eight-day Pacific cruise from Japan to Hawaii that will be programmed to cross the international dateline at midnight of December 31. This arrangement will enable the reveling passengers to witness "the earliest dawn of the year 2000 on the globe" and to continue their partying once they have crossed the dateline into the previous millennium.[6] Assuming that the *Queen Elizabeth II* is still seaworthy, it will be enlisted by the six-hundred-member Millennium Society, based in Washington, D.C., which plans to transport 1,750 people from New York City to Alexandria, Egypt, from which they will continue on land to the outskirts of Cairo, where they will celebrate the new year and new millennium at the Great Pyramid of Giza. The price tag for the Giza celebration is ten thousand dollars per person. The society is also offering satellite-linked parties in all twenty-four time zones around the world, at significant locations such as Stonehenge, the Eiffel Tower, the Acropolis, the Taj Mahal, the Great Wall of China, and Red Square. Of course, top entertainment is being lined up for each of these gala events. The Millennium Society's plans for its proposed "biggest bash" at Egypt's Great Pyramid of Cheops will feature both the Grateful Dead and the artist formerly known as Prince.[7] There can be no doubt that pop culture is going to make a very strong showing in the world's millennial celebrations.

The hotel industry from Istanbul to Times Square is frantically revving up to accommodate the thousands of reservation requests with which they have been barraged since the early 1990s. In Istanbul tour operators have already blocked rooms at the Swissotel, from which global-minded guests will be able to see the almost simultaneous dawning of the new millennium over Asia and Europe. The Savoy Hotel in London is already booked twice over and will have to draw lots to decide on its room assignments for the celebration. New York's new Marriott Marquis Hotel in Times Square has been booking reservations for December 31, 1999, even prior to the hotel's completion. In France, Euro Disneyland's most luxurious hotel is already booked solid, and for those who prefer to celebrate on the move, word has it that the Concorde will be holding a New Year's party at sixty thousand feet.[8]

Major cities and other tourist spots around the world are making their own plans for millennial celebrations. Sydney, Australia, is tying its promotion of the New Year's celebration with its role as host of the 2000 Summer Olympic Games. Edinburgh, Scotland, is preparing for a huge *hogmanay* (New Year's celebration) in 1999, and as part of the promotion is playing up the Scottish roots of the famous New Year's ballad "Auld Lang Syne." Greenwich, England, will open the doors of its colossal new Millennium Dome at the stroke of midnight 2000, and Germany's Expo 2000 is expected to draw forty million visitors.

New York City is making plans for "Celebration 2000," which is being billed as "the greatest party the world will ever see." Events will begin at 7 A.M. on New Year's Eve, 1999, and continue in one form or another throughout the year 2000. The highlight will be a Fourth of July tall ships flotilla from fifty nations to sail up the Hudson River from New York Harbor.

President Clinton, who plans to be present at the Fourth of July event, has reminded Americans that the millennium is no longer a distant future and urged them to "take stock" so as to "begin the world over again for our children and our children's children."[9] The White House has also set up a White House Millennium Program Website (www.whitehouse.gov.) and has invited electronic suggestions for the American millennial celebrations.

President Clinton is not alone in striking a serious note in preparing for the new millennium. Philadelphia — the City of Brotherly Love — has launched a New Neighbors in the New Century campaign, aimed at promoting multicultural sensitivity and addressing the issues that divide Americans. Other serious concerns over the approaching year 2000 include the much-touted computer glitch, the controversy over the 2000 census, and the relative merits of the class of 2000.

Computer experts are hard at work to try to correct the programming flaws whereby years are identified only by two digits, rather than four, producing a reading of 00 rather than 2000. Such an outcome could, of course, cause havoc in businesses, banks, travel schedules, credit statements, Social Security benefits, and water and electrical supplies, to name but a few problem areas. Preparing the world's computers for the millennium could run up a bill as high as $600 billion. Major financial houses are already insuring themselves at heavy premiums against possible litigations.[10]

Critics of the ten-year census contend that the 2000 census will be too costly (over $4 billion) and that, what's worse, the long form, in particular, is far too intrusive into the private lives of Americans. Assessments of the graduating high school class of the year 2000 seem to be mixed. The so-called turn-of-the-millennium generation is described by some as jaded, spoiled, cynical, unfocused, and uncommitted, but others see in the same group a deeper longing for direction and purpose, which will become their hallmark as the responsible adults of tomorrow, who will guide us through the imposing challenges of the new century.[11]

Obviously, concerns about the year 2000 easily slip into predictions. As is the usual case with millennial fervor, some of these predictions will invariably be somber, dire, and apocalyptic. Apart from the whole panoply of religious prophecies, which will be discussed in chapter 4, the last decade has certainly experienced no dearth of secular doomsday prognostications. Mihir Desai, of Harvard University, has drawn attention to the clear note of finality that characterizes so much of today's reading: there is the "end of history," the "end of architecture," the "end of science," the "end of sovereignty," the "end of marriage," or, in short, "the end of everything."[12] This sense of living in the shadow of the end is frequently expressed in forecasts of environmental catastrophe and deteriorating weather conditions. Even astronomers have joined the bandwagon with predictions of armadas of asteroids approaching the earth in August 2000 and a most unusual alignment of Mercury, Venus, Mars, Jupiter, and Saturn in May 2000.

The cultural setting of this secular millennial hype, with all its enthusiastic plans for travel and festivity, its anxious preparations for meeting impending problems, its predictions of future threats, and its historical sense of reaching the close of an epoch, remains aeons apart from the atmosphere of awestruck expectation that characterized the first human crossing of a millennial divide. Nevertheless, despite the colossal chasm that separates us from the world of the late tenth century, history still tends to repeat itself, and for this reason, it should prove instructive to us to try to reconstruct the religious atmosphere surrounding the first millennial turning.

Millennial Movements around the Year 1000

There can be no question that Europe underwent very dramatic (or should I say traumatic?) changes around the year 1000. What has been hotly disputed by historians, however, is the religious mind-set of the period. Was the year 1000 a "year like any other year" — that is, untouched by any special apocalyptic fear or fervor? Or was it a time of great apocalyptic agitation and hidden religious terrors? Until recently, the historical consensus favored the idea of an uneventful millennial crossing, dismissing the second view as the product of an overly vivid, romantic imagination. The pioneering work of French historians, such as Henri Focillon, Georges Duby, and Guy Bois, and an American, Richard Landes, however, has seriously challenged this conventional reading of the documents and has made a very persuasive case that the "period around 1000 may well mark one of the high-water marks" of millennial belief in the history of the West.[13]

While the vast majority of official church documents and chronicles are conspicuously silent about significant apocalyptic agitation or potent millennial movements at the time, there is also a significant record of unofficial (and therefore uncensored) reports which paint a picture of widespread religious tumult. Notable among these minority chroniclers is the Burgundian monk Rodulfus Glaber, who describes a time of frenzied popular expectation stirred by countless pilgrimages, mass gatherings of the peasants, and grassroots-inspired peace councils. Glaber's apocalyptic bias is unmistakable in his anxious admonitions that, with the end of the first millennium, Satan is about to be unleashed for the great struggle that is to precede the day of final judgment. For the new historians, Glaber's apocalyptic fears and trepidations are only a hint of a broad-based, popular religious expectation regarding the millennium.

In the closing decades of the tenth century, as often enough in the history of Christianity, millennial beliefs were viewed as politically dangerous by the ruling aristocracy and as doctrinally unsound by church authority. It was of obvious interest both to the surviving Carolingian aristocrats as well as to the new manorial lords to join forces with the official representatives of orthodox church teaching so as to downplay or to ignore any remembrances of millennial religious frenzy at the approach of the year 1000. Such beliefs and activities were regularly censored from official church documents. Both the religious and the secular establishment far preferred safe writings, such as the influential book the *Antichrist,* written in 954 by the monastic chronicler Adso, who not only disparaged end-time speculation, but made the claim that as long as the Carolingian Empire survived through the reign of the Frankish monarchy, there could be no appearance of the Antichrist. Clearly the book served well both the interests of church orthodoxy and the ambitious and imperial aspirations of the Franks.[14] The blatant bias of the official records makes it impossible to dismiss the Glabers of the day as bizarre crackpots or to discount on the basis of these approved accounts the recurring image of a widespread popular millennialism in the year 1000.

Such a heightened state of religious expectation makes even

Entrance to the main church of the Abbey of Cluny. Not only was Cluny a center of monastic renewal in the medieval period; it was also a center of a millennial peace movement.

more sense when seen in the context of the major political and social upheavals of the day. Historians have often noted a close connection between political, military, or moral upheavals and the emergence of unusual apocalyptic ardor.[15] The studies of the talented French historian Guy Bois on the international influence of the Burgundian Abbey of Cluny have made a convincing case for a European-wide cultural and political revolution in the latter years of the tenth century.[16] This revolution consisted in nothing less than the total collapse of the Carolingian Empire and with it the final demise of the ancient Roman system, with all its political and social structures.

Foremost among these was the ancient institution of slavery, which, under the impact of religious reformers at monastic centers such as Cluny, was rapidly unraveling. The two decades preceding the year 1000 witnessed an intense period of transformation, as slaves were freed from both monastic and aristocratic bondage, creating a whole new class of free townspeople. In the year 987 the last ruling Carolingian dynasty had fallen; Hugh Capet had assumed (many felt "stolen") the French throne; and insubordinate warrior lords began to exert their independence from both the king and the remaining Carolingian aristocracy. Unfortunately for the peasantry, their newly won freedom was quickly transformed into a new form of oppression at the hands of these increasingly powerful manorial lords. The Carolingian order was gasping for its dying breath, and the new feudal order was being created. It was a time of utter instability, anarchy, and violence.

It was during this unsettled period that heavily fortified castles began to dominate the landscape of the southern French countryside, and their masters, known as the "castellans" (Fr. *chatelains*), entrenched themselves as the despotic rulers of both the freed and servile peasants. These changes, which inaugurated the "new manorial regime," were widespread throughout the Frankish kingdom.[17] The resulting new order created far-reaching changes touching the very core of the social fabric. With good reason this has been called the beginning of the Feudal Revolution.

The castellans, for example, found it necessary to change the traditional laws of inheritance as a way of strengthening their newly won power. The result was the establishment of primogeniture, which passed the estate to the eldest son at the price of disinheriting the younger sons. This radical change only set the stage for further conflict and violence. The peasants, whatever their prior status, became servile and lived in terror of imprisonment and torture in the dungeons of the castellans. The pillaging and plundering of church property by the new warrior class became a commonplace event. Castellans and their armed horsemen (*milites*) regularly engaged each other in combat over land and authority, creating an atmosphere of continual fear for the defenseless population of laity and clergy alike.[18] In a word, the dark nights of pretechnological, forest-covered Europe were filled with dangers and terrors of all sorts. Within such a context questions about the imminence of the Last Days would certainly arise — and this all the more so as the calendar approached the millennial date 1000.

The Italian scholar Umberto Eco, then, is not indulging in romantic reverie when he claims that the years leading up to the second millennium were pervasively apocalyptic. He is historically accurate when he describes the period as "a time of failing harvests, recurrent famines, regular pestilences, droughts, floods, petty warfare and lawlessness."[19] In dramatic acts of repentance in preparation for the imminent day of judgment, people began to donate land, homes, and goods to the poor. Others canceled debts, forgave injuries, neglected businesses, and left their homes unrepaired and their fields unplowed. Flagellants in ever-increasing numbers mortified their flesh in the spirit of penitence in preparation for the final day of reckoning. Nor is journalist Russell Chandler conjuring up his own fantasy when he describes the scenario of New Year's Eve, 999 C.E., in St. Peter's Basilica in Rome as a night of fear and terror, followed by an outbreak of joy and euphoria as the new year dawned and the world continued to go on as before.[20] Focillon even goes so far as to claim that the sense of euphoria and new-born confidence created by the peaceful and uneventful passing of New Year's Eve 999 was a very important factor in the "building of the West" in the centuries that followed.[21]

As we will see in subsequent chapters, dedicated apocalyptists are not easily dissuaded or discouraged by failed prophecy. Accordingly, when the millennial year 1000 passed without incident, apocalyptists were quite ready to recalculate their end-time predictions. Furthermore, since all significant dates have an impact that greatly affects the periods that immediately precede and follow them, it is not surprising that Glaber depicts the whole period surrounding the "thousandth year of Christ the Lord" as a time of apocalyptic and millennial fervor. Accordingly, he and his fellow apocalyptics had no problem establishing new millennial deadlines, especially for the years 1010 and 1033.

The baneful mood surrounding 1010 resulted from the news of the destruction of the Holy Sepulcher in Jerusalem at the hands of Al-Hakim, the caliph of Cairo. The incident provoked fear as well as rage, as Al-Hakim was quickly identified as the Antichrist — the Nebuchadnezzar of Babylon — whose sacrilegious act in the Holy Land was a certain sign that the Last Days had begun.[22] The apocalyptic significance of the year 1033, on the other hand, was traceable to the Augustinian tradition, which assumed that

Jesus died in the year 33, and that the year 1033 would mark the "millennium of the Passion." Once the year 1000 (the millennium of the Incarnation, i.e., the birth of Christ) had passed without incident, the millennial calendar was revised to focus on 1033. Both of these "back-up" millennial dates were marked by intense religious as well as political agitation. (It is not unreasonable to anticipate a similar fluidity of prophetic dates as we once again cross a millennial divide into the year 2000.)

During the waning years of the tenth century, while violence, social dislocation, and anarchy were reaching a paroxysmal state, the general populace was caught in a kind of collective religious enthusiasm, which encouraged the discernment of apocalyptic signs amid the vicissitudes of the times. Apart from the collapse of the last Carolingian dynasty (987) and the general unraveling of the old order, the apocalyptic imagination of the populace was deeply stirred by such events as the appearance of Halley's Comet in 989, the betrayal of the last Carolingian pretender by the bishop of Laon in 991, the coincidence of the Feast of the Annunciation with Good Friday in 992, and the devastating effects of a plague which regularly ravaged southern France throughout this period.

The plague, then known as the *sacer ignis* (holy fire), was seen as a special divine retribution for human sinfulness and a clearcut sign of the impending end-time tribulations (much as some religious groups view the scourge of AIDS today). In modern times, the medieval plague has been identified as "ergotism," a pathological condition resulting from the ingestion of grain infected with ergot fungus. Ergotism has a certain hallucinogenic, intoxicating effect upon its victims and is capable of producing powerful hallucinations, including both terrifying visions of hell and glorious images of heaven.[23] It could well have played a significant role in fostering religious revivals and in raising the general level of apocalyptic consciousness. That such a scourge, as well as other omens, should appear as Christendom prepared for the imminent approach of the millennium of the Incarnation undoubtedly served to reinforce the sense of an impending doom.

Apocalyptic beliefs, on the other hand, are not limited to ominous predictions and doomsday forebodings. Combined, as they were, with a heavy dose of fear and trembling, there lies, nonetheless, at their very core an underlying conviction of unwavering hope. Among the most constructive and hopeful outcomes of the heightened millennial awareness of the period was the rapid growth and spread of the Peace Movement throughout Europe. In fact, according to Landes, the "Peace of God" current may well prove to have been "one of the most powerful and consequential chiliastic (millennial) movements in the history of the West."[24]

The Peace Movement, which took on official status as the Peace of God (later, the Truce of God), was in its origins a popular movement, emerging from the oppression and violence to which the common people were subjected during the anarchistic transition to the new order of the feudal age. In fact, even as it eventually became ecclesiastically organized around official Peace Councils, it always remained very much a movement of the people. The peasants, living in continual fear of the warrior barons, found natural allies in the reforming monks of centers such as Cluny, which through the tightly knit network of monastic orders was able to tap resources and win support in high places throughout the Latin West. But even this alliance would have been impossible without the pervasive religious enthusiasm which had been generated among the masses by the approach of the one thousandth anniversary of Christ's birth. This spiritual ardor found a powerful form of expression in the popular piety of devotion to the saints, and especially in the pilgrimages to their shrines and the highly elaborate cult of their relics. It was the monks who promoted these cult centers and protected the pilgrims who flocked to them.[25]

Since the age of the martyrs, Christians throughout the Roman Empire had maintained an ardent devotion to the relics of the saints, especially to those who had shed their blood in the name of Jesus. No doubt enthusiasm for the relics, particularly among the illiterate, had to be checked periodically by church authority, which viewed the populace as only too prone to enthusiastic exaggeration and to relapses into their pagan past. But if church authorities looked with a certain misgiving and suspicion on these expressions of popular piety, at the same time they promoted the cult of relics as a way of harnessing the religious zeal of the peasantry. The conspicuous rise in the popularity of relic devotion in the closing decades of the tenth century was also due, at least in large part, to the powerful apocalyptic significance with which the period was endowed by the faithful.

During the last decades of the tenth century, the gathering of revered saintly relics regularly drew massive crowds into the open fields in moving services of prayer and penitence. This new and powerful paraliturgical practice moved the relics of the saints from the remoteness of the crypt to the public view of the altar, and, as a result, their reliquaries became portable — ready to be brought to participate in these mass religious rallies or eventually in the major Peace Councils that would begin in the last few years prior to the new millennium. At these rallies the relics of the saints were raised up ecstatically for veneration, and given the millennial mind-set of the day, this literal "rising of the saints" was understood as the fulfillment of the end-time prophecies of the Book of Revelation. The "sociability" of the saints achieved through the gathering of the various relics (including those considered by the populace to be competitors) also helped create a certain conciliatory atmosphere for the participants at the Peace Councils.[26]

The first of the great Peace Councils was held at Limoges in Aquitaine in 994. Others would be held regularly well into the eleventh century. The idea of the Peace of God was not simply the outcome of the practical alliance of monks, peasants, and church authorities — it was also closely tied to the vividness of apocalyptic expectation. The program of the Council of Limoges was quite typical of the Peace Councils in general. It began with public and communal acts of penance in preparation for Christ's imminent return. It contained a service of healing in conjunction with the relics, especially of St. Martial, a very popular saint-martyr of the region. (Legend had it that he had been an apostle and companion of the Lord.) At least according to the records, the healing phase of the Council of Limoges proved to have been effective, curing many of the faithful of the horrible symptoms of the *sacer ignis* (the ergot plague). The council ended with an alliance of peace and truce, sworn to by all the participating lords. In the eyes of the millennium-conscious participants, this truce was seen as a powerful portent as well as manifestation of the end-times — a temporary realization of the "glory of God on earth."[27]

Commentators on the Council at Limoges described the results of the council in the messianic language of the classic peace passage from Isaiah: "And they [the nations] shall beat their swords into plowshares, and their spears into pruning hooks"

(Isa. 2:4). From beginning to end, the structure of the Peace Councils reflected an unequivocally millennialist flavor, moving from penitence and deliverance from divinely sent terrors (plagues) through the power of divine intervention (miraculous cures) to the construction of a new, earthly kingdom of peace, justice, and harmony.[28]

The initial effect of the Peace Councils was extraordinary: codes were set up to protect the unarmed citizenry — both peasants and clergy — from the armed mounted horsemen (the *milites*). The armed knights were given a legitimate place within Christian society and were expected to use their military skills in defense of the Christian people and ultimately for the liberation of the Holy Land. Severe church penalties were meted out to those who violated the truce. But by the third decade of the new century, the nobility had successfully co-opted the Peace Movement to serve its own interests and to bolster its own authority. Within a short time, the Peace of God lost its grassroots support and the armed knights returned to their warlike ways. In this sense, the Peace of God ultimately proved to be a failure, but not before it had helped produce, if even for a short time, a society which was thoroughly imbued with the millennial principles of peace, justice, and harmony in the world.

What Can We Learn from the Year 1000?

The social, political, and cultural context of the world at the approach of the first millennium seems light years away from our own situation. By today's standards, the world at the turn of the first millennium was technologically primitive, diseased and hungry, threatened with terrors both real and imagined. Even apart from the affliction of widespread superstition, all human concerns and cultural changes were surrounded by an all-embracing religious aura. Accordingly, the closest cultural counterpart in today's secular world to the mass, open-air, religious assemblies of the late tenth century might be the huge gatherings of fans at outdoor rock concerts or other celebrity performances, such as on the Great Lawn in Central Park. But despite the enormous cultural chasm that separates us from our millenarian ancestors of the tenth century, the above reflections on the events of the year 1000 can offer us some important insights and lessons that should make our crossing of a new millennial divide somewhat less hazardous.

As a starter, we can spare ourselves the distress and confusion experienced by our millennialist ancestors at the failure of their end-time predictions for the year 1000 by resisting the temptation to engage in fruitless speculation on naming end-time dates. Furthermore, we ought to prepare ourselves for an intensification and multiplication of doomsday and millennial prophecies as we get closer to the year 2000. Along these same lines, we can expect to see a marked increase in the spotting of celestial signs, in the sighting of UFOs, and in anguish about earthquakes, epidemics, and other global calamities. Finally, we ought not to be surprised if once having uneventfully passed the millennial landmark of the year 2000, those who were predicting either the day of wrath or the triumphant return of Christ will undauntedly sit down to recalculate their end-time prophecies. New millennial deadlines may also come and go at various times throughout the first half of the new century. The year 2033 (bimillennium of the Lord's Passion) is a very likely candidate as a backup date for millennial prediction.

But there is a far more important lesson to be learned from the history of the year 1000. The prediction of disasters, calamities, and global tribulations is never the last word in a genuinely millennial faith. Millennialism is in the long run optimistic. For the persecuted Christians of the first century church, the image of the millennium provided a vision of hope in face of their daily experience of suffering, danger, and desperation. This basic millennial theme should continue to serve as a powerful reminder that the forces of evil will ultimately be destroyed and that those who remain faithful will be vindicated upon the Lord's return. The key to millennial belief is that God is the Lord of History. Throughout the centuries, and especially in times of persecution and anxiety, Christians have found courage and consolation in the conviction that in the long run the power of God will prevail. In chapter 6 we will show that this belief is at the very heart of millennial faith.

The practical expression of this Christian hope around the year 1000 took shape in the courageous and unprecedented work of the Peace Councils. Today — as we get ready to cross another millennial divide — instead of giving way to the fear of doomsday destruction and predictions of global catastrophe, we ought to be looking for our own twenty-first century counterpart to the Peace of God. In the following two chapters we will attempt to reflect in broad strokes on the varieties of urgent challenges that face the human family in the century that lies ahead. Hopefully this will help crystallize for us a focus of moral commitment that is equivalent to the role played by the Peace Movement around the year 1000. And even if this new cause should, like the Peace of God, eventually collapse, history will still consider us blessed if, even for a brief time, we are able to make visible a little bit of the "glory of God on earth."

– 2 –

Food Scarcity and Technical Abundance

The events preceding the year 1000, to the extent that we can know them, might well give us a clue as to what to expect in the months and days preceding the year 2000. But whatever happenings, beneficent, banal, or catastrophic, might occur during this preparatory period as well as on New Year's Eve 1999, the problems and challenges we can realistically anticipate for the new century will remain with us in force long after the millennial hype has lost its steam. While it is impossible to predict today the exact nature and extent of these future challenges, certainly by carefully examining the trends and problems so evident at the end of the century, we should be able to make some plausible projections, at least into the first few decades of the twenty-first century.

In this chapter, then, I will try to identify and explore what I believe to be some of the most urgent of these future challenges. While my list of challenges is by no means complete, it will, hopefully, reflect the major types of global problems which are likely to continue to concern all of us who feel a responsibility for the human future. While many of these challenges have their origins in local situations, in today's interdependent world, their global implications easily become apparent. Political events in Moscow, for example, can have deep repercussions in Latin America, and economic trends in the Pacific Rim can have a powerful impact on the New York stock market. Who can question that we live in a globally interconnected society?

Apart from their global scope, another special aspect of these diverse future challenges is that they all seem to threaten some kind of disorder or disharmony on a grand scale. If this should prove to be the case, it may well suggest that the path to resolution will require serious effort toward creating a new order and a new era of cooperation and harmony for the human community. Among the types of global challenge that are likely to continue to catch our attention as we move into the third millennium, we do well to include the following: (1) food for the world, (2) the revolution in technology, (3) an ecologically sustainable economy, and (4) threats to life and social stability. The first two of these issues are the subject of this chapter, while we will address the remaining two challenges in the chapter which follows. We begin with the increasingly disturbing question of worldwide food scarcity.

Food for the World

Observers at the Worldwatch Institute, located in Washington, D.C., have recently made it clear that the world at the end of the twentieth century has moved into the very serious situation of food scarcity. As indications of the seriousness of this problem, they have drawn attention to the doubling of the market price of both wheat and corn between 1995 and 1996. They attribute this rise in cost of grain to a significant decline in the rate of food production, which has now fallen well behind the increasing demand for grain and grain products. The "unprecedented rise in affluence in Asia" (especially in China), in conjunction with the addition of about ninety million people a year to the world's population since 1985,[1] have contributed greatly to this imbalance of supply and demand.

It would be less than fair, however, to overlook the good news in the demographic situation, namely, that world population growth has actually slowed down from the high point of 2.1 percent annually in the 1960s to 1.5 percent in 1996. Fertility rates have also declined during the same period: 46 percent in Indonesia, 55 percent in Brazil, and 68 percent in China. But despite these significant positive developments, population growth worldwide continues to increase at far too fast a pace.[2] While population increase is traceable to a number of factors, by far the most decisive has been the unparalleled advances in health care and disease control throughout the world, especially through the use of immunization and antibiotics. In most instances, improved health care has made for an aging population, especially in the industrialized democracies. In the developing countries, it has reduced drastically the number of children who die in childbirth or during their early years. In Tunisia, for example, the infant death rate dropped from 138 to 59 (i.e., deaths per thousand live births) between 1970 and 1990, and the overall population of the country doubled in size from 1960 to 1990.

Since instances like Tunisia are not atypical, the effect of these local population increases are clearly reflected in global demographic statistics. At the beginning of the twentieth century the world's population numbered 1.6 billion people. By 1925 the number had reached 2 billion, whereas from 1925 to 1976 that number doubled to 4 billion. Statistics for 1990 put the global population at 5.3 billion, and even the most conservative estimates for the near future (the year 2025) project an ongoing mushrooming of the human planetary population to estimates ranging from 8 to 14 billion. (The World Bank forecasts a "stabilization" of these expanding figures at between 10 and 11 billion people by the middle of the coming century.)[3] To view the situation from a different angle, the annual addition to the world's population from 1955 to the present has jumped dramatically from 47 to 90 million. Even now more people are born worldwide each year than those who die. Despite efforts at population control and the loss of life through wars and disease, the overall population of the earth continues to grow at exponential rates.

What greatly exacerbates this serious problem of steady record growth in the world population is the fact that this proliferation of human life takes place in an alarmingly imbalanced way. The anticipated awesome population explosion of the coming century will occur at a much larger scale among the poor, developing nations (the South) than among the industrialized, affluent countries of the North. Again, by the year 2025 the population of the United States is expected to increase by 25 percent, and a number of European nations, such as Germany, expect a stagnant, if not negative, population growth. By way of contrast, Africa, the poorest of the continents, is expected to expand its population from 480 million to 1.58 billion. Clearly this disproportion of population growth will greatly exacerbate the huge economic gap that already separates the affluent from the poor of this world.

Ironically, the nations with the least amount of resources will have by far the greatest populations to feed. At the same time, because of the rapid developments in global communications and

A Bangladeshi mother carries her malnourished child. Despite the promise of sufficient food for all earlier in the century, famine stalks the world at the millennium as it has for ages. Photo by Hoosier.

media entertainment, this burgeoning population of poor people is continually raising its demands for greater consumption from the available food chain. Economic growth in Asia in the last two decades has far outstripped that of western Europe and North America in their heyday of industrialization. The Chinese economy alone, with that nation's current population at 1.2 billion people, has grown by two-thirds between 1990 and 1995. This translates into a 60 percent increase in income for this vast population, resulting in an unprecedented rise in demand for livestock products. Since all livestock products — meat, cheese, butter, eggs, and so on — depend on the supply of grain, China's consumption of that staple during that period increased by 40 percent.

Up until the middle 1980s the widespread use of fertilizer, improved irrigation, and modern methods of farming had doubled the world's output of grain, and the production of hybrid rice strains, dubbed "miracle rice," in Asia brought yields of two or three times more than the traditional varieties.[4] Since that time the tide has turned dramatically. Food productivity has been seriously undermined by loss of croplands through deforestation, overgrazing, and shortsighted use of irrigation. In fact, irresponsible irrigation, combined with waste and the industrial use of water, is quickly turning fresh water into a scarce resource. The use of fertilizer, so effective in the past, becomes less and less useful with the shrinkage of well-watered grainland. To make matters worse, the world supply of seafood is very much on the decline as a result of the great drain on ocean fisheries brought about by the substantial growth of trawling fleets initiated in the 1970s.[5]

Coupled with the growing human population, expected to produce three billion new mouths to feed within the next two decades, the general slowing down of food production is quickly moving the world into *an age of food scarcity*. Dwindling food supplies worldwide seem unable to keep up with the population increases, especially in developing countries. Drought seasons in developing countries can have devastating effects on infant and adult survival, as the recent events in North Korea have made clear. When the situation is further complicated by political tensions, the devastation is even worse. In major grain-producing countries like the United States, drought conditions affect world food supply by reducing carryover stocks of grain below the safety level required for global food security.[6]

Projections by the Worldwatch Institute and by individual governments, such as Japan, point to a coming food scarcity of such monumental proportions that only immediate and vigorous international attention can keep the situation from becoming a global tragedy.

The Technological Revolution

It is understandable that many look to the spectacular success of the late twentieth-century "technological revolution" as a major source of hope for resolving the awesome problems facing humanity at the turn of the millennium. Unfortunately, as we have seen in the case of food supply, agricultural technology has not been able to keep up with the population explosion. There can be no doubt that recent decades have witnessed major breakthroughs in physics, electronics, and biotechnology, producing spectacular changes in the shape of society and of the workplace. High-tech and electronic technology have taken over in areas as diverse as education, business, medicine, food production, financial markets, and personal communication. Most of us rejoice in the immediate benefits of the technological revolution in making our work more efficient, saving us from many time-consuming, menial tasks, and enabling us to do business across continents in a fraction of the time it would have taken several decades ago.

At the same time, however, even the most beneficial and useful technological advances, whether in communications, automation, or biotechnology, carry with them a whole range of negative side effects. Furthermore, the extremely rapid pace of these radical changes has left us reeling and confused about the cultural and ethical implications of their effects on society. While both the invention of the computer and the discovery of DNA represent major turning points in the history of science and technology, they also open up many new questions about the impact of the information revolution and of genetic engineering on our lives. A brief overview of some of these major technological developments will throw light on the issue.

The Age of Information

At the heart of the information revolution at the approach of the new millennium is the successful synergetic combination of photonics (the high-tech control of electrical energy) with the science of fiber optics, which makes use of minute filaments of glass that can transmit information at superefficient speeds. We are told, for example, that the combined text of the *Encyclopaedia Britannica* and the Bible could be transmitted around the globe in less than two seconds by way of fiber cable.[7] This technology continues to bring about major advances in TV, office machines, automobile instrumentation, and telephone communications. All together, these radical technological transformations have created what we now call "the age of information" — an age which is still in its infancy at the dawn of the twenty-first century.

The full potential of information technology is best summed up in the idea of the "information superhighway." The superhighway is not yet a reality, but is already anticipated in the current technology of "personal computers, multimedia CD-ROM software, high-capacity cable television networks, wired and wireless telephone networks," and above all in the Internet. According to Bill Gates, the Internet system is the principal forerunner of the coming superhighway, much as the Oregon Trail marked the pioneer beginnings of the modern automobile highway system. The construction of a "full superhighway" is an expectation of the near future, probably of the next decade. It will first require the creation of a whole physical infrastructure, including the wide-scale installation of fiber-optic cable and the development of the appropriate software platforms.[8]

The steps that have already been taken in building the infrastructure for the superhighway involve applications and services so attractive that Gates predicts that financial investment in the future superhighway is a sure thing. Within a decade this expanded infrastructure will create "the real information highway," which "will combine the best qualities of both the telephone and the cable network systems."[9] The current Internet must undergo many changes before it is transformed into the information highway, but even now it is rapidly evolving and quickly becoming the most inexpensive means of communication across vast distances.

As in the case of any other great technological advance, the creation of the information superhighway at the beginning of the third millennium will not be without its significant downsides. Even now the use of the Internet raises very serious questions about the preservation of privacy, commercial confidentiality, national security, and ethical abuse. These issues are not likely to diminish in the future. The danger of the loss of privacy through computerization of information has already been deeply felt over the last several decades. Detailed information on the personal lives of U.S. citizens is already stored away in as many as eighteen federal, sixteen state and local, and twenty-five private-sector computers.[10] It is also very likely that whole wireless networks will emerge from our present-day cellular systems, even though wireless service runs obvious risks regarding both privacy and security. Fortunately, even today computer manufacturers are avidly searching for new and more effective methods of encrypting radio signals and preventing all sorts of eavesdropping and electronic spying. Record-breaking investing in Internet-related industries shows great public confidence in information technology. At the same time, however, the looming fears connected with the Y2K problem serve as a vivid reminder that technology can also run amok.

While the integration and unification of communication systems are absolutely essential for an effective information superhighway, they also leave the door open for unscrupulous leaders to gain governmental control over news agencies and hence over the free flow of ideas.[11] Legislators will face the big challenge of mediating between government agencies pressing for more personal data in the name of security and private citizens insisting on the protection of their personal freedoms. Increasing instances of the ethical abuse of the Internet by preying pedarasts and other psychopathic sexual deviates have stirred heated controversy over censorship and First Amendment rights. In the long run, only careful vigilance on the part of a technologically informed public will stand in the way of both government abuse and unbridled corruption by purveyors of pornography.

Bill Gates draws our attention to an even more far-reaching ethical dimension of the information revolution by insisting that the real success of the information highway will depend upon its availability to every citizen and not just to the privileged elite. Otherwise the information highway becomes just another "private road." From a practical perspective, Gates also argues that if the information highway does not succeed in including the majority of eligible users — across the economic board — it will become too costly to guarantee good, solid content.[12] Perhaps this is one of those cases where ethics and practicality go together.

In principle, because of its low operating cost (i.e., beyond the original investments), as well as the astonishing speed of its connections, the information highway should be able to bring the best sources of information and of education to whomever can access a computer. In this way, the highway could serve to neutralize geographic and socioeconomic borders, which tend to keep both nations and economic classes separate and unequal as regards educational opportunities. In a word, the superhighway of the future has the potential of contributing to the material and intellectual enrichment of all people, and of helping to bridge the enormous economic gap separating the rich and the poor. On the other hand, it is just this equality which tends to make all nations and cultures look alike, and in this way the superhighway presents a serious threat to the survival of traditional,

Modern technology can be adapted easily in premodern cultures. These Kayapo Indians recorded proceedings at the first meeting of the Indigenous Peoples of the Forest at Altamira, Brazil, in February 1989. Photo by Kit Miller.

pretechnological cultures. There is already much resentment in several parts of the world over the importation of American pop culture, especially through the impact of satellite-transmitted TV shows. No doubt, a balance will have to be struck between the advantages of global homogeneity and the preservation of local cultures.

Robotology and Automation: The New Industrial Revolution

With all the current discussion of the revolution in information technology, one might mistakenly conclude that the age of industry is something of the past. However, even a superficial look at the great variety of manufactured goods around which our daily lives revolve — from automobiles to the steel girders of office buildings — should be enough to convince us that industry is not a relic of the past. Even the computers upon which the information technology rests have to be manufactured by someone somewhere. What radically separates us from the past industrial age are the manner in which goods are manufactured and the globally dispersed location of industrial plants. Actually, advances in information technology have made it possible not only to manufacture practically anywhere on the globe, but also to do so in automated, cost-effective ways not previously imagined.

Automation is not a newcomer to the workplace. Manual laborers of the nineteenth century feared and hated machines as a very real threat to their job security. Today, however, with the advances in computer technology, automation has jumped ahead by leaps and bounds. Compared with the factory system which has dominated manufacturing until recently, the new automation radically changes the way in which industrial goods are made. The First Industrial Revolution, which created the factory system, is quickly being supplanted by the so-called Second Industrial Revolution, in which factory workers are replaced by robots and other forms of computer-driven automation. The first revolution was led by England; the second is being directed by Japan.

Robots, which are basically a form of artificial intelligence, are designed to perform very different kinds of tasks, and for this reason fall into a variety of categories, the principal of which are industrial robots, field robots, and intelligent robots. Industrial robots are fixed machines programmed to perform a number of automatic tasks, such as welding, cutting metal, painting, and so on. Today they are mainly used in auto factories. Field robots are capable of moving around with the help of sensors, and are usually employed for operations too dangerous for human workers, such as mining, undersea work, and so on. In the near future they will be used in agricultural work, where they will be known as agribots, which can wander around the fields or orchards harvesting crops. Finally, the most recent robotic development is in the field of artificial intelligence, or knowledge-based systems; these robots are designed to do problem solving after the analogy of the human brain. The military employs a number of such robots, such as the "smart weapons," like the Patriot missiles, which achieved much prominence during the Desert Storm War.[13] Finance and industry are already beginning to use "neural networks" that imitate the synergistic operations of the brain and nervous system. Chase Manhattan Bank has such a neural-net system in place for detecting credit card fraud, and washing machines in Japan have been programmed to analyze laundry water so as to determine both the appropriate washing time and the proper quantity of detergent.

The remnants of the factory system created by the Industrial

Revolution are gradually disappearing in several industrialized countries, as factory workers are continually replaced by robots and other automated equipment. All this, of course, is done with a view to making manufacturing more efficient, productive, and cost-effective. In the long run, the decision to use robots is primarily economic. Japan's leading place in robotics — as compared with the United States — reflects the economic advantage of robotics for the Japanese industrial system. Highly competitive firms in Japan's auto and electronic industries drove each other to invest in new machines, including robotics and artificial intelligence (AI), in order to increase productivity. Japan was also greatly helped by its legendary tradition of cooperation and harmony between management and labor unions.[14]

The switch to robotics is also encouraged by Japan's deep commitment to maintaining a homogeneous culture and society, which makes it more than hesitant to hire foreigners in order to fill out its workforce. Finally, at least up until recently, the traditional large companies in Japan have fostered the policy of lifetime employment, so that when workers have been displaced by automation, they have been routinely retrained and relocated within the corporation. The fact that Japan has, by and large, a well-educated workforce also makes this transition more feasible. American labor unions, on the other hand, view robots as a serious and unambiguous threat to employment. They have good reason for this suspicion in that American industry ordinarily does not retrain "excessed" workers for new types of employment: they are simply *laid off*. The robotics revolution is likely to take off wherever there is a high cost of labor, a shrinking pool of skilled workers, and, in general, a well-established "engineering culture." Wherever unemployment is high, on the other hand, there will be an understandable resistance to the industrial use of robots.[15]

This last assertion fairly well excludes the likelihood that indigenous robotic industries are likely to find a footing in developing countries and also makes it very tempting for multinational corporations to establish their own automated manufacturing in these same countries, where assembling and packaging for export can be done by basically unskilled workers at low labor cost. While the presence of multinational companies in the developing world has, on the whole, contributed to a rise in living standards, the large-scale use of robotics might ultimately create social havoc in terms of unemployment patterns. Especially vulnerable is the large potential labor force of unskilled young men, whose economic frustration can clearly pose a serious threat to stability not only in the region but globally as well. If this should happen, the long-term implications of the robotics revolution would prove devastating to economic development and threatening to political tranquillity.[16]

At a completely different level, some observers see the future developments in robotology and artificial intelligence as posing a serious challenge to human dignity and to religious belief. In blurring the lines between sophisticated machinery and human intelligence, technology has already encouraged the creation of "semi-intelligent agents," as well as speculation on guarantees of human immortality by way of passing on the core of human intelligence to computerized robots programmed to perpetual self-duplication. There can be little wonder that in some religious quarters ambitions of this sort constitute "playing God" with the human future.[17]

Biotechnology: Path to Salvation or Height of Arrogance?

If for those familiar with the potential of robotics, automation represents a form of "playing God," yet for others it is the rapid and startling developments in biotechnology that constitute the most flagrant form of modern idolatry. Both the wonders and the risks of biological engineering were brought dramatically before the public eye in the spring of 1996 with the cloning of a ewe named Dolly. News reports in journals and on TV were filled with stories on the scientific and technological breakthrough, which was quickly compared with the splitting of the atom in terms of its far-reaching implications for the future of humanity. There is no question that the cloning of a lamb from the cell of an adult sheep represented an enormous advance in reproductive technology. The astounding breakthrough, which took place at the Roslin Institute near Edinburgh, Scotland, is the latest achievement of biotechnology, which has taken off with breathtaking gusto since the scientific discovery of the DNA molecule earlier in the twentieth century.

Dr. Wilmut, the chief researcher on the project, and his small team of scientists at the institute were able to remove the nucleus, with its DNA from an unfertilized egg cell of a Scottish Blackface ewe, and replace it with an adult cell taken from the udder of a Finn Dorset ewe. With the help of electric impulses, they were able to coax the two cells to fuse and unite just as they would in fertilization. The resulting embryo was implanted in the uterus of another Blackface ewe, who eventually gave birth to a baby Finn Dorset lamb, named Dolly (in tribute to the American country singer Dolly Parton). Geneticists had previously cloned live frogs from embryonic cells, but had never been able to reproduce cloned animals from an adult cell, because unlike the embryonic cells, adult cells have already been differentiated to produce particular body parts. Since only use of an adult cell gives science the opportunity to know what it is actually cloning, the results at Roslin were clearly revolutionary.

The cloning of Dolly — the exact genetic carbon copy of her mother — also set the stage for many new, socially beneficial possibilities in genetic engineering. With the help of this same basic technology science will be able (1) to reverse the loss of endangered species, (2) to engineer the production of milk laced with important enzymes and drugs for pharmaceutical use, (3) to breed a new generation of cows, sheep, and chickens with greater capacity for producing milk, wool, and eggs respectively, and (4) to meet the growing demand for replacement of human body parts. (Even now biotechnology is on the brink of using fetal surgery and tissue engineering to cure birth defects in infants and to produce parts for organ transplants.) While these examples alone dramatically illustrate the positive social and environmental potential of biotechnology, the fourth instance already implies the use of this technology in the awesome and chilling prospect of producing human clones. After all, if we can clone sheep, we can clone people too.[18] For that reason, no sooner had the news of Dolly hit the press than a very heated ethical debate began to rage throughout the media.

So overwhelming in scope are the implications of human cloning that Bill Clinton, the president of the United States, almost immediately called for a moratorium on the use of this technology in human experiments. Talk about the temptation to play God! There is little wonder that the cloning breakthrough created such widespread, emotional reaction. A rather thoughtful article in *Time* magazine zeroed in on the heart of the issue with the question, "Can souls be Xeroxed?"[19] Obviously, the whole idea of human cloning touches all of us in the human family and profoundly arouses our instinctive curiosity, our highest aspirations, as well as our deepest fears. It points very dramatically to the need of tempering the capacity of biotechnology with the demands of preserving human dignity and high ethical standards.

Biotechnology is a much broader category than genetic cloning, for it includes "any technique that uses living organisms or processes to make or modify products, to improve plants or animals or to develop microorganisms for specific uses."[20] It has already made significant contributions to the advance of modern medicine and is a very important player in the struggle to keep agricultural and other food production up to carrying capacity for the exploding population.

While it is commendable that governments are making significant capital investments in the biotechnological revolution, they ought not to overlook the negative side of the enterprise. We already know, for example, that growth hormones given to hogs have proven dangerous in human consumption and that the cultivation of a single genetically engineered species of plant runs the serious risk of losing a whole harvest through blight or disease caused by a resistant bacterial strain. Biotech agriculture can also serve as an excuse for ignoring environmental reforms in the hope that new crop species, able to survive even in poor environmental conditions, will be developed. Furthermore, biotechnology contains within itself the built-in temptation of treating all of nature, including biological mechanisms, as "raw material for social manipulation."[21]

There is no doubt a certain irony that in a society so technologically advanced, much of the world still goes hungry and that this situation is likely to deteriorate more in the foreseeable future. The twin challenges of feeding the world and of channeling the technological revolution in humanly satisfying directions certainly will continue as major concerns into the new millennium. In the following chapter we will examine two other areas of potential global disharmony that also present serious challenges to the human future.

– 3 –

Disharmony with Nature and Neighbor

Since the end of World War II, less developed nations throughout the world, especially in Asia, Africa, and Latin America, have been engaged in a titanic struggle to achieve modernization of their economy and development of their industrial output. Some of these nations have actually become significant industrial powers; others have made much progress; and still others have remained mired in traditional structures inimical to modernization. All have learned, however, that successful modernization carries with it some devastating consequences in terms of environmental destruction and exposure to new threats to human survival resulting from violence, racism, new diseases, and political instability. All these consequences suggest some growing form of disharmony either with nature or within society. We look first at the difficult relationship between economic globalization and ecological responsibility.

Economy and Ecology: The Delicate Balance

The ability of peoples throughout the world to take advantage of the new technologies discussed in the previous chapter depends very much upon their economic strength. Technology today, coupled with the current uneven patterns of population growth, will more than likely continue to produce both winners and losers.[1] Despite the startling advances in biotechnology, information communications, and global economics, the gap between the rich nations and the poor is likely to grow even larger. Since the end of World War II, the global economy has grown more than it ever has in all of world history. Between 1950 and 1980, for example, the world's real GNP quadrupled, from two trillion to about eight trillion U.S. dollars.[2] By and large, however, this growth and prosperity have benefited only people living on a small portion of the globe, primarily those in advanced industrial economies. The full significance of this resulting economic gap is well illustrated by the fact that we approach the twenty-first century with more than a billion people living in poverty, that is, people striving to survive on less than $370 a year. If this gap continues to grow, as is quite likely, the beginning of the new century will witness an enormous migration from undeveloped, overcrowded, economically dependent nations to the richer nations of the globe. We have already seen signs of this coming social upheaval and are beginning to detect in both Europe and America a strong backlash against what is perceived by many as a very serious cultural and economic threat. In the meantime, the continued advances in telecommunications will only increase the anger of the have-nots both in developing and in industrialized societies[3] by continually reminding them of the advantages and material goods which they do not share.

During the same period of economic growth following World War II, the economies of the world quickly became more global and interconnected. This came about not by chance but by the determination to set up a *world trading system* that would be free of undue protectionist restrictions and unhampered by economic and political instability. Reinforced by more recent advances in communications technology and the accompanying revolution in the world of finances, the economic system has evolved into a full-scale global network, in which industry and technology are mainly in the hands of a newly emerged business entity called the "multinational corporation." By definition the multinational corporation is a "borderless world," in which the only loyalties and commitments are to the corporation and not to the nation of origin or to the industrial locations in which it operates. The underlying theory is that anything can be made in any part of the world. As a result, international joint ventures in business have become more and more common as the pressure to compete globally is felt more sharply throughout the business world.[4]

In the present global marketplace, international finance has been streamlined and rationalized by the phenomenon of immediate electronic transactions. As a result trading goes on in major world markets twenty-four hours a day, creating a single financial market. This tight interconnection can be seen clearly in the powerful chain reactions to financial developments anywhere in the globe. A rapid growth in European and Asian markets immediately followed in the wake of the financial boom of Wall Street in the early months of 1997. But on October 23 of the same year a serious currency crisis in the Asian markets, starting with a dramatic plunge of Hong Kong's Hang Seng Index (1,212 points), drove markets down drastically throughout the globe. Loss of confidence in Hong Kong's economy and in the political stability of Thailand created a chain-reaction stock plunge in Japan, the United States, Germany, England, and Mexico, but especially in the newly emerging markets of Latin America. A similar monetary crisis hit the global markets the following year, following currency devaluation in Indonesia and economic meltdown in Russia. The speedy global impact of these financial debacles dramatizes the downside of economic connectedness.[5]

Enthusiasts of globalization claim that, in the long run, it will inevitably raise the standards of living in poor countries, while providing significant economic benefits to the citizens of developed nations. Critics, however, stress the dark side of globalization, depicting it as an ideology of the powerful and the wealthy which ultimately will only add to economic inequity as well as to cultural homogenization. What is certainly clear is that the rational market, left to its own devices, is concerned neither with social justice nor with fairness.[6]

Another big problem created by the globalization of the economy and the consequent emergence of a single world market is that this global market is basically indifferent to the necessity of maintaining "an environmentally sustainable economy."[7] As the cold, rational demands of the market economy and the advances in information technology continue to lay workers off or force them into low-paying jobs, there is often little sympathy among much of the population for reforms geared to protecting and preserving the *environment* — especially if they should be at the expense of employment and economic prosperity. Multinational corporations also have a record of establishing

A young woman and a child walk in a recently destroyed rain forest near Belim, Brazil. Photo by Sean Sprague.

plants in countries with the least demanding environmental restrictions. Globalization on the whole has not been friendly to the environment.

There is no question, on the other hand, that the growth of the global economy has contributed greatly to raising the standard of living in various parts of the world. But even a cursory look at the newly industrialized economies of East Asia shows that they have fully joined their European and American counterparts in a persistent demand for ores, gas, timber, and other natural resources from the developing nations. Paul Kennedy reminds us that once the average Korean reaches a European standard of living, he or she will consume the same amount of energy and foodstuffs and create an equal amount of atmospheric pollution. Should the Chinese join this company as well, their per capita consumption of resources could easily bring about an environmental crisis of enormous magnitude.[8] The whole issue of economic development and ecological damage is greatly exasperated when we recall that the world's population is expected to quadruple by the year 2025.

The rapid spread of industrialization, even to developing countries, and the large-scale use of industrial products such as fertilizer have wreaked all kinds of havoc on the environment. Ecological destruction also results from large-scale deforestation, the acidification of primal forests, the pollution of waterways and aquifers, the dangerous emissions of CO_2, methane, and other greenhouse gases into the atmosphere, as well as the disposal of hazardous wastes into the environment. The extent of this damage can be somewhat gauged by the ongoing loss of fifty thousand living species a year through the destruction of the tropical rain forests and of other natural ecosystems.[9]

The largest single threat to the thin "film of life" which covers this planet is what scientists and concerned environmentalists have been calling "global warming" — a direct consequence of economic activities. As a result of the greenhouse effect created by the emissions of CO_2 (carbon) and CFCs (chlorofluorocarbons), the overall global temperature has already jumped somewhere between 0.3 and 0.7 percent, and the rate of climate change going into the next century is predicted to be greater than any previous warming since the end of the Ice Age.[10] The effects of global warming on the earth's environment could prove devastating, causing the sea level to rise fifteen to ninety-five centimeters by 2100, creating enormous flooding and related damage. Many important ecosystems will decline or fragment, bringing about the destruction of innumerable species.[11] Finally, environmental damage never remains local but invariably has significant global repercussions.

After years of dispute, the reality of the greenhouse effect and its highly deleterious consequences for the planet were given official recognition by the world's leaders at the Rio Earth Summit of 1992. While much has been accomplished since Rio, the 1997 follow-up called Rio+5 also made it clear that the actual commitment of governments, including the United States, to take significant steps to limit the emission of greenhouse gases has been quite negligible. The results of the International Global Climate Conference held in Kyoto in December 1997 were at best ambiguous. While some consensus was reached on controlling the emission of specific greenhouse gases, sharp philosophical differences continued to divide the attitude of industrialized countries from that of their later-developing counterparts.[12] Basically, Third World and developing countries consider the steps taken by developed nations as inadequate for controlling the emissions of heat-trapping gases. Clearly, any successful program for the containment of environmental hazard will require the cooperative efforts of both rich and poor nations, but, even more, a proper moral frame of human communities throughout the globe.

Violence, Disease, and Other Forms of Destabilization

Of course, food scarcity, unemployment, human cloning, as well as environmental degradation are all in their own way serious potential threats to human life and survival. But here I want to focus on the more immediate forms of menace, such as violent crime, terrorism, religio-ethnic conflict, and epidemic disease. I will also include under this general heading potentially violent and always destabilizing threats to community cohesion such as racial intolerance, cultural conflict, and intrareligious tension.

Crime, Drugs, and Violence

Any analysis of the special problems facing the human family at the outset of the twenty-first century would be out of touch with daily living, both in developed and less-developed countries, if it did not address head-on the threat of violent crime. Even though recent statistics released by the U.S. Department of Justice show a slight decrease in violent crimes in very recent years,[13] polls are also showing that Americans feel more concerned than ever about the threat of violence to themselves and to their families. The ongoing prosperity of the security industry also serves as a measure of the extent of this anxiety about violent crime. The anxiety is not without basis, for even though the number of violent crimes in the United States decreased by 3 percent between 1994 and 1995 and the last several years have seen a distinct decrease of criminal assault in major urban areas, the long-term statistics from 1973 to the present, provided by the Bureau of Justice's *Criminal Victimization Survey,* show that violent crime — including rapes, robberies, murder, and assaults — is still very much on the increase.

Property crime in the United States in 1995 has been estimated at $15.1 billion. On the average, one murder was committed every twenty-four seconds, one forcible rape every five minutes, one robbery every fifty-four seconds, and one aggravated assault every twenty-nine seconds.[14] Over the past twenty years injuries to crime victims have increased by 10 percent, with an average of 2.2 million crime victims injured each year. The use of firearms in general and of hand guns in particular in the commission of violent crime has increased significantly over this same period. Apart from the questions of statistical reports and public sentiment on the issue, there can be no doubt that violent crime remains extremely costly in the United States, both in terms of personal suffering and in terms of financial burden. While violent crime has been on the decrease in general, it has been on the rise among teenage gangs, who increasingly create a serious safety problem, especially in the inner city of large urban communities. By the same token, this same age group is also the greatest victim of violent crime. For young African American males and females (ages fifteen to twenty-four), for example, homicide is now the leading cause of death.

The *National Crime Victimization Survey of 1973–1992* shows that a third of the victims of violence "perceived that the offender ... had been using drugs or alcohol or both at the time of the offense."[15] Alcohol abuse makes its own substantial contribution to violence, especially in the areas of spousal abuse, aggravated assault, and injuries resulting from drunken driving. The use and sale of illicit drugs, however, create a whole alternative culture which is inherently dependent on the use of criminal violence. According to the Government Accounting Office (GAO), 20 percent of men in prison in the early 1990s had been charged with various drug violations, and one of every three women in prison had been incarcerated for drug crimes. Since the 1970s, violent crime committed for the sake of a "drug fix" and deaths resulting from shoot-outs between competing drug dealers or with law officers have become a standard menace in our society.

Street gangs which thrive on the illegal drug trade are highly organized and are found in all major American cities, and when gang members are deported to their countries of origin, they often establish their local branches of the U.S. gangs.[16] Billions of dollars are spent each year in efforts at drug interdiction, especially in the seemingly hopeless war against international drug cartels. Yet since 1995 the use of illegal drugs has continued to rise rapidly, and there has been a steady increase of drug-related violent juvenile crime, which, if unchecked, will lead to a doubling of violent crime by 2010.[17] The dilemmas created by the war against drugs have produced a worldwide debate over the decriminalization of so-called recreational drugs and over the relative merits of drug interdiction and drug rehabilitation.

Terrorism and Religious Violence

Perhaps there has been no sadder nor more discouraging instance of religiously inspired violence in recent years than the assassination of the Israeli prime minister Yitzhak Rabin on November 4, 1995. Equally horrifying atrocities had been committed during this same period by extremist Arabs against Israelis and vice versa. But this was a Jewish leader — a much-decorated commander of the Israeli army — who was mercilessly gunned down by one of his own people. Rabin — in conjunction with the Labor Party and his foreign minister, Shimon Peres — had decided to take a risk for peace, and together with Palestinian leader Yasir Arafat and Jordan's King Hussein had shocked the world with the sensational news of a Palestinian-Israeli peace accord. This decision had created a euphoric state of hopefulness for peace-lovers throughout the world, but also generated intense opposition from many within Israel. The fatal shot of the fanatic's gun quickly turned that brief moment of light into one of dark despair and disbelief at the power and determination of the forces of destruction.[18]

The violent encounters between Muslims and Hindus over the Babri Mosque in the city of Ayodha, India; slaughter in the Golden Temple of Amritsar by Indian troops sent to crush Sikh nationalists holed up there; the Islamic Intifada in Palestine; the continued bloodletting between the Buddhist Sinhalese majority and the Tamil Hindu minority in Sri Lanka; the still-unresolved guerrilla warfare between Catholic IRA militants and Protestant extremists in Northern Ireland; bloody massacres of unarmed villagers by Muslim fundamentalists in Algeria; the recent vicious war between Russia and its Muslim minority in Chechen; as well as more current events, such as the blasphemous provocation by an Israeli woman who publicly depicted Muhammad as a pig and the summer 1997 suicide bombing by Hamas extremists in a Jerusalem market — these are among the many instances of religiously

Terrorists have at their disposal the means to strike at the interests of powerful states, thus raising the stakes in the search for security and spreading widely a sense that world order is precarious, as was dramatically shown in the August 7, 1998, bombing of the U.S. embassy in Nairobi, Kenya. Photo by Khalil Senosi.

inspired violence that cast dark shadows over human civilization in the closing decades of the twentieth century. Such episodes make it extremely likely that religiously inspired terrorism will remain a serious force of destruction as we move into the new century.

Terrorism, whether religiously based or otherwise, continues to present a very deadly and costly threat to human life and social stability in these waning years of the century. The menace of a terrorist use of biological, chemical, or nuclear weapons as well as the possibility of poisoning food or water supplies reveal the vulnerability of global society to terrorist attack. The bombings of the World Trade Center in New York in 1993 and of the federal building in Oklahoma City in 1995 brought the specter of "domestic terrorism" vividly before the eyes of the American public in an unprecedented way. The year 1996 has been recognized as a boon year for international terrorism. Today's citizens worldwide have good reason to fear the violence of terrorist and other criminal attacks.

Social Conflict: Racism, Ethnic Violence, Culture Wars, the Abortion Controversy

While the latter half of the twentieth century has certainly recorded marvelous successes in the fight against racism and the injustice that it breeds, new forms of racial tension continue to rise and to express themselves in violent ways. Despite real advances in civil rights for African Americans and other minorities in the United States, racial hatred in the form of black church burnings, police brutality, and racial rioting continues to create the deep divisions in American society that became so disturbingly apparent during the criminal trial of O. J. Simpson. Elsewhere, racial discrimination even in the so-called color blind societies of Brazil and the Caribbean islands continues to operate in subtle and not so subtle ways. Racism was clearly dealt a serious blow by the recent collapse of the apartheid system in South Africa, and the ongoing trials in the postapartheid period reveal the depths of cruelty and inhumaneness that had been practiced against the black majority. The indictment of four New York City police officers in August 1997 for the sadistic and brutal torture of Abner Luima, a Haitian immigrant, has provided yet another reminder that the ugly specter of racial brutality cannot be dismissed as a shameful memory from a remote past.

Apart from black-white tensions, our contemporary multicultural society has also experienced many other kinds of cultural tensions, ranging from horrific acts of genocide in Bosnia, to hostility and violence toward Arab and Turkish immigrants in Europe, to gender battles over women's rights, gay rights, sexual harassment, and the role of homosexuals and of women in the military. Even more persistent and equally visceral, in the United States, is the abortion controversy, which threatens to tear the nation apart, as religiously committed pro-lifers brand their pro-choice opponents as ungodly murderers of the innocent, and the defenders of pro-choice depict their adversaries as obsessive and violent fanatics.

On the religious front, Orthodox Jews have denounced as inauthentic the religious beliefs and practices of the other main Jewish branches. Internal dissensions have seriously beset a number of Christian denominations, including the Baptist Convention, the Presbyterian Church, the Episcopal Church, and the Catholic Church. The bitterness of this internal factionalism leaves little room for dialogue and gives scant hope for a harmonious resolution of these conflicts in the coming century.

The Devastation of AIDS and Other Infectious Diseases

Despite the enormous progress in medicine and in biotechnology during the latter part of this century, a whole host of new "infectious diseases" has created very serious health threats in both developing and developed countries throughout the world. Serious diseases, such as malaria, cholera, yellow fever, tuberculosis, and hepatitis, that were once considered under control are now reappearing in increasingly frequent incidences. Americans felt terrorized in 1994 by an outbreak of a flesh-eating infection called Step-A, and Europe has been in a health and agricultural turmoil since 1996 as a result of the spread of "mad cow" disease. Other devastating infections little known before, such as Ebola, Lassa, dengue, and hanta-virus, which produce a deadly pulmonary syndrome, producing hemorrhage, high fevers, and horribly painful death, are clearly on the rise, especially in the less-developed nations of the world.[19]

Through travel and commerce even these once exotic and rare diseases are easily spread worldwide. A recent statement of Nobel laureate Dr. Joshua Lederberg dramatically calls attention to the global health threat caused by these emerging diseases: "The microbe that felled one child in a distant continent yesterday can reach yours today and seed a global pandemic tomorrow."[20] We are also paying the price for the effective but unrestrained use of antimicrobial drugs (antibiotics) with the ever-increasing appearance of drug-resisting pathogens (the so-called superbugs), of the kind that cause malaria, tuberculosis, gonorrhea, pneumonia, and various hospital-acquired infections.[21] Today infectious diseases still remain the leading cause of death worldwide, and their economic cost in terms of direct treatment and of lost productivity reaches many billions of dollars annually.

By far the most devastating of the newly emergent diseases has been AIDS, which like TB is often transmitted through the infected needles of drug users. AIDS, caused by a human immunodeficiency virus (HIV), which leaves the body unable to fight sicknesses, has become *the* "plague" of our times. Since eight or nine years might pass before the symptoms of the infection will appear, it is very difficult to determine the demographic impact of the disease. It also means that many individuals, unaware of their own infection, pass on the virus to unsuspecting victims. To graphically illustrate the dilemma and the threat of the disease, Paul Kennedy compares those who have AIDS with the tip of an iceberg which floats above the water, whereas the much deadlier aspect of the disease comes from the many unknown HIV-positive persons who, like the larger part of the iceberg, remain unobserved and undetected beneath the sea.[22]

At the eleventh International Conference on AIDS, held in Vancouver in July 1996, it was announced that approximately twenty-two million people worldwide carry the AIDS virus and that about eighty-five hundred are infected each day. In the United States, about one person in three hundred is HIV-infected, whereas in the African countries of Botswana, Zambia, Zimbabwe, Uganda, and Malawi, at least one in ten adults carries the virus. Projections for AIDS in the coming century are truly frightening. The World Health Organization predicts that as many as forty million people will be HIV-positive worldwide by the year 2000. Some AIDS researchers are convinced that the infected population in Africa is so great that by the year 2010 the population of the continent will be on the decline. A recent Harvard epidemiological study expects the future devastation of AIDS to be even greater in Asia than in Africa.[23]

The cost of AIDS not only touches human life and health, but also places an enormous drain on the economy. For example, the cost of treating AIDS and HIV patients in the United States in 1995 was $15.2 billion. A full drug treatment for an individual AIDS victim costs up to $1,000 per day, and, in fact, about $38,000 dollars are spent annually on treating each AIDS and HIV patient in the United States. Experts at the recent World Economic Forum in Davos, Switzerland, estimated that by 2005 the cost of AIDS "could depress the global economy by as much as 4 percent of the US gross domestic product."[24] The irony of the situation is that the great majority of the victims of AIDS are in poor countries, where it is impossible to afford these skyrocketing financial costs. Most African countries, for example, can afford less than $10 per day for each AIDS patient.

Currently this inequity has set off a raging debate about a trial test for effectiveness of the anti-AIDS drug AZT for pregnant mothers in the Ivory Coast. In this test half of the AIDS-infected women were given a placebo in an experiment to assess the short-term use of the drug.[25] Most of the African mothers were happy to have the fifty-fifty chance that they otherwise would not have had. Such a test would hardly have been given in an affluent, developed country. Once again, with the issue of AIDS, the gap between rich and poor is drawn in an extremely dramatic way, and it is far from an exaggeration to say that AIDS is an epidemic or plague that threatens the very existence of human life on the planet.[26]

A Rallying Point for the Third Millennium?

These urgent problems which we face as we stand on the frontier of the new century are all very serious challenges which require a thoughtful, dedicated, and intelligent human response. Unanswered, each of these issues is capable of creating ever-increasing disorder and chaos. Because these challenges are so diverse and distinctive, they require a variety of specialized and expert responses, but taken as a whole, they all seem to reflect some fundamental discord or disharmony in nature and in society. For this reason any complete and adequate solution to these global concerns will require collaborative efforts toward constructing a more harmonious relationship with nature, the environment, the emerging technologies, the global economy, and among the diverse ethnic, racial, and religious components of the human family.

A high level of international cooperation toward guaranteeing an adequate food supply, despite the growing encroachments of industrialization and urbanization on productive crop land, will be extremely urgent. Similar cooperation will be required to achieve a greater balance between our natural resources and the growth of the world's population and between new agricultural and fishing technologies and the ability of the earth to refurbish its natural resources. A greater harmony is also needed between progress in information and biotechnology, on the one hand, and the obligation of preserving human dignity and legitimate cultural diversity, on the other. Automation in industrial production also demands new cooperative efforts between industry and labor, and enthusiasm for economic globalization will have to be balanced by concern for local development and ecological responsibilities. Managing the environmental threat calls for an unprecedented alliance between industrialized and developing nations, as well as a universal determination to respect the fragility of the earth.

The continuing menace of crime- and drug-related violence, especially in our urban centers, cannot be met by law enforcement alone but will require an equally resolute effort to attack the poverty, economic inequity, and drug addiction which nourish criminal behavior. Religious wars and ethnic strife will not be checked without a much more heightened awareness of the unity of the human family. Cooperation among the nations of the world will be an absolute prerequisite for combating the ruthless destructiveness of international terrorism. The control of the emerging infectious diseases is impossible without an extraordinary level of interaction between the medical profession and the world's political leaders. The battle against AIDS, in particular, requires a concerted effort from governments, the medical profession, religious organizations, caregivers, and all segments of the community.

Serious reflection on the challenges of the coming century makes it very clear that a model of universal harmony must replace one of conflict and competition if the new century is to see real progress in overcoming the discord and dissonance that pervade so many crucial areas of life in the late twentieth century. Global cooperation in responding to the Y2K crisis may well provide the first opportunity toward developing such a model.

We have seen that Christian Europe approached the first millennial divide joined in solidarity by an enthusiastic and devout commitment to promoting *the peace of God*. At the outset of the second millennial crossing, we stand in need of our own moral rallying point. What could be a better candidate for a new millennial banner to guide us and inspire us on our march into the twenty-first century than *the pursuit of global harmony*? The ramifications of such a pursuit will be explored in the closing pages of this book.

In the meantime, in the following chapter, we shall see that some religious leaders in the closing years of the twentieth century do indeed view the arrival of the new millennium as an occasion for a worldwide spiritual renewal and a corresponding commitment to seek solutions to the outstanding problems of our epoch.

Still other religiously based millennial movements look upon the goal of international cooperation and global harmony with suspicion and distrust — as unrealistic, illusory, and even dangerous. In fact, for them the whole ideal of global harmony is a great deception, totally in conflict with the expectations of apocalyptic biblical prophecy.

– 4 –

The Millennial Religious Response

Religious responses to the challenges of the third millennium or the bimillennial celebration of the "birth of Christ" vary greatly in outlook, interpretation, and practical planning. Despite this notable diversity in the way different religious groups are preparing themselves for the arrival of the new millennial divide, they usually share at least two common traits: (1) a powerful sense of urgency, based on the conviction that an epochal event is in the making, and (2) a sense that the arrival of the year 2000 has a profound religious significance requiring some sort of radical personal transformation. To better grasp this broad range of responses, it might be helpful to organize them into several clearly identifiable categories, such as fanatical or extremist responses, doomsday prophecies, grassroots apocalyptic beliefs, and mainline Christian preparations. In this chapter we will explore each of these types of millennial response in turn.

Reactions from the Fanatical Fringe

Recent years have witnessed several millennial-inspired apocalyptic movements that have shocked, terrorized, or disgusted decent people everywhere. The fanatical behavior these movements share has no respect for borders or cultural differences, and the tragedies they have produced are clearly global in range. Unfortunately, similar scenarios may well be repeated again in other world locations even before this book appears in print.

The Tragedy of the Solar Temple

The breaking story of a coordinated mass suicide/murder caught the world by shock in the fall of 1994. Members of a secret sect, apparently both religious and magical in nature, known as the Order of the Solar Temple had arranged for fiery holocausts to occur simultaneously both in Quebec and in Suisse Romande (French-speaking Switzerland). The organization, little known outside European occult and theosophic circles, mystically traced its roots back to the medieval monastic-chivalric order of the Knights Templar.

According to an old legend, a few of the knights had miraculously escaped from the brutal suppression of the order in the fourteenth century. In the year 1312, Philip the Fair of France, driven by envy and greed and with the spiritual support of papal authority, brutally suppressed the order and had fifty-four knights publicly burnt at the stake. According to the old Templar legend, the few knights who managed to escape found their way to Ethiopia. Some of the principal leaders of the modern Templar movement are believed to be the direct descendants of these knights. The power of the legend became evident in the 1994 coordinated "suicides," in which, had it not been for the unforeseen escape of one of the intended victims, the death toll would have reached exactly fifty-four — all by fiery conflagration.

The secret Templar societies date back hundreds of years in France, Belgium, Spain, and Portugal, but were reorganized and revitalized in the 1960s by the French charismatic leader Jacques Breyer, who not only reinforced the mythological links with the Knights Templars, but was also responsible for introducing a strongly apocalyptic worldview into the group by predicting the imminent end of the world and the glorious return of the "Solar Christ" for the year 1994.[1]

Unlike more typical apocalyptic groups, the membership ranks of the Solar Temple included a good percentage of elite professionals, including editors, public officials, journalists, physicians, and business entrepreneurs. The apocalypticism of the Solar Temple was both antinomian and anti-establishmentarian, despite the fact that its members were not primarily recruited from the economically and socially disenfranchised. Documents and letters discovered after the tragedy point to close similarities with the Branch Davidians and the Montana Freemen and other such millennial groups.[2] The mass self-execution of October 1994 has been shown to have resulted from a strong conviction in the imminent demise of the universe, coupled with a deep resentment against the powers of government. The act of self-destruction was at once an ill-contrived venture toward discovering a better life and a desperate protest against the world as it is.

Apocalypse on the Tokyo Subway

Less than a year after the Solar Temple catastrophe a nerve gas attack on the Tokyo subway, which left twelve dead and thousands injured, made it very clear that we had not witnessed the end of apocalyptic millennialism gone awry. Leaders of a bizarre, new, Buddhist-based sect called Aum Shinrikyo (Supreme Truth) were quickly indicted as responsible for this horrendous crime of public terrorism.

The principal defendant in the indictment is the charismatic, authoritarian cult leader, Shoko Asahara, who claimed extraordinary preternatural powers, such as levitation, and who attempted direct communication to the brainwaves of his disciples. Asahara suffered from a serious visual handicap and also lacked the intellectual abilities to gain admission into Tokyo University, which would have been his passport into the elite circles of Japanese society, which he soon began to hate with a vengeance. Asahara successfully won new recruits to Aum Shinrikyo, especially from among the newly emerging class called *otaku* — which is made up primarily of maladjusted young people who have been unable to find a place in the mainstream.[3]

Initially Aum Shinrikyo was passive and inner-directed, stressing a meditative discipline that would protect members from the evils and dangers of the modern world. Increasingly, however, Aum members became obsessed with the fear of a nuclear war between the United States and the Soviet Union, and Asahara began predicting a major nuclear holocaust for the year 1999. He found further justification both for his apocalyptic vision of the end-times and for a more aggressive response to what he felt was a hopelessly corrupt government and radically evil society. Once having concluded that only violence and destruction could bring down this evil system and prepare the way for a better world, Aum Shinrikyo did not hesitate to begin its violent campaign against the world with its deadly nerve gas (sarin) attack on the Tokyo subway. Amid the reams of evidence and the confusion of diverging reports which will no doubt accompany this Japanese trial of the century, it is important to keep in mind the observation of two prominent Japanese journalists that "the basic force behind Aum is to accelerate the advent of the millennium."[4] Millennialism always has the potential of being distorted into a force of destruction.

Comets, Spaceships, and Heaven's Gate

The force of the above statement was further confirmed by the mass suicide of thirty-nine members of the Heaven's Gate cult in late March 1997. Heavenly signs have played a central role in apocalyptic warnings and omens as far back as biblical times and beyond. Such was to be the case once again when the Hale-Bopp comet appeared majestically and vividly in the March night sky. At least for a small cult named Heaven's Gate, led by a certain Marshall Herff Applewhite, the appearance of the comet was a sure sign that "deliverance was near." Given the cult's unique mix of biblical belief and UFO theology, it was not inconsistent with its long-held tenets to expect salvation from a spacecraft that would take cult members to a higher dimension.[5]

Lutheran theologian Ted Peters had identified the sect as "a more virulent form of UFO theology" as early as the 1970s. In a very informative book, published in 1977, called *UFO's: God's Chariots?* Peters had identified Applewhite and his then partner, Bonnie Trusdale Nettles, as the leaders of the movement. The two leaders were known variously as "The Two" (derived from the two witnesses of Revelation 11) or as Bo and Peep (later to be changed to Do and Ti). Even in those early days, the cult was obsessed with spaceships and the Book of Revelation. They understood both the "cloud of light" in which Jesus ascended into heaven as well as the cloud on which the two resurrected witnesses of Revelation 11 were carried aloft "in the sight of their foes" (Rev. 11:11–12) as UFOs on a religious mission. The followers of "The Two" (later organized as Heaven's Gate) could expect a similar transformation from the human level to a higher level of existence on another planet, once again with the necessary transportation provided by a UFO.[6] Like other millennial groups, they felt the urgency for immediate deliverance from a worldly existence, in the conviction that the end-times predicted in Revelation were now at the threshold.

In late March the brilliant glow of the Hale-Bopp comet convinced these highly susceptible disciples — then living a strict communal life in the suburbs of San Diego — that a UFO was hiding behind the comet and would soon descend to earth to gather the faithful members of Heaven's Gate and transport them to their celestial abode. In order to be ready for this spiritual as well as physical voyage to a higher kingdom, they would have to shed their "containers" or "vehicles" (i.e., their physical bodies), which is just what they did with the help of phenobarbital-laced pudding chased with vodka. The theatrically orchestrated suicide of these thirty-nine cultists has left commentators deeply troubled about what other millennialist-inspired tragedies might lie in store as we get closer to the year 2000.[7]

Doomsday Preachers

Even Americans with little knowledge or little interest in biblical matters are at least vaguely familiar with the many evangelical preachers who conduct either TV or radio ministries. No doubt, too, the political initiatives of Pat Robertson and Jerry Falwell in recent years, as well as some of the scandals that have rocked these ministries as of late (the Jimmy Swaggart and Jim Bakker cases immediately come to mind), have called public attention to this significant religious presence in American culture. These sensational aberrations notwithstanding, there is no reason to believe that the majority of these prophecy teachers are not sincerely convinced of the message they so enthusiastically communicate.

Despite differences of style, the biblical prophecy preachers uniformly convey a message of imminent global catastrophe from which there is no chance of deliverance short of a sincere and fervent commitment to Jesus Christ as personal Savior. Across the board, these evangelists not only are apocalyptic in their doomsday preaching, but in varying degrees are also convinced millennialists who teach that the terrible tribulations which are inevitably on the near horizon will serve as a prelude to the return of Christ and the establishment of his triumphant millennial kingdom on earth.

Unlike many of their nineteenth-century predecessors, today's prophecy preachers, for the most part, avoid the temptation of making specific predictions of times or dates for the end-time scenario. They are, nevertheless, of one voice that the biblical predictions of impending apocalyptic calamities are poised to find their fulfillment somewhere around the year 2000. Today with the help of the modern media, doomsday prophecy preachers abound. A select few of them, such as Hal Lindsey, Jack Van Impe, John F. Walvoord, and Grant R. Jeffrey, have achieved such special status and respect, especially in evangelical Christian circles, that their theological speculations — even the seemingly far-fetched ones — strike a note of credibility among their followers and clearly respond to a real need at the grassroots congregational level.

These prophecy superstars display an extraordinary talent for communicating their message through live media, video tapes, and books. While each has his own special emphasis and particular style, as a group they show a remarkable convergence of ideas in their central prophecy teachings. The following sketch, drawn from the writings, tapes, and ministries of leading prophecy evangelists, is meant to give a representative picture of the core of these teachings today.

Perilous Times and Signs of the End

With the 1970 publication of his very successful and highly popular book, *The Late Great Planet Earth*,[8] Hal Lindsey won his fame as a leading prophecy teacher. His genius was his remarkable ability to relate biblical prophecy to the realities and the fears of nuclear holocaust. Lindsey, whose seminal work has set the tone for much subsequent biblical prophecy teaching, has recently attempted to revise and update his apocalyptic message in a new work entitled *Planet Earth — 2000 A.D*. In this latest application of biblical prophecy to current events, Lindsey looks even beyond the nuclear threat to our daily world of drugs, violent crime, ethnic cleansing, "twisted morality," false religion, natural disasters, and the global spread of AIDS and other infectious diseases to conclude that we are living in times of "unprecedented peril."[9] When we add to this the picture of political instability, especially in the Middle East, he is persuaded that we are now living in the biblical Last Days.

The Millennial Religious Response

In popular American religious culture, televangelism plays a major role in spreading millennialist interpretations of contemporary events. Ignored or disdained by the elites, televangelists such as Jack Van Impe have enormous impact on the way ordinary persons look at the millennium.

Jack Van Impe and his wife, Rexella, a very influential televangelist team, see additional unmistakable signs of global peril in the potential nuclear threat of a very unstable Russia, particularly in view of recent weapons agreements it has made with Iran. Russia, they claim, is still a very dangerous bear. Even more recently, the Van Impes have been viewing the ongoing Chinese military buildup, in conjunction with astounding economic growth, with increasing suspicion. Could it be, they ask, that it will be China that will supply the bulk of the military hordes who will attack Israel in the final Battle of Armageddon?[10] Across the board, prophecy evangelists strongly affirm that an array of current events — which they explore in detail — make it very clear that the biblical prophecies about the end-times "can't be talking about any other time in history but today."[11]

The global analysis of "signs," which is so characteristic of biblical prophecy preaching, is also tied to some form of worldwide "conspiracy theory," which over the decades tends to add new elements coming from changing current developments. Lindsey's earlier emphasis, for example, on the fear of a "giant world federation" orchestrated by the European Union is now complemented by similar suspicions about the dangers of a "one world environmentalist agenda." Whatever form the conspiracy theory takes, it is always based on the fear of a "one world government" which the prophecy evangelists believe is a sign of the coming Antichrist, who is to rule "over every tribe and people and tongue and nation" (Rev. 13:7). Prophecy teacher Grant R. Jeffrey[12] fears that the technology needed for the Antichrist's rule is already available in "smart cards" — electronic-chip ID cards (which have already been implanted in the bodies of pets) — which he views as the forerunners of a single monetary control suggested by the "mark of the beast" in Rev. 13:17.

Biblical prophecy teaching continues to view the establishment of the State of Israel in 1948 as a major sign that we are now in the Last Days. For this reason, "Israel watching" becomes a very important factor in establishing the biblical prophecy timetable. Today's prophecy evangelists regularly interpret "the desolating sacrilege" of Matt. 24:15 as the desecration of the Jewish Temple in Jerusalem — the final act of blasphemy and betrayal by the Antichrist, who, in their reading of the Book of Daniel, will deceive the Israelites through a false alliance in the Last Days (Dan. 9:27). Since no such desecration could occur without the presence of a new temple in Jerusalem, the prophecy preachers are typically quite firm in their conviction that the ancient Temple is about to be restored, thus setting the stage for the inauguration of the end-times.[13]

Premillennial evangelicals are very supportive of conservative Jewish organizations, such as the Faithful of the Temple Mount, who are actively involved in trying to restore the Temple on Mt. Zion and to reestablish the ancient Jewish Temple ritual. One requirement of the ritual is that Jews purify themselves with the ashes of a red heifer mixed with water before approaching the Holy Temple. Since the destruction of the last Temple in 70 C.E., not one red heifer was born within the confines of Israel until sometime in 1997, when a red heifer, named Melody, finally made her appearance on a farm in northern Israel. Prophecy preachers were not slow to hold up Melody as a concrete sign that the

Temple will soon be restored and that we are now at the threshold of the Last Days. At the same time, Lindsey and his colleagues warn against the "euphoria of a false peace" in Israel — a sure sign of the beginning of the tribulation.[14]

Timetables and Predictions

Despite the reluctance of contemporary prophecy preachers to name times and dates, Jack Van Impe interprets the biblical evidence as suggesting that the cataclysmic end-time scenario will get underway around the year 2001 (which happens to be the correct mathematical beginning of the new millennium). Van Impe also tries to add to the cogency of his biblical argument by borrowing predictions from other sources, such as Sir Isaac Newton and Nostradamus. His biblical argument, like that of many of his fellow preachers, is based primarily on the ancient "six-day theory," according to which each of the six days of creation stands for a period of a thousand years. Whence also the saying in 2 Pet. 3:8: "One day is with the Lord as a thousand years, and a thousand years as one day." Since Van Impe accepts the fundamentalist doctrine that the earth was created six thousand years ago, he concludes that in the year 2000 we stand on the edge of eternity[15] — an eternal sabbath to be preceded, however, by the catastrophes, conflagrations, and cataclysm of the end-time tribulation.

For his part, evangelist/journalist John Wheeler Jr., whose book *Earth's Two-Minute Warning* has been highly promoted by the Van Impes, takes an entirely different tack in attempting to establish a millennial timetable. His approach to the problem focuses on the Israeli recapture of Jerusalem in 1967 as the key prophetic sign of the approaching judgment. In the light of this historic end-time event, Wheeler finds new meaning in Jesus' declaration that "this generation shall not pass, till all these things be fulfilled" (Matt. 24:34). Basing his calculations on the assumption that a biblical "generation" refers to a period of forty years, Wheeler concludes that really big things (of the apocalyptic variety) are in store for humanity around the year 2007.[16] In his own version of "Israel watching," Wheeler, like Lindsey, warns against any illusions of false peace, for the time of tribulation is near at hand and to claim otherwise is to support the deception of the Antichrist.

Rapture and UFOs

If this prophetic future appears as a rather grim, if not dreadful, prospect, the prophecy evangelists are quick to appeal to the doctrine of the rapture — certainly one of the most pivotal teachings of end-time prophecy. This very popular teaching maintains that faithful Christians have nothing to fear, in that before the great tribulation begins they will be evacuated or *raptured* into heaven, where they will enjoy the blessings and joys of the heavenly banquet of the Lamb and prepare to return with the Lord to inaugurate his millennial kingdom on earth. Jack and Rexella Van Impe are even able to promise us "front row seats" for viewing the frightful end-time events.[17] Lest Jack and Rexella should appear somewhat hardhearted in their view of the "unfaithful" or "unsaved," they have shown their compassion for the latter group by producing a new video, called *Left Behind*, which provides guidelines and directions on how one can survive and still save one's soul even if you "miss the Rapture."[18]

Grant R. Jeffrey, one of the most biblically grounded of the prophecy evangelists, goes to some length to try to demonstrate that the key premillennialist beliefs, such as the rapture and the tribulation, formed a central part of Christian teachings starting from the earliest centuries. He also attempts to relate and integrate the "rapture" doctrine with the central thrust of New Testament teaching. He reminds the reader, for example, of St. Paul's insistence that before Christians are able to share in eternal life with God, they must first put on an imperishable and immortal nature (1 Cor. 15:53) and translate their corruptible bodies "into a glorious resurrection body." For Jeffrey, the purpose of the rapture is precisely to make this translation. For this reason he argues that the rapture must never be presented as a simple reward to faithful Christians in view of the good works they have performed.[19]

Since biblical prophecy is always fine-tuned to reading the "signs of the times," with a special predilection for heavenly signs, it is not too surprising that in recent years some leading televangelists have begun to pay serious attention to UFOs and extraterrestrial visitations. Unlike the followers of the Heaven's Gate cult, the prophecy preachers do not identify the rapture with any kind of spaceship escape from the earth. Nevertheless, not a few, including Hal Lindsey, "have become thoroughly convinced that UFOs are real" — that at least some of "these sightings... are of real spacecraft." At the same time, however, Lindsey's view differs sharply from that of secular "ufologists," in that he believes that the visiting extraterrestrials are actually demons — "spiritual beings at war with God." As the end-time approaches, the goal of these demonic beings is to create signs and false wonders that will serve to create the "great deception" found in Paul's Second Letter to the Thessalonians (2 Thess. 8:12). For Lindsey this deception consists in the forging together of "Hindus, Moslems, Buddhists, false Christians, et al. into a one-world religion."[20]

In the meantime, Jack Van Impe Ministries has also caught on to the apocalyptic dimension of the UFO phenomenon, as witnessed in its recent video entitled *Extraterrestrials: Global Invasion Approaching*.[21] Given the significant influence of these leading prophecy preachers, the UFO-demonic theory might very soon become a standard feature in evangelical Bible study classes. It would not be surprising if UFO spottings find their own place in grassroots preaching as one of the major signs that we are already in the Last Days.

Grassroots Believers: Evangelicals and Catholics

Grassroots or popular religion is always influenced by the official religious teachings of the authorized leadership, but as we saw in the religious situation preceding the year 1000, the interests and priorities of the two are not always identical. Oddly enough, both evangelicals and Roman Catholics zealously embrace apocalyptic and millennial beliefs at the grassroots level. Understandably, the expression of these popular beliefs and their relation to the teachings of the official leadership differ significantly in each case.

Grassroots Evangelical Millennialism

Randall Balmer of Barnard College, New York, a leading authority on evangelicalism in America, puts more stock in the millennial beliefs and teachings of the grassroots membership than in the statements of the televangelists or of the professors at major evangelical seminaries. The latter, he claims, get too involved in theological nuances on fine points of eschatology and also tend "to hide behind the verbal veil of prescribed answers."[22] Whatever validity there is to Balmer's claim, there is no doubt that ordinary, committed evangelicals have deep millennial convictions, which include a lively expectation of the imminent return of Christ. They also tend to downplay the importance of some of the fine theological details. But apart from such differences in style and emphasis, there does not appear to be any substantial difference between the end-time message of the local congregations as compared to that of the major televangelists.

A good case in point is the preaching and Bible study of Pastor Bob Coy, a very popular evangelical preacher at Calvary Chapel, Fort Lauderdale, Florida. The Calvary Chapel movement began as a mission to the hippies and drug addicts of southern California in the 1960s, and has since spread to middle-class communities across the country. Some of the most successful of these new communities are found in southern Florida, where blossoming churches have been established in Tamarac, Fort Lauderdale, and Pompano Beach. Pastor Bob Coy has been the guiding light at Calvary Chapel, Fort Lauderdale, since 1985, where he leads a very lively congregation in Sunday services, Bible study, video and audio instruction, and a wide variety of adult and youth ministries. Pastor Bob, as he is affectionately called by his flock, emphasizes the "plain" reading of the scriptures and for the most part avoids abstruse theological controversies.

In response to a persistent urging from his congregants, in 1996 Pastor Bob gave a series of Bible studies entitled "Jesus Is Coming Back Again" (subtitled: "A Study of End Time Events").[23] Having informed his audience that the doctrine of Jesus' Second Coming or imminent return is basic to all Christian faith, Pastor Bob did a masterful job of presenting the substance of premillennial teaching in language that was at once clear, down-to-earth, and challenging. References to the work of Lindsey and the emphasis of his message made it very clear that Pastor Bob is also an ardent follower of Lindsey, Van Impe, and the other "big wig" prophecy preachers.

Like the leading televangelists, Coy is a sharp observer of the "signs of the times," that is, the current events that point to the fulfillment of end-time biblical prophecy. Specifically, he relates the evidence of political instability and the ongoing threat of terrorism and international conflict to the end of the world descriptions found in Matthew 24, where Jesus points to the sign of "wars and rumors of wars" (Matt. 24:6–8). In addition, he cites the appearance of "false Christs," like David Koresh, but especially the gurus of the New Age religions, as an indication that we are in the Last Days, and that Christ is coming "very, very soon." In his emphasis on the "demonry" of the New Age movement, as well as in his frequent negative references to Russian leaders, to Yasir Arafat (whom he describes as "the guy who looks like Ringo Starr with the towel on his head"), and to Muslim nations in general, Pastor Bob reveals many of the same biases and provincialisms that too often typify the perspective of the televangelists.

As a spirited disciple of biblical prophecy, Pastor Bob accepts all the other key premillennialist beliefs, including the rapture, the great tribulation, the millennial kingdom, and the whole end-time chronology. It is apparent, however, that his main fascination is with the rapture, when the church of true believers will disappear and the faithful will have a "balcony seat" for Armageddon. When discussing this event, Pastor Bob assures his audience that he will be "outa here." The ever-threatening chance of a political explosion in the Middle East impels him to convey to his audience a sense of "the urgency of the times in which we dwell." While wisely resisting the temptation to predict the "time" of Christ's return, he nevertheless insists that we are in the right "season." Christ could return five years, ten years, fifteen years from now or at any moment. Everything is in place. The main thing is to be ready — to live holy and godly lives in waiting for his return (see 2 Pet. 3:11).

Catholic Apocalyptic: Visions of Mary

Much like the mainline Protestant denominations, official Roman Catholicism has tended to dismiss millennialism and apocalyptic as the stuff of wild-eyed sectarians and doomsday prophets. The new *Catechism of the Catholic Church* does tell us, however, that in the Last Days there will be a final assault by the powers of evil, which will ultimately end in divine triumph and the final judgment. But it does not say a word about an earthly kingdom to be ruled by Christ and his saints, clearly because of the Catholic insistence that "Christ the Lord already reigns through the Church."[24]

Despite the church's official teaching on the matter, many Catholics at the grassroots level seek Christ's earthly rule all the same. This deep-felt millenarian concern is most commonly evident in the messages connected with visions or apparitions of Mary, the mother of Jesus, that have been reported in many parts of the world with growing frequency since the early years of the nineteenth century. The sites of many of these proclaimed appearances remain very popular pilgrimage shrines, such as La Salette, Lourdes, Rue de Bac (Paris), Fatima, and Czestochowa. In recent years the reports of Marian apparitions have increased at such a startling rate that even the usually cautious Cardinal Joseph Ratzinger claimed that they must be counted as very important "signs of the times."[25]

Most recently, the hub and focus of worldwide "visitations" of Mary has been the small village of Medjugorje in present-day Croatia. Beginning on June 24, 1981, while Medjugorje was still part of Yugoslavia, two children, later followed by four more, claimed to have seen the Blessed Virgin Mary and, subsequently, to have received daily messages from her. Much like the evangelization of the "born again" evangelicals, these messages summon everyone to personal reconciliation with God and the cultivation of prayer and interior peace as a prerequisite for world peace. If Mary's plea is not heeded, however, the world will be punished with a terrible chastisement in judgment for its sins. This idea of a universal chastisement is without any doubt the Catholic version of the tribulation.

Not surprisingly, the admonitions of Medjugorje are tied to the doctrinal and religious practices of Roman Catholicism, stressing the importance of frequent confession, regular recitation of the holy rosary, and constant remembrance of the poor souls in purgatory. A distinct feature of the Medjugorje message, however, is the importance of remaining open to the presence and power of the Holy Spirit, especially at the dawn of the new millennium.[26] This last prescription appears to provide a certain common ground for Christian millennialists of many different stamps.

The admonitions of Marian visionaries from the world over make it very clear that the Marian apparitions serve as a kind of

Between 1981 and 1992 an estimated twenty million pilgrims visited the shrine of Medjugorje, in the former Yugoslavia. There and in the literature of the Medjugorje movement they encountered a message to repent and pray that human beings would be open to the meaning of the "millennial" chastisements visited upon earth in the twentieth century.

Catholic apocalyptic, complete with speculations as to the identity of the beasts of Revelation. Through the century, for the majority of Marian visionaries, the prime candidates have been Communism and Free Masonry. In fact, the latter group also finds a place in the Catholic version of "conspiracy theory," as the alleged organizer of a worldwide movement to undermine the faith in the Last Days. While the Marian messengers, for the most part, avoid naming dates for the end-time events, a few, like Christina Gallagher of County Mayo, Ireland, claim that the punishments predicted by Mary will occur before the year 2000.[27]

Despite the dire predictions of the Marian visionaries, Catholic optimism still prevails, for though the chastisement will be great and swift, it not only will mark the end of this sinful age, but at the same time will inaugurate the start of a new epoch — "the era of peace." This seems to be as close as grassroots Catholicism gets to an earthly millennial kingdom, but then again, it is pretty close indeed.

Mainline Millennialism and the Renewal of Faith

For some time now, the mainline Protestant churches in the United States have been suffering a serious decline in membership, and Roman Catholicism, while more stable in numbers, is nevertheless experiencing an almost catastrophic shortage of clergy. By way of contrast, the evangelical and "born again" communities are dynamic, strong, and flourishing. While all Christian communities profess the basic creedal doctrine of the Second Coming of Jesus Christ, mainline churches usually lack any sense of urgency or immediacy about this belief. In Pastor Bob's words, they proclaim that "Jesus will come again — ho hum." With the approach of the anniversary year 2000, however, many mainline Christians — Protestant and Catholic alike — are finding a new stimulus to energetically confront the challenges of the coming millennium with renewed faith and zeal.

Protestant Liberalism and the Recovery of Hope

Church historian Martin Marty has recently remarked that the sadness of our fading century can be seen in the fact that we are inclined to poke fun at our forebears, who only a century ago were filled with hope for the human future. In preparation for the coming millennial landmark, Marty is proposing an effort to recapture some of the optimism and progressivism that characterized the faith of our recent ancestors. In a brief editorial written for the *Christian Century*, Marty authentically reflects the liberal Protestant attitude toward the approach of the year 2000. He has no interest in millennial or apocalyptic Bible predictions for the turn of the century, but, very much in line with mainline Protestant leadership, he sees the millennial anniversary as an occasion to renew faith commitment to the transformation of society and culture.[28] Despite some murmuring from the grass roots, demanding answers to detailed questions about the return of Christ, the mainline progressive leadership forges right ahead with a spirited pursuit of its religious and social agenda.

Without a shadow of doubt, the principal religious priority of mainline Protestantism clearly lies in the area of ecumenism, that is, the movement dedicated to the unification of the separated Christian churches. The prayer of Jesus that "they all may be one" as he is with the Father is resonating within these "oldstream" churches with a growing sense of urgency as the bimillennial celebration of Christianity grows closer. Both the enthusiasm and the expectations have reached sufficient pitch that participants will not be satisfied with any goal short of *full communion* — which means a mutual recognition of baptism, exchange of ministers, joint liturgies, and especially a sharing in the Lord's Supper. Furthermore, none of this, in the view of participants, has to wait for the cumbersome process of official church mergers.[29] Recently, the Evangelical Lutheran Church in America (ELCA), the Episcopal Church, and several Reformed churches have been working diligently toward this goal of full communion. Fruitful dialogue with the Roman Catholic and Orthodox churches continues with vigor. For many mainline Protestants, in the United States and overseas, the approach of the year 2000 heralds what has been called "the ecumenical moment."[30]

It is impossible, on the other hand, to single out any distinct challenge that liberal Protestants embrace as the unique or special focus of their practical social commitment. Recent works in mainline theology tend to emphasize a variety of different issues, such as those described in the two previous chapters. What is ironic is that some of the favorite themes of liberal theology, such as gay liberation, feminism, and ecology, are the very issues fundamentalism cites as apocalyptic signs and portents that the end is near. A recent work by Catherine Keller, who teaches at Drew University's School of Theology, gives us a pretty good sense of the theological priorities of mainline American Christianity as it undergoes self-review on the threshold of the next century.

In her delightful, if recondite book, entitled *Apocalypse Now and Then,* Keller addresses the question of millennialism by challenging what she calls fundamentalist *retroapocalyse*. By this she means "looking back" (retro) at the ancient biblical texts as if their message had been addressed directly to our present-day situation with all its problems, dangers, and moral confusion. Her bottom-line critique of literalist millennialism is that by its own inescapable logic it necessarily encourages a "spiral of violence" as well as a pessimism about all human attempts to save the world as it is.[31] She offers her own book as a kind of *counter-*

apocalypse, which intends to replace doomsday fatalism with a realistic and responsible theological defense of environmentalism, feminism, and the struggle for economic justice and peace. The key challenge of the new millennium is to address these issues by working against selfishness and individualism in order to create what she calls a "spirit-centered" community.[32]

Vatican Millennialism: Jubilee 2000

As early as 432 C.E. the Catholic Church at the Council of Ephesus rejected the literal reading of the millennial text (Revelation 20) as "a deviation and a fable." To this day the Catholic churches — Roman, Anglican, and Orthodox — have steadfastly upheld this view as their official position and continue to discourage any prophetic speculation about a coming thousand-year reign of Christ on earth. Jesuit theologian Brian Daley appeals to the authority of Augustine in support of the official teaching. It was Augustine who had written that it is better "to profess an ignorance that is careful than a knowledge that is false." Augustine's "studied ignorance," claims Daley, well suits the Gospel exhortation to continued vigilance, in that it is a constant reminder that we know neither the day nor the hour (Matt. 24:36).[33]

Official Catholic rejection of end-time speculation is not meant to undermine the importance of millennial symbolism. This helps explain Pope John Paul II's exuberant enthusiasm in preparing for the celebration of the bimillennium of the birth of Jesus in the year 2000, as well as his cautions lest this approaching date should encourage any "fanciful" end-time speculations. At a personal level, the pope from Poland, from the time of his papal election in 1978, has felt a special providential call to lead his church into the third millennium, and in his 1994 apostolic letter "On the Approach of the Third Millennium" (*Tertio millennio adveniente*), he invited the entire church to a three-year spiritual preparation for celebrating the "Jubilee Year 2000."

Pope John Paul borrows the idea of a Jubilee Year from the Old Testament notion of setting aside a special season of the Lord's favor. In the Bible the Jubilee Year was a time of forgiving debts, liberating the poor, and ministering to the sick and the captives (Isa. 61:1–2). For this reason, the Holy Father would ban all Christian triumphalist posturing as incompatible with the spirit of the Jubilee and encourages all Christians to prepare for the millennial celebration in prayer, examination of conscience, and a renewal of trust in God's lordship over history.[34]

At the practical level, the pope believes that Vatican Council II (1962–65) was a providential milestone directing the church in its remote preparations for the Jubilee Year 2000. For this reason he sees Jubilee 2000 as an occasion for renewed commitment to achieving the ideals and principles that were laid down at Vatican II. Among these great themes, the pope singles out those of church unity and of openness to the world as the central goals to be highlighted at the Jubilee celebration.[35]

Like mainline Protestantism, the Catholic Church sees the new millennium as a unique occasion to advance the cause of harmony and solidarity among the diverse Christian communities. At the same time, it is to serve as a catalyst for Christian witness to the world through the pursuit of human rights, peace, and economic justice — all building the foundations for a "civilization of love." Commenting on Pope John Paul II's apostolic letter "On the Approach of the Third Millennium," Jesuit theologian Avery Dulles remarked that the solemn Jubilee of the year 2000 is meant to open up "a new Springtime of the Christian life under the power of the Spirit."[36] The invitation to celebrate Jubilee 2000 is essentially a call to global community as the path to "reestablish the unity of the human race."[37]

As we reach the end of this chapter, it has become quite evident that religious responses to the approach of the third millennium are very diverse indeed. From the fanatical fringe we learn to be on guard against the destructive extremes that so easily distort millenarian thinking. Beyond this the fringe has no positive lesson to offer. Among the ranks of biblical believers, the "doomsday preachers" and the grassroots millennialists anticipate the beginning of dire apocalyptic scenarios for the year 2000 or thereabouts. Their literalist reading of the biblical prophecies which support this perspective offers detailed knowledge of the human future with few loose ends left to the imagination — this is its strength and appeal. On the other hand, it offers little incentive for protecting and caring for the world or for healing the wounds that divide nations, races, and religious and ethnic groups. For its part, the mainline religious response to the new millennium lacks the clarity and, at times, even the urgency of the fundamentalist message, but it has the merit of proposing a more compassionate and positive agenda toward the world and toward our fellow human beings.

Since these diverse forms of religious millennialism have their roots in the Christian scriptures, it is to these biblical sources that we now turn.

– 5 –

On Reading the Book of Revelation

The diverse religious responses described in the last chapter all share the common conviction that in some way the arrival of the third millennium has a very special religious significance. While for some the year 2000 marks the beginning of an apocalyptic time of tribulation, for others it represents a unique opportunity for a renewed commitment to the Christian Gospel. As in the past, so also today this current wave of both millennial hopes and millennial fears is rooted, in one way or another, in the teachings of the last book of the New Testament, called the Apocalypse or the Book of Revelation.

The Book of Revelation is without doubt one of the most controversial books of the Bible. Its rich and complex imagery has left it open to a wide variety of interpretations. The book was widely and hotly debated in the early church, and it took several centuries before it found an undisputed place in the canon of the church's inspired writings. Even this hard-won victory was not to last, as Martin Luther, Ulrich Zwingli, and other Protestant Reformers of the sixteenth century once again questioned the book's legitimacy as a witness of Christian revelation. Since then the book has been both widely ignored by large segments of mainstream Christianity and enthusiastically embraced as the key to all scripture by a number of sectarian, fundamentalist, and evangelical groups. Its powerful symbolism has provided an endless source of artistic expression, inspiring such great works as Michelangelo's *Last Judgment* in the Sistine Chapel, the woodcuts of Albrecht Dürer, and the cantatas of Johann Sebastian Bach. Its trenchant critique of the powers of this world has served as an inspiration to both religious and political reformers through the centuries, and the allure of its message is still evident in recent novels such as Umberto Eco's *The Name of the Rose* and films such as Francis Coppola's *Apocalypse Now.*

A Question of Artistic Style

Together with several Old Testament books, such as Daniel and parts of Ezekiel, the Book of Revelation belongs to a type of literature, called *apocalyptic,* that was widely known in Jewish circles for several hundred years prior to and following the time of Christ. It also includes a variety of noncanonical Jewish writings such as the First Book of Enoch, 4 Ezra, and the Testament of the Twelve Patriarchs, as well as a number of works discovered more recently among the Dead Sea Scrolls. This whole category of writings takes its name (apocalyptic) from the Greek title of the Book of Revelation, that is, the Apocalypse of John (*apokalypsis* is the Greek word for revelation).

A genre or literary form represents a particular style of writing or of literary expression. The apocalyptic genre is characterized by a variety of special traits which distinguish it from other literary forms. Basically, these include such features as (1) a narrative framework (i.e., a story form), (2) the reception of a heavenly message through the mediatorship of an angel or some other celestial being, and (3) a set of insights, derived from these heavenly revelations, regarding the meaning of God's plans for the ultimate outcome of human history. For this reason apocalyptic literature shows a twofold thrust: a *vertical* direction, which emphasizes the unveiling of heaven's secrets through the medium of dreams and visions, and a *horizontal* direction, which is concerned with interpreting the course of history and its ultimate consummation.[1] The setting for the visions of Daniel in chapter 7, for example, is clearly that of the divine throne room (vv. 9–10), but the message relates to the historical destiny of four powerful earthly kingdoms, the Babylonian, the Median, the Persian, and the Seleucid Greek Empire. The visions of their demise in chapters 8 to 12 and the coming of the kingdom of God described in chapters 2 and 7 serve as a sign of hope for the Jews oppressed during the reign of the Seleucid king Antiochus IV (symbolized by the little horn of the fourth beast). Apocalyptic, in a word, is concerned both with ecstatic vision and with world transformation.

Since the Book of Revelation, like Daniel and parts of Ezekiel, belongs to the general category of apocalyptic literature, any valid reading of this difficult work will necessarily bear in mind the general literary characteristics of the genre and avoid confusing them with the religious message or theme of the particular book in question. An awareness of the highly creative use of imagery and ancient legends found in both Daniel and Revelation as belonging to the idiom of apocalyptic literature will preclude any literalistic or journalistic type reading of these symbols. To do otherwise would be to miss or distort the religious and prophetic message of the inspired authors. When, for example, the author of Revelation describes the triumphant Christ as a warrior arrayed for battle against the armies of the beast in chapter 19, he is clearly making the point that the course of history is firmly in God's control and even the power of Satan cannot prevail against God's plans for the human future. To take the image literally, on the other hand, would be to negate the dominant theme of Revelation — the meek Lamb of God's triumph over evil through his sacrificial death — and would, in fact, run counter to the Christ-image portrayed throughout the rest of the New Testament.

In his very thoughtful and pastorally sensitive commentary, *Approaching Hoofbeats: The Four Horsemen of the Apocalypse,* evangelist Billy Graham calls attention to the "clanging symbolism" of the Book of Revelation. He reminds his readers that John of Patmos wrote Revelation "in a certain type of poetic language known as apocalyptic language" — a language that uses "vivid imagery and symbolism to speak about God's judgment and the end of the world." Graham makes no bones about the difficulty we have today in interpreting the "word pictures" of Revelation, which, nevertheless, were perfectly clear to the readers in John's day. Not only were the symbols and images employed in the text familiar to the readers; they also referred to real events of their own time. They had no need of decoding. But if all the images of Revelation are not apparent to us today, the "grand design of the prophet's vision" as well as "the urgency of his warning" still come across loud and clear. As Graham puts it, the abiding message of Revelation is "one of both warning and hope — warning of the coming judgment and hope of Christ's inevitable triumph over evil."[2] He cautions us against obscuring the full impact of this message by confusing it with the rich details of the imagery.

The Core Message of the Book of Revelation

As Graham suggests, interpreting Revelation requires real fidelity to the historical setting of the Christian communities of Asia Minor to whom the book was addressed. The book was written *about* these communities and the events which deeply affected them. At the same time, however, it was also written *for* people of all time.

The Book of Revelation was addressed to a group of churches in western Asia Minor (modern-day Turkey), whose members were mostly converts from Judaism. It was written by a local church prophet, named John, who had been exiled by the Roman authorities to the desolate island of Patmos, toward the end of the reign of Emperor Domitian, around the year 95 or 96 C.E. Compared to other emperors of the period, including his father and his brother before him, Domitian was not a particularly cruel or ruthless ruler, though there is good reason to believe that he actually killed his own brother, Emperor Titus. On the whole, Domitian's reign was beneficial to all classes of Roman citizens. While there is no evidence that Domitian conducted any systematic or wide-scale persecution of Christians, the record does show that under his rule the Roman practice of emperor worship was definitely given a new impetus, as suggested by the title *dominus et deus noster* (our Lord and our God) with which he began all decrees. Throughout Asia Minor, in particular, the local population had deep resentment for Christians because of their refusal to participate in civic rituals in which the emperor was worshiped as a god and the city of Rome (Roma) as a goddess. The Christian abstention from public worship very likely also had a significant economic impact, reducing the sale of religious articles and undermining a variety of commercial enterprises tied in with the civic ritual.

Chapter 13 of Revelation strongly hints at the insidious role of an unnamed local official who had become an energetic supporter of the emperor cult, accusing Christians of impiety and disloyalty. He is described by John as "another wild beast come up out of the earth," who used the authority of the first beast (i.e., the emperor) to promote its interests by making the world and all its inhabitants worship the first beast (Rev. 13:11–12). The text also clearly implies that at least economic sanctions were imposed upon Christians for their failure to observe the state religion, for the beast "did not allow a man to buy or sell anything unless he was first marked with the name of the beast or with the number that stood for its name" (13:17). It was to these churches, experiencing persecution or the threat thereof, that John sent his pastoral letters of encouragement and assurance. This message, with all its apocalyptic symbolism, would have been very clear to the Christian communities to which it was addressed, as well as to any local Roman official who might have chanced upon it.[3]

John of Patmos was a *biblical* prophet — one who sees the divine plan behind the realities and appearances of this world and lays it bear for all to hear. In this sense, the book is about the experiences, the fears, and the hopes of a specific group of Christians who lived in Asia Minor at the end of the first century of the Christian Era. For this reason, it is right to say that it is a book about past events, and any responsible reading of Revelation will never divorce itself from this original historical context.

At the same time, however, it is a book that has a powerful message for today's readers. As part of sacred scripture, it is a book about our present and about our future. The message it continues to transmit is that God is ultimately the Lord of History — "the King of Kings and the Lord of Lords" (Rev. 19:16) who will, in the last analysis, bring vindication and victory to his faithful followers. This is a message with as much meaning for the contemporary world as it had for the seven churches to whom John first disclosed his visions. Despite the dire ring of some of its passages, the Book of Revelation is ultimately an optimistic message of hope for those whose experience gives little reason for optimism.

Just as in Daniel (chap. 7) the figure of the Son of Man appearing in the clouds is the vindicator of all those who presently suffer trials by reason of their fidelity to God, so also the Christ will come in power and glory to bring judgment to the wicked and reward to the righteous. The identification Daniel's Son of Man with Jesus as the triumphant judge of the end-times (Rev. 14:14) illustrates the transformation of the Jewish apocalyptic tradition under the influence of the new Christian experience.[4] Within this new context, the resurrection of Jesus was the first in the series of end-time events.[5] It is God's vindication of his Holy One and the guarantee in advance that the victory has already been won. Just as death did not ultimately prevail over Jesus, so also in the end evil will not prevail against the power of God. Revelation, we can say, has a twofold thrust: a message of hope for the oppressed and a warning of judgment for the oppressors of all ages.[6] While preserving both the present and the future significance of the book, it remains crucial, nevertheless, to keep this reading firmly anchored in the original historical circumstances. Otherwise, interpreting the Book of Revelation can quickly deteriorate into a matter of subjective fancy.

A Book of Violence and Revenge?

There was much resistance to acceptance of the Book of Revelation in the early church because of its frequent appeal to images of violence, terror, and vengeance. Typical of the language of Revelation is the description in chapter 14 of the lot of those who submit to idolatry in the form of emperor worship: "If anyone worships the beast or its image,... he too will drink the wine of God's wrath, and he shall be tormented with fire and sulfur in the presence of the holy angels and in the presence of the Lamb" (Rev. 14:9–10). At first blush, such imagery seems quite incompatible with the claim made above that the book is guided by the central Christian theme of faith in the Risen Christ — the meek and merciful Lamb of God, slain for the sins of the world. The hostility and the vindictiveness of the book's language may be explained, in part at least, by the social situation of the Christian communities in Asia Minor.

We have already seen that despite the ongoing animosity of local people toward Christians in Asia Minor, there is no historical record to support the claim that under Domitian, Christians were subjected to a large-scale oppression or persecution. Nor from the social-historical perspective is there any reason to believe that the members of these Asian churches belonged to an economically disadvantaged social class. In fact, information supplied by the historian Pliny suggests that Christians in Asia Minor were drawn from all ends of the economic spectrum, including both the wealthy and the slaves. In Revelation itself, in the letter to the church in Laodicea (chap. 3), it is clearly implied that the Christian community there is a very prosperous one. John contrasts its enthusiasm for gold and fine garments with its lukewarm commitment to embrace the demands of the Gospel. Despite Revelation's scathing critique of the Roman Empire as the representative and functionary of the powers of Satan, it is not at all likely that the author is a spokesman for some radical group of political or economic dissidents. Most early Christian writers urged Christians to support the empire with their prayers and to live in peace with their pagan neighbors.[7]

On the other hand, apart from economic or social status, all Christians constituted a distinct minority in terms of religious and moral beliefs. Following the destruction of the Temple by the Romans in 70 C.E., the Christians of Asia Minor, who were primarily of Jewish origin, became more and more isolated from their own Jewish roots and estranged from the rest of the Jewish community. Yet these roots were deep enough that they persistently used Old Testament symbols to define their faith in Jesus Christ. They were, at the same time, isolated from the broader pagan society because of their resistance to the renewed practice of emperor worship. Still haunted by the memory of severe persecution under Nero in the 60s, the Christians of Asia Minor lived in tension with the majority view of Roman citizens, whose view of reality was quite at odds with their own. It came quite natural for them to plug into their inherited Jewish apocalyptic imagery — with its emphasis on coming tribulations — to define and clarify their own situation. As a "cognitive minority" (a group whose views run counter to the widely accepted public knowledge), their opposition to the controlling majority took on extreme expressions of hostility and negativity, as witnessed in the description of the fall of Babylon, the biblical symbol for Rome, in Revelation 18: "Fallen, fallen is Babylon the great!... Pay her back as she paid others; pay her double for her deeds! Pour into her cup twice the amount she concocted.... She shall be consumed by fire for mighty is the Lord God who condemns her" (vv. 2, 6, 8).

In a similar fashion, John uses the literary device of seven bowls and seven trumpets to create a terrifying picture of the plagues and trials that are to come. We can well understand the difficulty of the early church in squaring the violent and vengeful tone of Revelation with the Gospel message of love and forgiveness. But despite its sometimes gruesome features, the Book of Revelation is not a book of gloom. It is a book written to provide consolation, encouragement, and strength to a community already in torment and anguish over what appears to be a situation of powerlessness against the evil forces of the surrounding society. The scenes of battle and of torment are amply balanced by hymns of victory such as that of chapter 12: "Now the salvation and the power and the kingdom of our God and the authority of his Christ have come, for the accuser of our brethren has been thrown down" (v. 10).

Historians may well continue to dispute whether the Book of Revelation was written to a Christian community actually tormented by the trials of serious persecution. The uncomfortable situation of a religious minority suffices to account for the polarizing and hostile language against the larger Roman society. As we have already seen, the Jewish-Christian communities of Asia Minor had ready at hand the powerful and dramatic rhetoric of apocalyptic literature to express their opposition to the idolatry of emperor worship and to the arrogance and injustice that dominated the public order.[8] It would be a serious misreading to confuse this rhetoric with the religious message of Revelation, whose focal symbol is the slain Lamb of God, who has already conquered the forces of evil through his sacrificial death and his resurrection. Revelation is an appeal to Christians to patiently endure their present suffering in the conviction that they will survive the great period of trial by "washing their robes in the blood of the Lamb," who "will lead them to springs of life-giving water, and God will wipe every tear from their eyes" (Rev. 8:14, 17). Only a distorted reading of the Book of Revelation can make it out as a work of vindictive violence.

A Book of Prophecy

Since the Book of Revelation is an apocalypse, we can expect it to contain all the dramatic and poetic features of that type of literature. But it is not only an apocalypse; it is also a book of prophecy. In fact, scholars have often said that apocalyptic is the "child of prophecy" — and therefore will contain a number of prophetic traits. The biblical notion of prophecy is not the same as the current popular idea, which understands prophets primarily as forecasters of the unforeseen future. The biblical prophets, on the contrary, were mainly concerned about *contemporary* events. Amos, Isaiah, Jeremiah, and Ezekiel, for instance, were all particularly sensitive to the social, political, and religious context in which they lived. They all served as "watchmen," to use the image of Isaiah himself (21:11–12), over the developments in society and in religion in their own day.[9] The prophets are the vigilant ones who see what others refuse to see beneath the appearances of the world around them and challenge people to change what is not in accord with God's will and the moral order. Amos, for example, cried out against disregard of the oppression of the poor during a time of great prosperity and sometimes ill-gotten riches in eighth-century Israel. What the prophets want to change, in other words, is not some aspect of the distant future, but rather some deeply felt concern of the present moment. In our day, leaders like Martin Luther King Jr. are properly called prophets in the true biblical sense of the term. To borrow a phrase from the English Baptist biblical scholar D. S. Russell, the biblical prophet is more accurately described as a "forth-teller" than a "foreteller,"[10] insofar as biblical prophets deal primarily with their own current situation, bearing witness to God's will and God's judgment over present events (i.e., events of their own day).

But just as the Book of Revelation has a message for today, so also its predictions and prophecies have a meaning for the contemporary reader. In other words, the prophecies of John also have something to say about the future. We have already seen that the Book of Revelation proclaims a guarantee of ultimate victory over the powers of evil in this world. But it also proclaims the prophetic promise of a human future in which God reigns in peace and justice even within the confines of history. This remains a message of hope and consolation for people of all times who are subjected to injustice and oppression. While Revelation, then, has a keen interest in the outcome of human history, it was not written to provide precise details about the human future. It is rather geared toward motivation and encouragement to fidelity to God in spite of the opposition of powerful evil forces. In a word, the hope-filled message of the Apocalypse is that God is the Lord of History.

Reading the Book of Revelation is particularly frustrating to anyone with a strictly logical and historical mind-set — to anyone determined to uncover a clear-cut, chronological time line of events. The apocalyptic style is notoriously repetitive and spiral in its description of end-time catastrophes. The circularity of this style defies any attempt at chronological sequencing, but guarantees that the reader will not miss the central message of both judgment and hope. The account of the breaking of the sixth seal in chapter 6 (vv. 12ff.) provides a good example of repetitive circularity. Certainly it would seem that the devastation described in this passage could hardly be more complete: the sun turns black; the moon turns red as blood; the stars fall from the heavens; the sky disappears. Yet after all this the narrative continues (with the sun once more shining in the heavens), and life goes on amid a new set of apocalyptic disasters described through the literary device of the seven trumpets. It is obvious that we are dealing with a poetic narrative — albeit a very powerful and beautiful work of artistry. The narrative scheme is much more influenced by the author's predilection for mystical numbers than by any desire for sequential consistency. To describe the end-time events in terms of three sets of seven disasters sent from heaven is clearly far more important for John than any attempt at precise chronology.[11]

While the biblical prophets, including John of Patmos, do have much to say about the future, they have little interest in exact predictions or the setting of timetables. John's concern is fully in line with that of Jesus: to proclaim "the hidden beginning of God's rule and the glorious kingdom of God to be expected at the end — despite all opposition."[12] Certainly some early Christian groups were tempted to use Jesus' message to satisfy human curiosity and to look behind the curtain of the future. For this reason, it is not surprising that at the approach of the third millennium, today's Christians also feel the allure of a similar kind of speculation. The evangelists strongly resisted such calculations about the end of the world and the Lord's return, reminding their readers that the Son of Man is coming "at an unexpected hour" (Luke 12:40) and recalling Jesus' own words of caution: "As to the exact day or hour, no one knows it, neither the angels in heaven nor even the Son, but only the Father" (Mark 13:32). The real point of the prophecies of Revelation, like those of Daniel before it, is to proclaim that God will continue to be in control in the historical future.

Mystical Numbers and "Clanging Symbols"

The prophetic message of the Book of Revelation is regularly expressed in very rich and powerful poetic imagery and also through a constant play on sacred or mystical numbers. The use of both media of expression is characteristic of Jewish apocalyptic literature. The language of apocalyptic is very far from descriptive or referential newspaper language, and for this reason should not be read as providing some kind of "pseudoinformation" either about the cosmos or about the world's historical future. The symbolic character of John's visions is obvious. In fact, John often decodes the symbols for us, as when he explains the meaning of the seven stars in Rev. 1:20. The symbols he employs are derived primarily from the rich imagery of the Jewish prophetic and apocalyptic writings, and to a lesser degree from a transformed pagan mythology. They reflect the interests as well as the creative skills of an elite group of Jewish-Christian scribes. These skills include both an extraordinary command of picture images as well as an expertise and fascination with the symbolic interpretation of numbers.

The Power of Numbers in Revelation

I have already pointed out how the concern for employing a group of sacred numbers regularly takes precedence over any attempt to provide a chronological time sequence. There can be little doubt that the author as well as his readers were fascinated by the mystical meaning of numbers. Numerology is a very ancient art and was very popular in both the Jewish and Gentile world of New Testament times. John not only has a deep affection for numbers, but uses number images as the symbolic network around which the book is organized.

The structure of the book revolves around John's favorite number, seven, which stands for fullness, totality, perfection, or even divinity. While this favorite biblical number occurs fifty-four times throughout the work, its most important role is to provide an organizing principle for the prophetic narrative. It begins with (1) letters to seven churches of Asia Minor and continues with (2) the opening of seven seals, (3) the angels blowing seven trumpets, and (4) the pouring of the seven bowls of wrath.

Some scholars also see the remaining chapters as containing the seven end-time events: the coming of God's word (19:11–16), the last battle (19:17–21), the binding of Satan (20:1–3), the millennium (20:4–6), the defeat of Satan (20:7–10), the last judgment (20:11–15), and the new Jerusalem (chaps. 21–22). In this way, the new Jerusalem would be the seventh event in yet another septet. In any case, there can be no doubt that the author has a very special predilection for the number seven and that it carries primarily a symbolic significance.

When, for example, John addresses the seven churches of Asia Minor, it might well be that he has seven specific churches in mind, but it is more likely that his use of the number seven implies that his message is addressed to the "whole" church of his time. The same kind of reading must be given to the other sacred or mystical numbers used throughout the book — such as "half" or "three and a half," referring to a limited time, for example, the silence of about a half an hour in Rev. 8:1; a thousand, to signify a large multitude, as in "thousands and thousands of angels" (5:11); or twelve (and its multiples, as 144), to indicate the original tribes of Israel in continuity with the full community of the elect (144,000), whose robes have been made "white in the blood of the Lamb" (Rev. 7:14).[13]

An even more widely known use of number symbolism in the Apocalypse of John centers on the number six, which, as one less than seven, is the traditional numerical representation of imperfection and therefore of evil. Obviously, this idea of evil is magnified by any replication of the number, as in the famous combination 666. After describing the beast from the sea, who has power over the nations, demands to be worshiped, and economically exploits his subjects, the author identifies him cryptically by stating that his number is 666 (Rev. 13:18). Interpreting the code of this mysterious number and identifying its bearer has been a favorite pastime of believers, serious scholars, as well the fanatical fringe over the course of the centuries.

Since in the ancient world numbers were written as letters, every number had a letter equivalent and any combination of letters had a numerical value. This equivalence would vary, of course, depending on which alphabet one was using, for example, Hebrew, Greek, Latin, or Aramaic. In the case of Rev. 13:18, an additional problem arises from the fact that a number of Greek manuscripts contain the divergent reading of 616 rather than 666. Nevertheless, since the title Caesar Nero in Hebrew letters happens to produce the numerical equivalent of 666, and given the lively legends of rebirth that surrounded the memory of this ruthless emperor, the text has been widely interpreted as referring to Nero, reincarnated as Emperor Domitian.[14] While any such interpretations cannot be certain, it is clear that John had in mind a public figure *of his own day,* connected with Rome and its emperors. He certainly was not referring to any personage of later history, whether it be Frederick II, the Saladin, Hitler, Mussolini, Henry Kissinger, Pope Paul VI, or Bill Gates — to mention but a few of the many candidates for Antichrist to be put forward by preachers, televangelists, and other apocalyptic enthusiasts through the centuries (as well as more recently by religious surfers on the Internet).

Over the course of history, the beast of Revelation has also been commonly fused with the image of the Antichrist, a mysterious figure mentioned only in the letters of John: 1 John 2:18; 4:3; and 2 John 7. This identification, however, is not totally inappropriate, for the beast of Revelation is both an enemy and a parody of Christ, mirroring the attributes of Satan the way the Son mirrors those of the Father. The same image of the Antichrist is also frequently tied to the enigmatic personage mentioned in 2 Thess. 2:8 — the "lawless one," who in the Last Days will deceive people with demonically inspired signs and wonders. So even though the term *Antichrist,* as such, is not used in the Book of Revelation, it is often identified with it, and on this account, it constitutes one of the historically most powerful and enduring picture images connected with the work.

The book is also replete with many other forceful and alluring images that have consistently captured the religious imagination through the centuries. Certainly any creditable list of such images would have to include the battle of Armageddon, the parousia, the whore of Babylon, the great tribulation, and the Lamb of God.

Key Picture Images of Revelation

Armageddon, which appears exclusively in Rev. 16:16 to describe the location of the final end-time battle between the followers of the Lamb and the followers of Satan, is, in all likelihood, an allusion to the region of Megiddo in the biblical Plain of Esdraelon, where the armies of ancient Israel defeated the forces of the Canaanites (Judg. 5:19). Despite its very modest mention in the Book of Revelation, it has assumed a very prominent place in several more recent schools of millennialism. These subsequent interpretations expand on John's original prophecy, depicting Armageddon as the final cosmic showdown between the forces of good and evil.

The Second Coming of Christ (the *parousia* in the original Greek) was a bedrock belief of the early Christian communities and is a dominant theme in the Book of Revelation. It is tied to the Jewish prophetic expectation of a coming messianic rule, and as such reflects the imagery borrowed from the Book of Daniel in describing the triumphant return of the Risen Christ on the clouds of heaven (e.g., Rev. 1:7; Dan. 7:13). Revelation, like all early Christianity, expected an imminent parousia, and many New Testament scholars hold that the greatest challenge to the survival of early Christianity was the delay of the parousia.

Babylon, the ancient Mesopotamian capital, where the Jews had been brought in chains after the destruction of the Temple, became a standard Jewish metaphor for the epitome of wickedness (see the Tower of Babel story in Genesis 11). In the Book of Revelation the image is embellished as the "whore of Babylon," and described by the author as "Babylon the Great, the mother of harlots" (Rev. 17:5). From the context, however (e.g., the harlot is drunk with the blood of the martyrs, and sits on seven hills), it is evident that for the Christians of Asia Minor Babylon symbolizes the Roman Empire, with all its power, corruption, and idolatrous emperor worship. In chapter 18 the whore of Babylon is repaid for her sinfulness and infidelity with total destruction through fiery conflagration.

The word *tribulation* (*thlipsis* in Greek) is found forty-five times in the New Testament, and carries with it the connotation of oppression, affliction, or trouble. It represents a theme quite typical of apocalyptic scenarios, based on the underlying conviction that the present evils are such that they cannot be overcome except through a great catastrophe that destroys the present order. In Revelation 7, for example, the earth will be destroyed in punishment for sin, and only those who are washed in the blood of the Lamb will survive. Since Jesus in the Gospel of Matthew speaks of tribulation as a prelude to the end-time events, the "great tribulation" of Revelation is often read as a distinct period of incomparable disaster, persecution, and suffering which must precede the final events of God's deliverance and the parousia or return of Christ.[15] The scourges or punishments themselves (as in Revelation 8 and 16) are often described in terms which evoke the ten plagues of Egypt — thereby relating the present sufferings of the saints to the oppression of God's people in Egypt, from which they were liberated (against all odds) by the power of almighty God.[16]

The overriding positive theme of the book is particularly evident in the dominant role given throughout the work to the figure of the *Lamb* — the image of the Risen Christ — who like the Passover lamb of Exodus had been slain to save his people from the slavery of sin. The idea of the sacrificial paschal lamb and Isaiah's notion of the Suffering Servant of God are brought together in this image of the Lamb who receives worship standing near the throne of God (Rev. 5:11–14). The promise of victory is now extended beyond Israel to all the nations, which in the new heavenly Jerusalem walk with the twelve tribes of Israel in the light of the Lamb (Rev. 21:24). Revelation encourages no acts of vengeance; with the victory of the Lamb there is no further need of vengeance. Nor does it wallow in disaster and suffering, but rather serves as a powerful reminder that God is in control of the world's history and will not abandon those who put their trust in him. When correctly understood, then, the Book of Revelation is not primarily a harbinger of doom and destruction, but rather a proclamation of hope and encouragement in the face of overwhelming evil. As we have seen earlier, Revelation transmits this message through a rich use of symbolic language and ancient imagery. History has shown that whenever readers lose touch with the poetry of Revelation's imagery, literal readings have consistently produced bizarre, fanciful, and, only too often, terribly destructive interpretations of the book.

Of all the images of Revelation, however, the one that has proven most powerful, controversial, and influential through the centuries is that of the *millennium*, or thousand-year reign of Christ. This image, which is the main focus of the present work, is the subject of the following chapter.

– 6 –

The Reign of a Thousand Years

The image of the millennium is given only a very brief and passing mention in the Book of Revelation, and is altogether unknown elsewhere in the New Testament. Yet despite this scant scriptural attestation, the image has nevertheless had an astounding influence on religious and secular thought through the centuries, inspiring pious and saintly believers as well as religious fanatics and violent revolutionaries. The idea of the millennium or thousand-year reign of Christ at the consummation of human history is found uniquely in chapter 20 (vv. 1–10) of the Book of Revelation. Since the various millennial and apocalyptic movements to be discussed in the subsequent chapters rely so heavily on their reading of the message contained in these verses, it is worthwhile citing the passage here in full:

> [1]Then I saw an angel coming down from heaven, holding in his hand the key of the bottomless pit and a great chain. [2]And he seized the dragon, that ancient serpent, who is the Devil and Satan, and bound him for a thousand years, [3]and threw him into the pit, and shut and sealed it over him, that he should deceive the nations no more, till the thousand years were ended. After that he must be loosed for a little while.
>
> [4]Then I saw thrones, and seated on them were those to whom judgment was committed. Also I saw the souls of those who had been beheaded for their testimony to Jesus and for the word of God, and who had not worshiped the beast or its image and had not received its mark on their foreheads or their hands. They came to life again, and

reigned with Christ a thousand years. ⁵The rest of the dead did not come to life until the thousand years were ended. This is the first resurrection. Blessed and holy is he who shares in the first resurrection! Over such the second death has no power, but they shall be priests of God and of Christ and they shall reign with him a thousand years.

⁷And when the thousand years are ended, Satan will be loosed from his prison ⁸and will come out to deceive the nations which are at the four corners of the earth, that is Gog and Magog, to gather them for battle; their number is like the sand of the sea. ⁹And they marched up over the broad earth and surrounded the camp of the saints and the beloved city; but fire came down and consumed them, ¹⁰and the devil who had deceived them was thrown into the lake of fire and brimstone where the beast and the false prophet were, and they will be tormented day and night for ever and ever.

The Meaning of the Millennium

The chaining of Satan for one thousand years is depicted as the consequence of Christ's glorious return or parousia. The beast and the false prophet, agents of Satan (the very personification of evil), have already been cast into hell by the power of the returning Christ, symbolized by the warrior on the white horse in chapter 19. While the sealing of Satan in the abyss in chapter 20 clearly indicates Christ's victory over the ultimate source of evil, John wants to make it clear that the final effect of this victory is not immediate, but is delayed for a definite period of time — one thousand years. During this time, the triumphant Christ will reign, together with the martyrs, that is, "those who had not worshiped the beast or its image and had not received its mark on their foreheads or their hands" (v. 4). The number 1000, we have already seen, frequently symbolizes a large number, multitude, or (in this case) a significant period of time.

John borrows this notion of the millennium or thousand-year reign of God from the Jewish apocalyptic expectation of a coming messianic kingdom. This tradition commonly understood the days of creation as periods of a thousand years each, and the seventh of these "world-days" was considered the time of the Messiah (see above the "six-day theory" discussed in chap. 4).

A classic rendition of the millennial paradise in the painting known as *The Terrestrial Paradise,* by the Limbourg brothers, in *Très riches heures du Duc de Berry* (1410).

For the Jewish-Christian readers of Revelation this image evoked the notion of a thousand-year Sabbath, and suggested a restoration or return to the original order and harmony of God's creation. In this respect, the use of the term "that ancient serpent" in verse 2 is an allusion to the story of the fall in Genesis 3 and implies both "the removal of the curse and recovery of the tree of life."[1] In a word, the inauguration of the messianic kingdom is a return to the beginning—the inauguration of a new creation.

This millennial passage, like much of the Book of Revelation, is heavily indebted in its imagery to Old Testament and other ancient Jewish sources. The thrones of the martyrs in verse 4 are a reflection of the scene of divine judgment in Dan. 7:9, in which thrones were placed before "the ancient of days." The key theological point John is making in introducing the image of the millennial kingdom at this juncture of his work is that the saints and martyrs who had suffered for their resistance to idolatry (the rule of Satan) will ultimately triumph and rule with Christ. The destiny of the martyrs is carefully presented in such a way to contrast with the fate of the beast described in chapter 19. The beast had been thrown into the lake of fire (19:20), which is understood by John as the "second death," whereas the martyrs, once restored to life, will not be subject to the second death, but shall reign with Christ for a thousand years (v. 6).

Furthermore, in order to indicate that the triumph of Christ's kingdom is irreversible, John gives Satan a last chance to deceive the nations — represented by the countless forces of "Gog and Magog" (John's adaptation of the mysterious apocalyptic figure, "Gog of Magog," who marches against Israel in Ezekiel 38-39). By an act of God these armies of Satan are totally annihilated, and Satan himself is consigned to eternal torment in the "lake of fire and brimstone where the beast and the false prophet were" (v. 10). Even the most formidable forces of evil must fall before the power of Christ's peaceable kingdom. At the same time, the temporary binding of Satan also serves as a reminder that there is no let up in the struggle against evil until this world as we know it comes to an end. In the meantime, great victories — as important as they are — are not to be seen as final.[2]

John of Patmos, then, has borrowed heavily from Jewish apocalyptic traditions — both canonical and noncanonical — to paint the picture of a millennial kingdom established in the Last Days by the triumphant Christ, who rules together with his martyrs and saints. This imaginative scheme functions as a vision of hope, encouragement, and guidance to small communities of Christians besieged by a basically hostile society. Apocalyptic imagery aims at depicting meaning, rather than predicting details. While the millennium of Revelation 20 stands for the vindication of the martyrs, it does not predict "the manner of this vindication."[3] For this reason, it is misguided to attempt to predict the time of the kingdom's arrival or to interpret its details as literal information about the future.

Harmony as a Sign of the Kingdom

While the millennial kingdom is barely mentioned in the New Testament, it really represents a very important aspect of a much more central biblical image, namely, that of the kingdom of God. This symbol, the kingdom or reign of God, is a controlling theme throughout both Old Testament and New Testament theology. It was the principal theme of the Hebrew prophets and constituted the key motif of Jesus' preaching. While the Book of Revelation is not particularly fond of this term as such, it is frequently alluded to throughout the work, as, for instance, in the vision of heavenly worship before the divine throne in Revelation 4 and in frequent references to the reign of God (e.g., in 12:10) or to Jesus as "King of Kings" (e.g., in 19:16). In the Old Testament or the Hebrew Bible, the kingdom of God, especially in the early prophetic writings and in the Psalms, often suggests God's sovereignty over both nature and history. Psalm 47, for example, proclaims that "God is the King of all the earth" and that he also "reigns over the nations." The reign of God means a period of peace and justice on earth, with peace and harmony among the nations and between humanity and nature. Among the great prophets of the exile, the image of the kingdom of God also begins to express more and more the hope for a future world, for "new heavens and a new earth" where no more shall be heard "the sound of weeping and the cry of distress" (Isa. 65:19).

For the later prophets the harmony of the kingdom was viewed as a state of reconciliation and peace between Israel and the nations, who "shall beat their swords into plowshares, and their spears into pruning hooks" (Isa. 2:4). The messianic age will bring the gathering together of all the nations in Jerusalem, and the lion will lie down with the lamb (Isa. 11:6). This hope for such a future kingdom of righteousness becomes even more pronounced in the apocalyptic literature which began to appear around the second century B.C.E. Only by this time, this hope begins to transcend the limits of life in this world and gradually includes belief in a future resurrection of the just. Both the prophetic expectation of a this-worldly rule of justice and the apocalyptic vision of a future life in the heavenly kingdom are brought together in the symbol of the reign of God — the proclamation of which was the core message of the preaching of Jesus. The millennial symbolism of Rev. 20:1–10 draws attention to the this-worldly, inner-historical dimension of that kingdom, by envisaging a time period permeated with the biblical ideals of righteousness, justice, and harmony.

The theme of universal harmony is carried over from Jewish prophetic literature, where it finds very eloquent and powerful expression in the Book of Isaiah. This is all the more remarkable since it is generally recognized by scholars that Isaiah is the work of at least three different authors, living during different historical periods, before, during, and after the exile of the Judeans in Babylonia (597–539 B.C.E.). Some of this thematic consistency was obviously achieved by the work of the final editor(s), who took great care to repeat the same idyllic picture of harmony and peaceful cooperation (as in Isa. 11:6) in the closing chapters of the book:

> The wolf and the lamb shall feed together,
> the lion shall eat straw like the ox;
> and dust shall be the serpent's food.
> They shall not hurt or destroy in all my
> holy mountain, says the Lord. (Isa. 65:25)

In a word, this picture of natural harmony is an extension of the theme of peaceful political collaboration, a crucial issue in the early chapters of Isaiah, where the prophet envisages a time of political harmony between Israel and its Gentile neighbors, who would no longer "lift up sword against nation...nor learn war anymore" (Isa. 2:4). In chapter 25, following the fearful prophecies of what is called the "Little Apocalypse," Isaiah unambiguously proclaims God's intent to bring salvation to the Gentiles as well as to the Jews: "On this mountain the Lord of hosts will make for all peoples a feast of fat things, a feast of wine on the lees, of fat things full of marrow, of wine on the lees well refined. And he will destroy on this mountain the covering that is cast over all peoples, the veil that is spread over all nations" (vv. 6–7).

In the New Testament both in the teaching of Jesus and in the preaching of the early church, the Old Testament understanding of the kingdom of God was always taken for granted. For this reason, it is difficult to pin down a specific content-determined description of the meaning of the kingdom anywhere in the New Testament. Like the rest of the New Testament, the Book of Revelation assumes the traditional biblical meaning of the kingdom. The millennium scenario of Revelation 20 presupposes the vision of the just, righteous kingdom of Jewish messianic expectation, alluding to the quality of harmony by proposing a nonauthoritarian, tension-free sharing of the martyrs in the ruling power of the triumphant Christ. That "they shall be priests of God and of Christ" suggests a role of mediators between the divinity and the human family.[4] Mediation is itself always aimed at producing a situation of harmony. For the rest, Revelation reserves the explicit vision of perfect harmony to the description of the heavenly Jerusalem in chapter 21.

The New Testament, in general, portrays the Christian communities of the day as harbingers of the coming age, and encourages them to serve as both a sign and an initiator of the final manifestation of the reign of God. According to Revelation, while presently suffering and oppressed by reason of their fidelity to God's law, the Christian churches that remain faithful will serve as witnesses to the power of the kingdom that is already breaking into human history. Suffering persecution for Christ becomes the principal sign of acceptance of the kingdom.

The Acts of the Apostles gives us an ideal image of what the Christian community should be like, if it is to be a faithful witness to the coming age. Acts 4, in particular, gives the reader an image of the primitive church as a "community of believers" who "were of one heart and one mind" — reflecting in their own lives the harmony that will prevail when Christ returns to rule gloriously with his saints. It is no wonder that many millennial communities through the centuries have looked to the Acts of the Apostles to find the model for their own experiments in Christian communal living. By imitating the spiritual, economic, and social harmony depicted in Acts, these communities sought to bear witness to the imminent approach of the reign of God.

Raptures and End-Time Predictions

Although the image of the millennium in the Book of Revelation says nothing about a "rapture" or "taking up" of faithful Christians to meet Christ in the heavens upon his glorious return, large groups of evangelicals and other Christian believers have made this belief an essential component of millennial doctrine. This is particularly true of the very influential dispensationalist movement, which began to flourish in the United States during the traumatic era of the Civil War and the unsettled times which followed in its wake. (Dispensationalism will be discussed in some detail later in the book.)

Religious rapture has been a characteristic of American religion going back to colonial days and the ecstatic, emotional outflow of religious enthusiasm that characterized the First Great Awaken-

The Reign of a Thousand Years 89

A range of artifacts exemplify, concretize, and nurture millennialist belief in such doctrines as that of the rapture, portrayed in this postcard.

ing. It appears to have returned with a vengeance during the final quarter of the twentieth century.[5] But beyond the everyday kind of rapture that is part and parcel of the experience of charismatic Christians, many Christians expect the ultimate rapture which is expected to accompany the end of the age and the Second Coming of Christ. Since this belief is based on a rather abstruse and mysterious passage in Paul's First Letter to the Thessalonians, it might be well to reflect a bit on its meaning.

This letter, written to a newly founded church in Thessalonica, in northern Greece, is the earliest Christian writing to survive. It was very likely written around 50 C.E. to this neophyte church of converted Jews and Gentiles whom Paul and his missionary companions, Timothy and Silas, had to leave rather abruptly after riots broke out over their preaching. Paul, concerned lest the fledgling church had not been given sufficient grounding and might collapse under the stress of persecution or the confusion of false doctrine, sent Timothy from Corinth to visit the new community. Timothy brought back with him a glowing report about the fidelity of the church at Thessalonica, but he also brought with him a question that was deeply disturbing this community of ardent new converts. Paul surely had attempted to impress on the new church the main elements of the new faith: that there was one true God; that Jesus was his Son; and that Jesus had died for them and was raised from the dead in order to put right their relationship with his heavenly Father. From the emphasis of this letter, however, it would seem that what struck them most deeply was the conviction that Jesus was soon to return from heaven in order to bring the world to judgment.[6]

Had Paul instructed them sufficiently as to the time of Jesus' return? Had he prepared them for dealing with the death of loved ones while waiting for the parousia? Had he given them any guarantees that their departed loved ones would not miss out on the joy and victory of Christ's return? It might well be that his sudden departure from Thessalonica had prevented him from clarifying these fine points of his eschatological teaching. What is clear, at any rate, is that the main thrust of this letter was to convince the Thessalonians that those who had died would share equally with those who remained alive in the event of Christ's return. With this in mind he writes:

> [14]For if we believe that Jesus died and rose, God will bring forth with him from the dead those also who have fallen asleep believing in him. [15]We say to you, as if the Lord himself had said it, that we who live, who survive until his coming, will in no way have an advantage over those who have fallen asleep. [16]No, the Lord himself will come down from heaven at the word of command, at the sound of the archangel's voice and God's trumpet; and those who have died in Christ will rise first. [17]Then we, the living, the survivors, will be caught up with them in the clouds to meet the Lord in the air. Thenceforth we shall be with the Lord unceasingly. [18]Console one another with this message. (1 Thess. 4:14–17)

In this letter as elsewhere Paul remains primarily the practical and concerned pastor, more interested in bringing guidance and comfort to his flock than in providing theological precision. The theological core of his message remains constant: the future hope of Christians is inextricably tied to belief in the saving death and resurrection of Jesus. Perhaps during his stay in Thessalonica he had failed to make it clear that the resurrection is the guarantee of their own future resurrection and that at the parousia, those who had died in Christ would be the first to be raised. This, he tells them, is as true as if it had come from the Lord himself.

As for the dramatic scenario which depicts the survivors being caught up in the clouds with the resurrected just "to meet the Lord in the air," this clearly reflects a heavy borrowing from Jewish apocalyptic imagery. Clouds, for example, often represent the dwelling place of the Almighty or the adornments of the Divine Presence. In Exodus, it is a cloud which manifests God's protective presence in the desert; in Dan. 7:13, the mysterious Son of Man will appear in the clouds of heaven (in contrast to the beasts, who emerge from the earth); and in the Acts of the Apostles, Jesus is raised into heaven upon a cloud. Of course, trumpets and archangels are regular trappings in apocalyptic literature, and some scholars have even noted in this text literary similarities with Hellenistic scenes of secular parousias, that is, the arrival of princes and kings in great cities of the day.[7]

Whatever the sources of Paul's powerful imagery, the essential ingredient of his response is the guarantee that somehow "we shall be with the Lord unceasingly." On the other hand, Paul's description of all believers, the newly risen as well as the survivors, as being "snatched up" cannot be dismissed as window dressing. By way of contrast to the deputies of a Hellenistic city, who venture on their own to meet the arriving dignitary, the Christians here are transported to meet their Guest. This means that the meeting with Christ at the parousia is an act of divine initiative both for the survivors as well as for those who had previously died in Christ.[8] Paul, then, through the powerful language of apocalyptic, is reinforcing the fundamental biblical conviction that the kingdom of God cannot be achieved through human effort. To read the passage as a detailed literal description of Christ's return is to involve the reader in pointless speculations which may very well obscure the real theological message of the text.

The temptation to spin a whole doctrine of the rapture out of this isolated statement becomes particularly strong during difficult and uncertain times, when all of us welcome an escape from the challenges and dangers of the present moment. It is not surprising that "rapture" theology has had a boom during the twentieth century, with our world wars, economic depressions, terrorist strikes, and the constant threat of nuclear holocaust. But, if fidelity to the *spirit* of the text requires us to resist any such literalist spin-offs, with all the more reason should it deter us from getting caught up in the seductive trap of speculating about the timetable of the rapture and of similar end-time events. For this we have Paul's own warning in the very next verse of the text: "As regards specific times and moments,... we do not need to write you. You know very well that the day of the Lord is coming like a thief in the night" (1 Thess. 5:1–2). Here, no doubt, Paul is reflecting Jesus' own cautionary reminder that we know neither the day nor the hour of the Lord's return (Mark 13:32; Matt. 24:42).

Millennial Expectation in the Early Church

If evangelical, fundamentalist, and sectarian Christianity continues to put a central value on millennial beliefs, the mainstream churches, Protestant and Catholic, have been known to spiritualize, dismiss, or even ridicule these same beliefs as the staple of religious fanatics or obsessed anarchists. Whatever may be the value of that assessment, this view was not shared by the persecuted churches of the first Christian centuries. According to scripture scholar Geoffrey Wainwright, millennialism or chiliasm (from the Greek *chilioi:* thousand) provided these oppressed churches with "a promise of deliverance and of ultimate security" as an antidote to fear and anxiety.[9] In fact, chiliasm quickly became a vital focal point for doctrinal, liturgical, and moral life. Certainly in the Greek or Byzantine church, chiliasm was initially the normative belief of hierarchy, laity, and theologians, and it would remain a vigorous and persistent religious force throughout the first four centuries.

A clear, written record of chiliastic belief is found in the works of a number of significant early Christian writers. Papias, for example, who wrote around 125–30 C.E., and who seems to have had direct links to the teaching of the apostles, staunchly defended the imminence of Christ's personal reign on earth. His descriptions of this millennial rule were influenced by Isaiah's vision of universal harmony — which included both peace among the nations and concord throughout the animal kingdom. Justin Martyr, who wrote a few decades after Papias, identified Jerusalem as the site of the thousand-year reign, and, like Papias, stressed the image of earthly harmony in which "the animals will live at peace with one another and with human beings."[10]

Because of his theological stature in both East and West, there is no doubt that the most important witness of early Christian millennialism was Irenaeus. Having his origins in Asia Minor, Irenaeus eventually became bishop of the newly established Christian church of Lyon in southern France. His elaboration of millennial belief came out of his opposition to Christian heresies, especially gnosticism, which was causing much confusion in the church of the second century. By and large, the gnostic sects rejected the material side of creation and with it the resurrection of the flesh. Their idea of salvation was a purely spiritual existence freed from the encumbrances of the body. Of all the chiliastic writers, Irenaeus was the most balanced, consistent, and profound, firmly anchoring his millennial teaching in the apostolic conviction that in Christ all creation will be restored. In this context of his debate with the gnostic heresy, he presented belief in the coming millennium both as the fulfillment of God's promise and as an affirmation of the inclusion of the material side of creation in God's plan for salvation. In continuity with the Christian belief that the Word of God became flesh, the chiliasm of Irenaeus confirmed the ultimate "harmony of flesh and blood with spirit."[11]

Unfortunately, not all early chiliasm remained as balanced as that of Irenaeus. The Montanists of Asia Minor, for example, proclaimed that their leader, Montanus of Ardabau, was the prophet of the Holy Spirit, who was about to initiate the Last Days. They thoroughly expected that the heavenly Jerusalem was about to descend in the little town of Pepuza in Asia Minor. Others, like Cerinthus and Nepos of Arsinoe, taught a kind of crude chiliasm, with an emphasis on sumptuous dining and erotic pleasures. As a result, chiliasm fell more and more into disrepute and was strongly opposed by major Christian writers such as Jerome, Tyconius, and eventually Augustine. It was Jerome (347–420 C.E.) who wrote: "The saints will never have a terrestrial rule, but only a heavenly one. So let's stop with this whole fable of a thousand years."[12] Following the lead of the African theologian Tyconius, the great Augustine (354–430 C.E.) rejected any futuristic interpretation of the thousand-year reign and equated it with the present age of the church. Given the enormous influence of Augustine on doctrinal matters, this "spiritualization" of the thousand-year reign effectively smothered the millennial fervor of the early church and, for the most part, still continues to dominate the orthodoxy of mainstream Christianity even to the present day. For centuries following Augustine any historical reading of the millennial symbolism was forced into the popular underground or to the sectarian fringe — that is, until the resurgence of millennialism in the Middle Ages, especially under the leadership of the twelfth-century Calabrian abbot Joachim of Fiore.

Building the New Jerusalem

Despite the Augustinian effort to stamp out millennialism from church life, the scriptural basis for the doctrine remained inscribed in the canonical text of Revelation 20. Not surprisingly, then, it took the work of the very gifted twelfth-century biblical scholar Joachim of Fiore (1135–1202) to bring fresh understanding to the Book of Revelation and in the process to bring new vitality to the ancient millennial doctrine. Joachim was able to make his original and creative contributions by combining his unique method for understanding the scriptures with a trinitarian interpretation of world history derived from the early Greek theologians. In reading scripture, Joachim used a principle he called concordia, that is, the notion of harmony or parallels between world history (which he found in the books of the Old Testament) and the salvation history of the New Testament from its very beginning to the final parousia. By drawing parallels between the two testaments, Joachim claimed to identify a general pattern in history, which he believed represented the irruption of the divine life of the Trinity itself into the heart of human affairs.[13]

Accordingly, for Joachim, all history is divided into three stages: the age of the Father, the age of the Son, and the age of the Spirit. Using the scriptures as a chart of history, Joachim concluded that his own generation was at the threshold of the final epoch of the human narrative — the age of the Spirit. Without contradicting the authority of Augustine, who had identified the millennium with the age of the Son (i.e., the church), Joachim proposed that Satan had been only partially bound during the age of the church and would suffer complete defeat only in the age of the Spirit.[14] For this interpretation he could appeal to Revelation 20, where Satan is loosed after the thousand-year reign, only then to be finally crushed by the divine power and "thrown into the lake of fire and brimstone" (v. 10).

Since for Joachim the unfolding of history reflected the inner life of the Trinity, it was reasonable for him to expect an increasing purification and amelioration of both church and society as history advanced through its progressive stages. The age of the Spirit, whose imminent arrival he fully expected, was to be a time of reform and renewal — an immediate preparation for the eternal fulfillment beyond history, symbolized by the descent of the heavenly Jerusalem (Revelation 21). God's plan, in other words, called for a final stage within history — a historical Sabbath which was to be ushered in by truly spiritual persons. Such a scenario was consonant with the goals of the religious reform movements of the day and at the same time effectively brought about an extraordinary revival of millennial belief.

Since Joachim viewed history as contributing to the building up of the new Jerusalem, he was deeply concerned with what kind of society would be required to support this formidable task. The practical-minded abbot did not balk at providing a detailed blueprint for the ideal human society in the age of the Spirit. As a visual thinker, he even designed elaborate architectural plans and detailed blueprints for the organization of his millennial community. The most complete of these designs, entitled *Dispositio Novi Ordinis* (The arrangement of the new order), is found in figure 12 of his amazing book, *Liber Figurarum* (The book of figures).[15]

The whole organization of Joachim's ideal community was meant to reflect the peace, harmony, and righteousness of the heavenly Jerusalem (Revelation 21), for which it was the preparation. At the heart and physical center of the plan was the main oratory or house of prayer where the spiritual leader of the whole community together with his most advanced monks lived a life completely dedicated to prayer and contemplation. From this spiritual epicenter roads led to the oratories of working monks, who mainly cared for the agriculture and livestock, the quarters of the secular clergy, who were charged with instructing the laypeople, and finally the homes and dormitories of lay workers and artisans, who were the main contributors to the economic viability of the community. From the spiritual leadership of the central oratory the vitality of faith was to permeate throughout the whole community, while at the same time each sector or order experienced special gifts of the Spirit, so that all could draw spiritual sustenance from the entire body.[16]

The community was to be a living sign of the coming heavenly Jerusalem, as well as a restoration of the original apostolic community of the early church (Acts 4). As such, it was to be marked by the spirit of harmony and loving cooperation. Joachim's designs indicated a diversified but unified society, cooperating in all its parts and functions. It entailed a harmony of economic and spiritual life, social and political life, monastic and family life, and — at an even deeper level — a harmony of body and spirit by encouraging "all senses and parts of the body to be devoted to the praise of God."[17] Joachim actually attempted to establish just such a society around the monastery of Fiore in the rugged Sila Mountains of Calabria. Like all utopian enterprises, Joachim's monastic-centered organization never fully reached its goals. Nevertheless, the ideal of societal harmony proposed by Joachim at both the theoretical and the practical level recaptures the spirit of Isaiah and the Hebrew prophets as well as the aspirations of the early church, and has in this way left posterity with a constructive, dynamic, and biblically based notion of the millennium.

Men and women of today, as we approach the third Christian millennium, perhaps more than ever, stand in need of prophetic visions, such as Joachim's vision of the age of the Spirit, to experience the challenge to a renewed pursuit of global harmony in terms that are spiritual, ecological, social, political, and economic. In the following four chapters we will examine a variety of historical millennial movements, especially in the United States, from colonial times to the present. Not all of them will stand up to the image of balance and constructive harmony bequeathed to us in the millennial vision of Joachim of Fiore.

– 7 –

America's Millennial Vision

At a recent academic conference on religion, I presented a paper on a millennial community from Germany which had established itself in the western frontier of the United States at the beginning of the nineteenth century. During the discussion period which followed, one of the many college professors in the audience expressed great disappointment about the loss of millennial fervor and purpose in this country. While an objective look at the record of U.S. millennialism would hardly justify any undue grief at its demise, the professor was nevertheless correct in recognizing that the United States of America had been from its very inception a nation thoroughly driven by a powerful millennial vision.

A Chosen Nation

Even the earliest colonists, such as the Puritans of New England, had come to the New World with well-established millennial beliefs. We will see subsequently how these very beliefs of fellow Puritans in the Old World had served to spark the ardor and vehemence of the English Revolution. When the Puritans migrated to New England in 1630, under the leadership of John Winthrop, they had a clear sense of mission to establish a new society in conformity with the demands of God's kingdom. As Winthrop read the Book of Revelation, the Puritans were called to the New World to create a new Jerusalem — guided by the famous image of the "city upon a hill" (Rev. 21:10), which would one day become so dear to President Ronald Reagan. The Puritans saw the New England settlements as prototypes of Christ's millennial kingdom, which they believed was soon to appear in the New

World. The famous Puritan divine Cotton Mather, in his popular work *Magnalia Christi Americana* (The great American works of Christ), predicted the fast approach of Christ's Second Coming. In general, belief in the imminent coming of the millennial kingdom was the rule rather than the exception among the American colonists.

For colonial religious leaders, millennial expectations often included some very down-to-earth expectations. The same Cotton Mather, for example, was known to preach that "Christ's Kingdom would bring economic justice, social harmony, and the downfall of dishonest merchants and politicians."[1] Jonathan Edwards, the most famous as well as the most exciting of the Puritan preachers, taught a brand of postmillennialism which featured America as both the central locus as well as the primary power source for the breakthrough of Christ's messianic rule on earth. This teaching was very much in harmony with the sense of chosenness and the optimistic belief in progress which marked the colonial worldview. Edwards further enriched his millennial vision by connecting it with the Great Awakening, a movement of spiritual renewal and deeply emotional conversion that was spreading across the American frontier in the years just preceding the revolution of 1776. Indeed, Edwards pointed to this great religious revival, with all its ecstatic excitement and emotional enthusiasm, as the proof of the outpouring of God's Spirit on the whole land.[2]

The beginning of the American Revolution occasioned an even sharper rise of millenarian fervor. Both the spiritual revivalists as well as the more traditional Congregationalists supported the revolution by appealing to the image of America as a chosen nation whose ultimate victory would serve to initiate Christ's millennial reign. This close connection between the revolutionary cause and the religious millennial hope marked the beginnings of what was later to be called "American civil millennialism." During the final months of the war, Ezra Stiles, then president of Yale, typified this politically directed theology in a famous sermon called "The United States Elevated to Glory and Honor," in which he expressed the hope that the revolution would lead to the establishment of an earthly millennial community right in America.[3]

The stressful and turbulent years of the revolution saw the

flourishing of many ecstatic millennial congregations, especially in the rural areas of New England and upper New York State. These groups (known collectively as "The New Light Stir"), unlike Stiles and the mainline Congregationalists, were unambiguously premillenarian in their beliefs. For them humanity was so depraved and sinful that only the destruction of the present order through Christ's triumphant return would make possible the establishment of the millennial kingdom. The Revolutionary War itself was seen as another powerful omen of the final tribulations predicted for the Last Days. Joseph Meacham, leader of a New Light millenarian sect in New Lebanon, New York, had raised the expectations of his followers to a feverish pitch in predicting the return of Christ in 1779. The failure of this prediction brought confusion and depression to Meacham and his followers and led to the disbanding of the New Lebanon congregation. At least some of the survivors of this debacle joined the more established Shaker community, whose millennial commitment is unabashedly reflected in its own official title: The United Society of Believers in Christ's Second Appearing. Unfortunately the disillusionment experienced by the New Lebanon community was not atypical of the fate of the New Light communities of the revolutionary period.

The waning millennialism of the late eighteenth century was to receive a new and unexpected invigoration through the impact of the dynamic religious revival that swept the new nation in the early decades of the nineteenth century. This "era of camp meetings and revival"[4] also corresponded with a large-scale westward expansion of the new republic. The result was a proliferation of millennial communities, many arriving from Germany and eastern Europe, such as the Rappites, the Zoarites, and the Amana community. On the other hand, some other very significant and dynamic millennial movements were strictly products of the native soil. Among these, perhaps the most colorful, controversial, and durable was the Church of Jesus Christ of Latter-day Saints, more popularly known as the Mormons.

The Gathering of the Saints

The Mormons were not only products of spiritual revivalism; they were also significant players in the settlement of the West. They were the spiritual descendants of an earlier Vermont-based sect

Joseph Smith (1805-44). The movement that began in 1830 when Joseph Smith published the Book of Mormon, which is central to the beliefs and practice of the Latter-day Saints (the Mormons), has brought a distinctively American element to the globalization of millennial beliefs.

called the New Israelites, who in their apocalyptic zeal had predicted the end of the world in 1801. Once again the experience of failed prophecy produced profound religious disillusionment, and the sect was quickly disbanded. Some of its leaders, however, migrated to upper New York State, where the religious fervor of the Vermont experiment was picked up by Joseph Smith Jr., the son of one of the remaining New Israelites. After almost a decade of unusual religious experiences, the younger Smith discovered some gold plates in the hills near Manchester, New York. These contained, in his view, an ancient document written in "reformed Egyptian," which was divinely inspired and delivered to him through the angel of Revelation 14, the guardian of "the everlasting gospel."

Through the various revelations of which he was the recipient, Smith was convinced of the widely held nineteenth-century millenarian view that the deterioration of religion and culture had so advanced that the end of this age was about to take place and the world would be visited with severe divine judgment. When Smith issued the famous Book of Mormon in 1830, he presented it as a sign that the end was nigh and that the millennial kingdom of Christ was about to begin.[5] For Sidney Rigdon, one of the most influential interpreters of early Mormon millennialism, the world was so steeped in wickedness that all human efforts at Christianizing the world would eventually come to naught. While the Saints were to prepare the way for Christ's imminent return through the ministry of apostles, prophets, and evangelists, nothing less than the power of Christ himself could cut off the power of "ungodly men" and consign to perdition "all those who resisted the restored gospel."[6] The Mormons had clearly developed their own brand of premillennialism.

The harshness of the coming judgment preached by Smith and Rigdon was greatly softened, on the other hand, by the unique Mormon emphasis on the "gathering of the Saints." According to Rigdon, the Saints would be gathered "from every nation, tongue, language and kindred, under the whole heaven unto places appointed," where they would find "defense and refuge" from the great wrath and destruction that would be "poured out over the whole earth."[7] The gathering of the Saints was in preparation for the establishment of the millennial kingdom, and would take place both in Jerusalem (for faithful Jews) and in America (for both Mormon converts and their Indian neighbors). There is no doubt that for the Mormons, America was viewed as a chosen land where God had planned the building of a New Zion — a new civilization in the wilderness, to be structured in the image of God's coming kingdom on earth.

When Joseph Smith was killed in a riot in Illinois in 1844, one of his disciples, Brigham Young, led the Mormons to Utah, where they founded Salt Lake City and acquired ownership of large tracts of land. There can be no doubt that the wanderings of the early Mormons and their final settlement in Utah correspond to their sense of a millennial mission of establishing a gathering place for the Saints in the heart of the New Zion, which is the United States of America. While expectation of an imminent day of judgment would be gradually modified as the church developed, there can be no doubt about the unambiguous millennialism of the early movement. Even their official title of "Latter-day Saints" serves as a reminder of their original sense that time was running out and of their identification with the saints of Revelation 20, who will ultimately rule with Christ in his millennial kingdom.

But if the Mormons were guided by a very specific millennialist doctrine of their own, the years just preceding the Civil War witnessed an overriding, if somewhat vague, millenarian spirit which permeated most of the churches and wielded a powerful influence on many aspects of American life. The dominant strain of millennialism in America in these years was still the gradualistic postmillennialism of the Jonathan Edwards variety. It often provided a powerful religious incentive for commitment to a variety of social reform movements, such as the cause of temperance. Most significant, however, was the role of this new religious vitality in providing a theological foundation and justification in the struggle for the abolition of slavery. Certainly for a large number of Northern preachers the institution of slavery stood as the principal obstacle to the advent of Christ's millennial kingdom. A number of major Christian churches were to become sharply polarized and divided over the issue of slavery. By the time the Civil War broke out both the Northern and the Southern churches were making claims to represent the true notion of Christian civilization, and several large churches — such as the Presbyterian, the Methodist, and the Baptist — were increasingly torn from within. As the carnage and fratricide of the war multiplied and increased in ferocity, the apocalyptic images of postmillennial belief came even more to the fore, reinforcing if not producing a catastrophic view of the end of history.

The Civil War as Apocalyptic Event

Military leaders on both sides were often guided by "an apocalyptic script"[8] which worked to make the war more total and more destructive. The most popular Northern marching song was the apocalyptic hymn "Mine Eyes Have Seen the Glory of the Coming of the Lord," and Northern preachers regularly espoused the theme that the war was a "climactic test of the redeemer nation and its millennial role."[9] Lincoln himself, who described the war as a "fiery trial" through which the nation must pass, regularly used a rhetoric that was replete with apocalyptic and millennial imagery. For many religious folk the Civil War was indeed an "American Armageddon."

The assassination of Lincoln was itself widely viewed as an apocalyptic event and quickly took on the aura of a millennial myth. The shedding of his blood was understood as a redemptive act that was a necessary price for the breakthrough of the new dispensation, for the sake of which the war had been fought. The "martyrdom" of Abraham Lincoln cast a heavy shadow over the optimistic American hope that the blood shed in the apocalypse of the Civil War would usher in a time of peace and harmony — a true millennial kingdom. In the long run, however, even the terrible tragedy of Lincoln's murder would not ultimately stand in the way of God's plans for his newly chosen nation — the United States of America. This more optimistic perspective was succinctly expressed by the preacher Charles S. Robinson on the Good Friday that Lincoln was shot. In the end, proclaimed Robinson, "over the sad pall that covers our buried hopes bloom the bright flowers of resurrection."[10] As a result of the assassination, Lincoln soon became a central and integral part of American millennial mythology and a major factor in the establishment of an American "civil religion," through which political heroes and national goals are given a religious aura and legitimization.

At the same time, Lincoln's violent death at the very moment of national triumph was the first in a series of setbacks that were to raise great doubts about the inevitability of a millennial outcome to the apocalyptic tribulations of the Civil War. This sense of cosmic disappointment was further aggravated by the Southern white backlash against the freed slaves, the second phase of industrialization with its accompanying social ills, huge population shifts from south to north and from east to west, the rapid emergence and growth of cities, and the new large-scale wave of immigration which upset the very fabric of American society. The combination of these ills, disappointments, and social changes did much to tip the scale of balance in American millennialism from the more gradualistic, optimistic postmillennialism to the hell fire and brimstone catastrophic expectations of the growing premillennialist movement.[11] On the other hand, postmillennialist progressivism continued to find its own forms of expression in the latter decades of the nineteenth century, continuing to support various causes of social justice and to provide theological support for the still-flourishing foreign missionary movement. The striking success of the movement began to convince many believers, such as the Reverend Jedidiah Morse, that "the millennium cannot be far distant."[12] Precisely because scriptural prophecy required that the Gospel be preached to all nations before Christ's glorious return, the vitality and success of the church's missionary activity at this point in history were seen as harbingers and signs of the Second Coming. There can be no doubt that the missionary enthusiasm of the late nineteenth century was powered by a powerful millennial undercurrent.[13] This same missionary zeal also encouraged interdenominational cooperation in the field and eventually was most instrumental in producing a genuine ecumenical movement among the Christian churches. But if biblical millennialism evolved in several directions in the wake of the Civil War, the same period also saw the continued growth of a secularized American version of millennialism, closely tied to the "martyrdom" of Lincoln and later widely known as "American civil religion."

Millennialism in Support of the American Dream

The post–Civil War period, then, saw the revival of the belief in America as an "elect nation" with a special God-given mission to the world. Already in 1845, we see evidence of this patriotic trend in an address by Mark Hopkins, president of Williams College, who expressed his confidence in the construction of an American society "as perfect as we can conceive in the present state when the Kingdom of God shall be set up, and his will shall be done on earth."[14] But it was especially in the period following the Civil War that this "civic millennialism" found concrete popular expression in the doctrine of Manifest Destiny, whereby the United States declared its right and duty to expand its territory as well as its influence throughout North America. The doctrine was used to justify both the conquest of the West and the Spanish-American War of 1898.

Certainly, from this point on, typical American millennial visions frequently combined U.S. national interests with a sense of special divine destiny. As Arthur Schlesinger Jr. has pointed out, the drive across the continent of an energetic and acquisitive people was not really hard to explain; it was somewhat more difficult, however, to find religious or religious-sounding justification for the expansion.[15] A transformed millennialism went a long way to providing such justification and legitimization with the necessary theological trappings.

As the United States became a world power in the twentieth century, the same kind of secularized, patriotic millennialism continued to function as a justification of America's world-saving mission. The biblical, religious roots of millennialism still remain quite evident in the writings of Walter Rauschenbusch, the most famous advocate of the Social Gospel movement. Rauschenbusch was a postmillennialist who urged a gradual transformation of society by Christian social action as a prelude to the ultimate reality of God's kingdom. The civic and patriotic quality of this transformation becomes far more evident in President Woodrow Wilson's insistence during World War I on America's divine destiny to save the world and, after the war, on the urgency of the establishment of the League of Nations as an important providential step toward bringing about a millennial age of peace on earth.

Following World War II, President Dwight D. Eisenhower regularly spoke of the United States as a "shrine or instrument of God" and his secretary of state, John Foster Dulles, did not hesitate to refer to the nation as the "savior of the world." Ronald Reagan was able to win the presidency by a landslide in 1984 by retrieving and co-opting the Puritan millennial vision of America as the anointed city on the hill, "set apart with a special love and faith and freedom."[16] While belief in America's divinely appointed destiny had received support at various times from both the postmillennialist and the premillennialist worldview, it was premillennialism that turned out to be the nation's staunchest and most enduring theological ally in its pursuit of the American dream.

Premillennialism and the Divine Dispensations

The premillennialist strain that had emerged so strongly following the Civil War and the assassination of Lincoln had clearly begun to dominate over other varieties of millennialism in both Britain and the United States. With its characteristic stress on biblical prophecy, it was soon to become fully incorporated into the belief system of American evangelicalism and even found a much wider diffusion among many members of the mainstream Protestant denominations. Premillennialism had experienced periods of both astonishing vitality as well as conspicuous decline during the early decades of the twentieth century. Initially, the horror and devastation of World War I had occasioned a heightened interest in biblical prophecy, and the premillennialist worldview even began to win significant public support. With the end of the war, however, the doomsday prophecies of premillennialism began to lose their appeal, and religious anxiety about the end of the world quickly began to yield to a new religious controversy — the struggle over evolution. Premillennialist thought was forced to take a back seat in the religious market for a while until the economic, political, and social unrest of the 1930s would reinstate the popularity of apocalyptic predictions.

The American premillennialist spirit, which, as we have seen, had found its roots in the horror and disillusionment of the Civil War, had been further reinforced and given specific theological content through the ministrations of the English preacher John Nelson Darby (1800–1882). Darby, who as a young man in England had been appalled by the secularism and unbelief that followed in the wake of the French Revolution, developed his own brand of biblical interpretation, based on the notion of seven divinely established historical dispensations. Darby's seven dispensations were conceived very much in the spirit of Joachim of Fiore's ages of the world, though the Englishman's dispensations were far more specifically defined. Darby, who preached his "dispensationalist" doctrine on several visits to America both during and after the Civil War, effectively transformed the American premillennialist tradition with his new biblical approach.

The Darbyian version of premillennialism reached new heights of influence and popularity with the publication of Cyrus I. Scofield's *Scofield Reference Bible* in 1909. Scofield's detailed commentary, which included both the biblical text and his own comments on the same page, could easily mislead a theologically untrained readership by indirectly suggesting a parity or even a confusion between the commentary and the scriptural text. The *Scofield Reference Bible,* following Darby's teaching, presented the return of Christ as occurring in two stages: (1) the secret spiritual rapture of the saints, to be followed by seven years of catastrophic events called the tribulation (1 Thess. 4:17; Mark 13:3–27); and (2) the return of Christ in visible power and glory at the end of the time of tribulation, the effect of which would be the defeat of the evil forces of the Antichrist and the establishment of the millennial kingdom on earth (2 Thess. 2:4–12; 1 John 2:18). The commentary was an immediate success, and over the subsequent years more than ten million copies were published. Through the combined contributions of Darby and Scofield, the rapture and the tribulation became doctrinal centerpieces of English-speaking premillennialism, and the commentary became "a major conduit for disseminating premillennial dispensationalism throughout the world."[17]

By the 1930s the premillennialist message once again gained a new wave of popularity as it addressed its doomsday predictions to the awesomeness of the new technologies as well as to the growing fears emerging from the increasing global unrest. Popular novels, like F. L. Oilar's *Be Thou Prepared for Jesus Is Coming*, described in dramatic detail the impact of the rapture on a typical American city as well as the extreme barbarity and oppression of the reign of the Antichrist. As the threat of fascism continued to accelerate in Europe, new sightings of the Antichrist became very common. Benito Mussolini, the new ruler of Rome (who had also signed a concordat with the pope — the traditional Protestant prime choice as Antichrist), emerged as the prime candidate. He seemed to best fit the image of the demonic end-time leader who would lead the forces of a revived Roman Empire.[18]

The Alliance with Fundamentalism

Late nineteenth-century developments, such as the growing influence of Darwinism in the schools, the dominance of liberal theology, historical-critical scholarship in the seminaries, and the progressivistic millennialism of the Social Gospel movement, had placed many religious Americans in a state of spiritual siege. In response to these threats the evangelical churches and the premillennialist tradition had formed a powerful and durable alliance by century's end. If the conservative evangelicalism of the alliance had been shored up by the success of the *Scofield Reference Bible*, it found additional support and strength in the publication of a series of twelve pamphlets called *The Fundamentals* between the years 1910 and 1915. The series was intended as a codification of the basic "unnegotiable tenets" of the Christian faith, with a special emphasis on biblical inerrancy over against the perceived claims of modern biblical scholarship.[19] When major leaders of the premillennialist movement throughout the country, including Cyrus Scofield, strongly endorsed this attempt to return to the "fundamentals," the fusion of premillennial dispensationalism with a vast grassroots evangelical movement was complete. As a result, the Darbyian dispensationalist approach to biblical prophecy ceased to be just a particular method of biblical study and soon became an essential component of a large-scale, grassroots evangelical movement which now began to be known as *fundamentalism.*

The tie with dispensationalism undoubtedly gave fundamentalism a more apocalyptic thrust through the conviction that the world is now near the end of the Sixth Dispensation — an age that is more than ripe for God's terrible judgment. Within this frame of thinking all contemporary human tragedies, such as war, terrorism, disease, and economic decline, become signs of the imminence of Christ's return and millennial rule on earth (i.e., the Seventh Dispensation). In good Darbyian fashion, fundamentalists also put special emphasis on the rebirth of the State of Israel in 1948 as a biblical sign (see Isa. 66:8) of the speedy coming of God's kingdom. At the same time the premillennialist scheme anticipates the conversion of the Jews to Christ in the Last Days. Hence the ambiguity, even today, of the relation of fundamentalism to the Jewish community and to the State of Israel.

Armageddon and American Politics

In recent years, it is this dispensationalist brand of premillennialism which has provided the strongest theological base for the promotion of civil religion and its patriotic version of millenarianism. The explosion of the first nuclear weapons at Hiroshima and Nagasaki gave premillennialism not only a new impetus and credibility, but also a radically different kind of end-time scenario to relate to biblical prophecy. No longer was it a question of earthquakes, famines, hailstones, and plagues. Premillennialists now had to make sense of the possibility of the total annihilation of the human future.[20] Dispensationalist preachers did not fall short of the challenge, but were quick to focus on this most frightening prospect, frequently reminding their audiences that only the touch of a button separated them from the horror of a nuclear holocaust. Writers for the *Moody Monthly,* the famous fundamentalist publication from Chicago, quickly adjusted to the drastically enlarged dimensions of apocalyptic expectation, claiming that the Bible had long foretold the coming of nuclear disaster.

Despite their commitment to literalism, prophecy preachers creatively transposed ancient biblical end-time descriptions into fascinating, if not fantastic, nuclear predictions. The wooden weapons of the forces of Gog described in Ezekiel 39 were conveniently modernized by the gratuitous claim that the wooden spears and arrows would be nuclear tipped — well adapted to "close-up fighting." Other commentators felt free to metamorphose Ezekiel's bows and arrows into "launchers and missiles."[21] It became a standard practice among dispensationalists to interpret the biblical hordes of Gog from the north as divisions of Soviet troops, while Ezekiel's Meschech was translated as Moscow and his Tubal was understood to mean the modern Siberian city of Tobolsk. With this wealth of imagination, there can be little surprise that dispensationalism remained a vital religious force throughout the Cold War period. Among the most successful representatives of this "nuclear-Armageddon" theology were John F. Walvoord, the former chancellor of Dallas Theological Seminary, and Hal Lindsey, the prolific writer of modern biblical prophecy.

Walvoord's revised edition of his very popular book, *Armageddon, Oil and the Middle East Crisis,* published shortly before the outbreak of the Persian Gulf War, sold over one million copies. In it the author claims that events in the Middle East make it clear that the "final stage" of the prophetic calendar is now set; the prophetic drama leading to Armageddon is about to unfold, and the rapture of the church "may be expected momentarily."[22] Hal Lindsey, for his part, has been dubbed "the Geraldo Rivera of millennialism." His writings are amazingly adept at interpreting biblical prophecy in a way that reflects the realities of nuclear war. For him the "fire, smoke and brimstone" of apocalyptic prophecy is a clear reference to "nuclear explosion, radioactive fall-out and melted earth!"[23] His 1970 work, *The Late Great Planet Earth,* sold more than fifteen million copies and successfully brought the premillenarian message into the mainstream of American futuristic thought by changing the Book of Revelation into a guide for the nuclear age.

The impact of Lindsey and other premillennial preachers has not only affected the religious beliefs of millions of people, but has also found its way into the inner chambers of high political power. Former president Ronald Reagan, whose confidants included Billy Graham, Don Moomau, Pat Boone, and other prophecy believers, had drunk deeply from the draughts of dispensationalist theology and was known to express frequently his private conviction that we find ourselves at the very brink of the Last Days. He was particularly intrigued by the prophecy about the forces of Gog from the north in Ezekiel 38, which premillennialists like Lindsey identified with the Soviet Union. Reagan's secretary of defense, Caspar Weinberger; his secretary of the interior, James Watt; and his surgeon general, C. Everett Koop, were all fervent prophecy believers who expected the imminent apocalyptic destruction of the world.[24] Lindsey was the most popular author both at the White House and at the Pentagon.

This unprecedented influence of religion on the highest authority in the land proved very disturbing to both religious and secular critics. Ironically, it was a coalition of several evangelical groups that, fully understanding the implications of the dispensationalist worldview, presented some of the most passionate objections to having a premillennialist president in the White House. Their fear, of course, was that a president who firmly believed in the inevitability of nuclear conflagration might be much less hesitant to push the much-feared nuclear button. They called upon President Reagan to repudiate the dispensationalist dogma that "nuclear holocaust is foreordained in the Bible." On the more secular side, the evangelicals were joined by the liberal lobby People for the American Way, which strongly assailed the underlying "Armageddon theology" as a blatant disdain for peace.[25]

Lindsey's pop approach to biblical prophecy has been challenged on scriptural grounds by a number of highly qualified critics, such as the Mennonite biblical scholar Dale Aukerman and the Lutheran theologian Ted Peters. The most basic and trenchant objection, however, is that expressed by Harvard theologian Gordon Kaufman, who argues that Lindsey's fatalistic view of biblical prophecy essentially cuts the nerve of human responsibility by teaching "that nuclear cataclysm is inevitable."[26] In view of this criticism, noted premillennialist preachers, such as Jerry Falwell, Pat Robertson, and Billy Graham, have softened their stand on the inevitability of nuclear holocaust.

Since the publication of Lindsey's best seller, a number of world developments have further undermined the accuracy and validity of his predictions. His identification of the European Common

Market with the ten horns of the beast of Revelation 13 lost some credibility when the organization expanded to twelve and more member nations. His naming of the Soviet Union as the demonic army of Gog and Magog in Revelation 20 hardly seems convincing today after the collapse of the Soviet Empire. Premillennialists, however, have rarely been deterred by discordant factual data. Jack Van Impe, the popular prophecy preacher, still insists that Russia is the most likely candidate for representing the biblical armies of the north at the battle of Armageddon. In a recent edition of his ministry magazine, *Perhaps Today,* he argues the Vladimir Zhirinovsky, the recent hard-line Communist candidate, will eventually lead Russia into a massive attack on Israel, issuing in the end-time events described in Ezekiel 38–39.

If the Armageddon theology of dispensationalism has served as a biblical legitimization of U.S. foreign policy, including nuclear preparedness and a one-sided focus on American national security, it will become apparent in chapter 9 that, with a slight twist of interpretation, premillennial thought is also capable of underwriting a virulent revolutionary and antigovernment mentality. Before examining that other side of the premillennialist coin, however, it is important to address the question of failed prophecy and the spiritual disillusionment which follows in its wake.

– 8 –

A Story of Hope and Shattered Dreams

What is obvious at this point is that millennialism is a highly diversified phenomenon which embraces many different forms and styles. Certainly, not all millennialist thinkers are given to the pessimism or fatalism so characteristic of the dispensationalist view. The millennial mind, as we have already seen in the case of Joachim of Fiore, is also capable of producing very noble and inspiring visions of the human future. But whether or not millennialist belief is hopeful or terrifying, it all too frequently succumbs to the compelling temptation of announcing in specific detail (year, date, and often location) the arrival of the end-times. Such brash attempts at forecasting the human future fly in the face of biblical admonitions and usually end in embarrassment and disillusionment for those who heed these messages. Nevertheless, even the eventual dissolution of millennial movements as a result of failed prophecy does not necessarily undermine all the worthy aspirations they might have embraced during their lifespan. Each of the millennialist experiments described below has been deeply shaken if not destroyed by unfulfilled prophetic expectations. Yet it will be argued that at least one of them has bequeathed to posterity an important and inspiring vision of human community.

The Rappites of New Harmony, Indiana

Early nineteenth-century America saw the establishment of numerous and diverse millennial movements, each with distinctive theologies, but all with a strong utopian bent. Many of these groups came from Europe, where for many people the French Revolution and the upheavals of the Napoleonic era had marked the end of the old European order. For a number of sectarian Christian groups these turbulent events also served as harbingers of the end of the present age and the inauguration of Christ's millennial kingdom. In coming to America, these religious communities were also hoping to escape from the controls of repressive state religion and discover an environment more suitable for preparing for the coming of God's kingdom on earth. Among the most fascinating and instructive of these immigrant millennial communities were the Rappites from southern Germany, who are best known for their settlement in New Harmony, Indiana, between the years 1814 and 1824.

The Rappites, who were so named after their visionary founder, George Rapp, are also known as the Harmonists, having established themselves as the Harmony Society through acts of association drawn up in Pennsylvania in 1805. The previous year, Rapp with about eight hundred followers had settled on the American frontier in western Pennsylvania, where they cleared the woodland and established a self-sufficient farming community. Unhappy with unfriendly neighbors and needing better soil for the cultivation of the vine, they moved farther west in search of a new safe haven where they could prepare for the return of the Lord in diligent work and the perfection of "brotherly harmony." In 1814 they found their new site along the Wabash River in southwestern Indiana, where they purchased thirty thousand acres of untouched woodland with easy access to navigable waterways. Here they established the village of New Harmony, which over the next ten years was to become one of the most successful of the many communitarian experiments that had sprung up along the American frontier.

Outside observers (including Friedrich Engels, the coauthor of the Communist Manifesto) had nothing but the highest praise for New Harmony, which in so short a time had become a thriving agricultural community, whose farm products, linens, flannels, and wine were highly prized and used throughout the American West. Both in Europe and in America, New Harmony had gained high approval for its social and economic organization. What the worldly observer often missed, however, was the centrality and the driving force of the community's millennial conviction in the imminent return of Christ on earth. In commenting on this essential aspect of life in New Harmony, a team of astute historians has remarked that "religious belief...was the invisible framework that held the Harmony Society together and supported virtually every building and activity that could be observed in New Harmony between 1814 and 1824."[1]

The Harmonists understood themselves as a chosen millennial community, modeling themselves after the early Christians of the Acts of the Apostles, who were "of one heart and soul," sharing everything they possessed in common (Acts 4:32). George Rapp closely identified the migrations of his community with those of Abraham in Gen. 12:2-3, whose offspring God had promised to make into a "great nation" in which "all the families of the earth shall be blessed." Accordingly, the Harmony Society felt driven by an inexorable divine call to live a community life that would serve as a model for the ultimate reconstitution of the human family. Rapp had often argued that if only one such society exists in the world, it will inevitably draw people from all nations to unite with it. However small and insignificant their own community might appear — hidden away in the woodlands of Indiana — it was nevertheless destined for nothing less than the regeneration and restoration of all humanity in Christ's millennial kingdom. This conviction so totally permeated every aspect of the Harmonists' life that none of their activities could accurately be described as purely secular.

One of the Harmonists' most popular biblical passages was Mic. 4:8, which contains a prophecy about the coming restored Davidic kingdom. According to Luther's German translation of the text, the prophet was foretelling a time when God's faithful community will receive the golden rose — the symbol of God's universal rule in Jerusalem. This symbol was stamped on all the Harmonist goods as a continual reminder to the members of the ultimate goal and purpose of their labors. To outside merchants and traders, however, the golden rose simply became a widespread symbol of high-quality merchandise.

Notwithstanding their extraordinary religious zeal, these peasants from Württemberg in southern Germany were a preeminently practical people. The notion of harmony was never just a spiritual and interpersonal ideal — though it certainly was all that. Harmony also meant a "prudent regulation of industry and economy," which was to help provide the foundation for a veritable "heaven on earth."[2] Even during the economic depression which began in 1819, the Harmonists were able to provide for all their own needs through agriculture and still sell more than twelve thousand dollars worth of agricultural produce annually. Their general store was especially popular, for it always managed to offer a wide selection of quality goods "produced by the Rappites' own fields and woodlands, mills and factories." Their fine cloth, especially their flannel, was highly prized both at home and abroad, and, of course, all their goods bore the Harmonist trademark of the golden rose. By 1820 their manufactured goods were valued at fifty thousand dollars annually, and in 1824 "Harmonist commerce reached to twenty-two states and ten foreign countries."[3]

The Rappites knew that the harmony of their communal life depended very much on their strong work ethic. When all one's possessions and all the fruits of one's labor are held in common, there is no place for laziness or gold bricking. All the Harmonists were expected to work hard for what today would be considered long hours (ten to twelve), depending on the demands of the season. On the other hand, all members of the society, whether living in married households or in the celibate dormitories, were provided with adequate rations of milk, food, and clothing. In general the Harmonist workday was a communal activity and was so arranged as to provide a sense of joy and fulfillment for all participants. Every day but Sunday, the villagers were summoned to daily work by the sound of French horns, which awakened them between five and six o'clock each morning. Apprenticeships were encouraged so as to maintain the various skills necessary for the successful management of a completely independent community. Whenever possible, work assignments were varied in order to combat the boredom of routine. Harvest time, in particular, was celebrated as a "grand communal occasion," in which all able hands, men, women, and children, would march off singing to the fields, where they would work for long hours, sometimes accompanied by the sonorous tones of New Harmony's well-trained band playing on some nearby hillock.[4]

Despite the practical communal character of the Harmonist activity, both their productivity and special lifestyle were inextricably tied to the community's whole millennial belief system, without which it would have had neither meaning nor vitality. There can be no doubt that the Harmonist communal living required a great deal of self-renunciation and the forgoing of many worldly pleasures. On the other hand, the community's rejection of worldly vanity and luxurious superfluity was fully expected in the long run to relieve the members from all want and material anxiety. As Frederick Rapp, George Rapp's adopted son, later put it: in New Harmony "diligence and labor are amply rewarded,"[5] for the surrender of earthly goods was directly aimed at producing a "freer, better and higher enjoyment" that is experienced "only in the unselfishness of harmonious sharing."[6] In a word, the self-discipline and sacrifice of life in New Harmony were intended to produce nothing less than Rapp's longed for "Heaven on Earth."[7]

In view of the life-affirming nature of Harmonist asceticism, it is not surprising that they took great pains to foster cultural and educational interests. They were particularly well versed in classical music, and Sunday religious services were often complemented by concerts given by the highly skilled New Harmony band. They strongly encouraged the reading of good literature, the composition of poetry, and the practice of the visual arts, but above all they excelled in music, producing both their own hymnal as well as their own secular compositions. All their creative work revealed a profound love of nature, which was also expressed through the tender care with which they protected the environment.[8] Each of the Harmonist settlements, including New Harmony, contained a labyrinth park, which they used for entertainment and relaxation, but also as a symbolic reminder of the obstacles and difficulties they must face each day on their spiritual journey toward the millennial kingdom.[9]

On the whole, the religious community of New Harmony, Indiana, offers a very positive and constructive variation on the millennialist tradition. The Harmonists' commitment to make this world a better place was based on their powerful sense of a sacred mission to restore lost harmony to God's creation. This powerful vision affected every aspect of their lives: personal, social, political, and economic, *transforming the notion of harmony into a very effective organizing principle, as well as a final ethical criterion for meeting every moral challenge.*

Unfortunately, the Harmonist experiment was eventually to be undermined by the authoritarian manner of its charismatic leader, George Rapp, who in his religious zeal for the kingdom had strongly urged the practice of evangelical celibacy among all members of the society. Ultimately, the recruitment of new members did not keep pace with the attrition which the community experienced through death and defection. But even more fatal to the Harmonist movement was the literalist belief in the imminent, physical return of Jesus Christ on earth. Continued delays in this vivid expectation eventually created an overwhelming sense of disillusionment, which finally caused the society to disband by the beginning of the twentieth century.

Even to this day, the visitor to the burial grounds of the millennial community at the historic village of New Harmony, Indiana, experiences a mixed sense of peace and sadness in contemplating the unmarked graves of the Harmonists who had long ago been laid to rest in the joyful hope of hearing the blast of the angelic trumpet, summoning them to greet the Lord upon his glorious return.

The Great Disappointment and the Rise of Adventism

The disillusionment of the Harmonists with the continued delay in the expected return of the Lord was gradual and undramatic, yet it eventually brought about the dissolution of the society. A much more dramatic disappointment took place in the middle of the nineteenth century as a result of the biblical prophetic predictions of the charismatic teacher William Miller. The Millerite movement began in Vermont and in New York in the early 1840s. Like the Mormons, whose origins were only slightly earlier, Millerite millennialism had found powerful inspiration and support in the Second Great Awakening, which had energized religious life throughout America in the early decades of the nineteenth century (see previous chapter). Given the camp meeting atmosphere — with its convulsive conversions, spiritual swoons, and "night cries" — that characterized this early revivalist scene, there is little wonder that it sometimes spawned more fanatical millennial movements, uninhibited in their speculations about the end of the world. William Miller, a self-taught prophecy teacher from Vermont who predicted that the end of the world would take place in 1843, was the charismatic religious leader of just such a millennial movement.

Returning from the War of 1812, during which he had served in the Vermont Militia, Miller underwent a profound religious conversion at a revival meeting in 1816. Despite his lack of formal training, Miller, a bright, hard-working farmer, began an intense but private study of the sacred scriptures, with a special passion for discerning the meaning of biblical prophecy. Threatened by the sense of a growing secularization and a moral decline in the general culture, Miller, like other traditional Christians, began to pay special attention to prophetic passages about the end-times. In his own efforts to interpret these apocalyptic passages, Miller relied on the chronological calculations of Bishop Ussher, a seventeenth-century Reformed theologian from Ireland. According to Ussher's computations, which were influential enough to have been inserted in the margins of the King James Bible, the date of creation was to be fixed at 4004 B.C.E. Ussher also held the widely accepted millennial view that the world would last six thousand years (and on this basis had predicted that the world would end in 1996).

Relying especially on a passage in the Book of Daniel, in which the heavenly voice assures Daniel that "the transgression that makes desolate" will last "for two thousand and three hundred evenings and mornings; then the sanctuary shall be restored to its rightful state" (Dan. 8:14), Miller set out to correct Ussher's calculations. Starting with the assumption that the biblical prophecy dated from 457 B.C.E., and understanding Daniel's 2,300 days as years which must pass before the earth could reach its final cleansing, Miller subtracted the 457 years from the prophetic 2300 to reach the number 1843. Once convinced of the correctness of these figures, Miller argued that Ussher's calculation of 4004 for the beginning of creation must be slightly off and changed it to 4157 B.C.E., thus providing exactly six thousand years from the beginning of creation to the end of the age.[10] Obviously, the most significant and ominous of these calculations for Miller's contemporaries was the determination of the year 1843 for the end of the world. Since Miller began to preach and circulate these ideas in 1831, those who accepted his teaching were convinced that the world was already in its Last Days.

Miller's lectures on the coming millennium, given in New York City in 1840, caught the attention of the press, and within a very short time Millerism became a hot national issue. Miller's millennial message received powerful endorsement from the very influential Boston pastor Joshua Himes, who had been won over by Miller's calculations, and who used his significant publicity skills to foster the cause. Himes immediately established an eight-page newspaper called *The Signs of the Times*, followed shortly by the *Philadelphia Alarm*, to help spread the word about the imminent return of the Lord. Apart from newspaper circulation, Himes was also a master at organizing large camp meeting revivals, featuring tents that could shelter between three thousand and four thousand people.

As hundreds of prominent preachers joined the movement, the expectation of Christ's Second Coming spread like wild fire through religious publications, Sunday sermons, and highly organized camp meetings across the country. As a result, both ministers and laypersons and urban as well as rural Christians from all branches of Protestant denominations joined this vast millennial movement. Historians estimate that by 1843 hard core Millerites numbered well over fifty thousand and that as many as a million Americans took seriously his predictions on the imminent end of the world.[11] As the fateful year approached, Miller first specified the end-time as between 1843 and 1844. By March 1844, Miller had to recheck his calculations and reset the date for October 22.[12]

When this latter date also passed without any visible sign of Christ's Second Coming, many abandoned the movement, experiencing what has been called "the Great Disappointment." Others, including Miller and Himes, convened meetings to try to salvage their millennial convictions despite the obvious error of their predictions. As a result of such meetings, Millerism split into a variety of offshoot churches, collectively known as Adventist.[13]

Attempts to reinterpret and save the Millerite predictions were at times quite ingenious. Joseph Turner of Maine, for example, argued that Christ had, indeed, returned in 1844, but in the heavenly realms and, though not visible, had set into motion the "millennial sabbath." Others, like Hiram Edson of New York, added the notion that on the same prophetic date Christ had cleansed a "heavenly sanctuary" (Heb. 9:24–28) rather than an earthly one. Most of the splinter groups that emerged from these diverse interpretations of the failed Miller prophecy did not survive beyond 1920, but a number of Adventist churches did eventually fully recuperate from "the Great Disappointment," and they continue to prosper today. The largest and best known of these churches is that of the Seventh-Day Adventists.[14]

The Seventh-Day Adventists refused to abandon the prophecy of Dan. 8:14 and the 2,300 days that had so obsessed Miller, though they recognized that he had mistakenly interpreted its meaning. They accepted Hiram Edson's view of the cleansing of a heavenly sanctuary as the correct meaning of the passage, so that Jesus was now in the holiest place in heaven, preparing for his Second Coming to earth. This new Advent was still imminent, but it was now clear to the descendants of the Millerite tradition that "no human should set a precise date for it."[15]

Perhaps no one did more to salvage Millerite disciples and other Adventists from gloom and depression after the Great Disappointment than one of his former disciples, Ellen G. Harmon. Through a series of ecstatic experiences she soon won the reputation of a great Adventist prophetess and successfully absorbed many of the disillusioned Millerites into her "Sabbatarian" movement. Sabbatarianism was a medieval doctrine, revived by the English Puritans, which held that the fourth commandment required that the Lord's Day be celebrated on the Jewish Sabbath. Through her own personal visions she came to understand that the warning of the third angel in Rev. 14:9 referred to those who violate this true Sabbath observance. She also concluded that the day of the Lord's return on earth had been delayed precisely because of the wide-scale violation of the Sabbath commandment by Christians everywhere. Through such a strategy, Miller himself was also indirectly exonerated from his failed prophecy.

Because of this insistence on the scriptural precept of observing the seventh day as the Lord's Day, the group began to go by the name Sabbatarian Adventists. Ellen Harmon had married James White, a former Millerite preacher, in 1846, and together they organized the group into an official denomination in 1860 at Battle Creek, Michigan. It was from this point on that they went by the new name Seventh-Day Adventists. The Whites, who were very interested in healing the body as well as the soul, followed in the footsteps of the controversial Presbyterian minister and evangelist Sylvester Graham, who had pressed the value of a strictly vegetarian diet and with that goal in mind had invented and manufactured the famous Graham cracker. So in addition to providing headquarters for the Seventh-Day Adventist Church, Battle Creek also served as the site for the church's new Western Health Reform Institute. One of Mrs. White's disciples from the medical profession, Dr. John Harvey Kellogg, who no doubt is best known for his famous health cereal, Kellogg's Corn Flakes, helped the White's to transform what was originally an Adventist water-cure center in Battle Creek to an internationally renowned health spa. The health-minded Adventists were strictly opposed to the use of liquor, tobacco, coffee, and tea, and they also opposed dancing and popular entertainment. In the tradition of the Reverend Graham, they encouraged the adoption of a bland diet as the best way of avoiding masturbation, which Mrs. White blamed as "the root cause of imbecility, dwarfed forms, crippled limbs, misshapen heads, and other deformities."[16]

Adventists' concern for the advancement of human health in the present order, however, did not in any way diminish their original millennial enthusiasm. Unlike their spiritual ancestors, the Millerites, Adventists insist that the exact time of Jesus' Second Coming cannot be ascertained from the study of biblical prophecy. This position obviously protects them from the kind of debacle the Millerites experienced when they predicted the exact date of Christ's return in 1844. Nevertheless, they fully believe that we live in the Last Days and are committed to regular observations and updated interpretations of the "signs of the times." They see their own millennial role as that of the faithful remnant. They alone bear the "seal of God" because of their faithful observance of the Sabbath command, and will have a special role to play in the final great battle against the armies of Gog and Magog after the establishment of Christ's millennial kingdom. The other Christian churches, Catholic and Protestant alike, bear the mark of the beast, and unless they convert to true Sabbath practice, they will ultimately share in "the defeat of Satan and the destruction of the unredeemed."[17]

The Adventist appraisal of the American republic is no more flattering than its view of other Christian bodies. Its stance in this regard sharply separates it from earlier forms of American millennialism, for which, as a rule, the United States had a very privileged place in the millennial scheme, or at very least provided the location for the establishment of Christ's earthly kingdom.

For the Adventists, on the other hand, America will in the long run become the ultimate adversary and will serve as an instrument of the Antichrist until his final destruction at Christ's coming.[18] These "antipatriotic" views did not tend to endear the Adventists to the bulk of the American population, and this might account to some degree for the greater success of Adventist missionaries overseas than in the United States. In fact, after her husband's death, Mrs. White lived for some time in Switzerland and in Norway, where she helped spread the Adventist message, and before the end of the century she had brought her medical missions to Australia and New Zealand. In 1988, Seventh-Day Adventists numbered 588,536 in the United States and some 5 million members worldwide. They have a highly organized church administration, and their medical facilities have won worldwide recognition.[19]

But if the Seventh-Day Adventists have assumed a more restrained outlook toward end-time predictions, the same cannot be said of another late nineteenth-century millenarian group, namely, the International Bible Students Association — or, as they have subsequently become known, the Witnesses of Jehovah.

Watching from the Tower of Zion

This now-popular organization was founded by Charles Taze Russell, who was born in Pittsburgh in 1852 — only eight years after the Great Disappointment of the Millerites. Russell is clearly not to be counted among those who were disillusioned by the Great Disappointment or otherwise discouraged from the practice of end-time prophesying. From the time of their founding in 1872, the Witnesses, as they call themselves, have, like Russell, not hesitated to set specific dates for end-time predictions. Nor have they been discouraged when these forecasts failed to materialize.

Russell, who grew up as a haberdasher in his father's stores, did not have the opportunity for any formal training in religion, neither at college nor in a seminary. He was, however, a very astute and intense student of the Bible and in his early twenties had organized a number of very successful Bible study groups. In 1879, in conjunction with other study groups, he organized a publication called *Zion's Watch Tower and Herald of*

Christ's Presence, later to be called simply the *Watch Tower.* By 1884 he had founded the Watch Tower Bible and Tract Society, which was also known as the International Bible Students Association. In 1931, under the leadership of Russell's successor, Judge Joseph Rutherford, the movement took the new name of Jehovah's Witnesses.

The new title reflected their conviction that the only proper biblical name for God is Jehovah, and that the truly biblical name for those who worshiped him was "witnesses," rather than "Christians."[20] While Russell insisted on a very dedicated and careful study of the Bible, which enabled him and his followers to establish a detailed biblical chronology and history, they did so while totally ignoring, if not despising, the findings of critical biblical scholarship over the previous one hundred years.

The basic doctrines which Russell drew from his biblical studies closely resembled those of the Adventists and other millenarian teachers who had preceded him. On the other hand, Russell did give this indigenous millenarianism his own particular spin. Jehovah was the one, supreme, and universal deity; yet Christ was important as the first of God's creation and the mediator through whom the Witnesses were to pray to Jehovah. Christ died for us at the stake (not the cross) as a ransom for sin and after his death rose as an immortal "spirit person," who continues his presence in the world. *History had run its course and the time of the end was near at hand.* For this reason, witnesses must remain apart from the world "and observe only those secular laws and follow only those practices of faith that are in conformity with the society's understanding of the Bible."[21]

Russell was typical of most millennialists in taking literally the 144,000 saints of Rev. 7:4 and Rev. 14:1, but he interpreted these as a small flock of believers taken from the whole of history, who are the true spiritual Israelites. These alone were the elect who would reign with Christ in heaven. The rest, "the great multitude" of Rev. 7:9, will remain on earth, where Christ will have established his millennial kingdom. This thousand-year period of peace will come to a violent end with the great battle of Armageddon. This end-time conflict will separate the faithful followers of Jehovah from those unfaithful ones whose lives will be destroyed in the final reckoning between good and evil. After this final triumph of Christ and his Witnesses, Christ's earthly kingdom will be brought to its consummation and, in a word, "heaven will be established on earth."[22]

The Jehovah's Witnesses have consistently argued that the United Nations, the world's religious leaders, and the United States itself will, in the Last Days, fight on the side of Satan in the battle of Armageddon. Even now the present order of national states is under the rule of Satan, and for this reason Witnesses are forbidden to salute any national flag or serve in the military forces. These practices have frequently put them in conflict with U.S. law and have made them the object of ridicule and persecution both here and abroad. During World War I, Judge Rutherford and other leaders of the movement were sentenced to twenty years in federal prison. For the Witnesses, however, the wars between earthly governments were basically acts of murder in which they must refuse to participate.[23]

The energizing power behind the Witnesses' zeal is their literal belief in the imminent coming of Christ's millennial kingdom. This central conviction of their faith impels them not only to prepare themselves through prayer in their "kingdom halls," but also to spread the word of their teachings through a massive publication campaign as well as through their all-too-familiar door-to-door visitations.

From the beginning of the movement the Witnesses have also been quite persistent in making specific predictions on the apocalyptic calendar. Initially, Russell rather cautiously argued that the parousia or Second Coming of Christ had already begun by way of Christ's invisible presence in 1874. He also predicted that the harvest of the elect 144,000 saints would be completed by 1881, and even more boldly declared that the power of the "Gentile nations" would end in 1914, but only after great tribulations on earth. This would be the prelude to the battle of Armageddon in 1918. The outbreak of World War I at this time temporarily bolstered the cause of the Witnesses, but when Russell died in 1916 and was not taken up physically to heaven, as he had foretold, the faith of the Witnesses was deeply shaken for a time. But Russell's successor, Judge Rutherford, was quick to make his own predictions, declaring that "Abraham, Isaac and Jacob and other faithful Israelites would return to earth in 1925."[24] In preparation for this event, the Witnesses built a mansion in San Diego to provide housing for the patriarchs upon their arrival. While the returning patriarchs were never seen, Rutherford did spend the last years of his life in splendid isolation at the mansion.[25] Even more recently, the Witnesses earmarked 1975 as the year the millennium would begin. Overall, the society has shown an amazing resiliency in the face of frequent failed expectations. As journalist Russell Chandler has recently put it, the Witnesses seem to have the uncanny ability to simply "reschedule doomsday and hit reset."[26]

History has shown quite decisively that there is great risk in attempting to predict the timetable for the Last Days. While the Jehovah's Witnesses have found a way to survive continual failures, they do so through isolation from the larger culture. For the vast majority of millennialists, failed prediction has caused profound spiritual and psychological harm, as in the case of the Great Disappointment. History will never know just how many of the Indiana Harmonists eventually experienced the pangs of disillusionment or even the loss of faith as their lively hopes for millennial fulfillment met with the frustration of continual delay. What does seem clear, however, is that the proclaiming of specific dates for the start of the millennium proves far more traumatic to the community of believers than a more general heightened awareness of living in the end-times.

As I mentioned at the beginning of the chapter, even millennial communities that ultimately fall apart because of unfulfilled prophecy may, nevertheless, leave behind an important spiritual witness and a legacy of human achievement. I have no doubt that the Millerites in their time encouraged many followers to a more conscientious observance of the moral life, and that the Jehovah's Witnesses even today continue to uplift the destitute and the dissolute from lives of degradation and despair. On the other hand, the reckless practice of casual end-time predictions causes too much human pain to be dismissed as a harmless theological fancy.

The millennialism of the Rappites in Indiana, for its part, had a very different thrust. Harmonist belief in the imminence of the kingdom produced very positive, community-building attitudes, encouraging an excellence-oriented work ethic and a deep sense of communal responsibility. For them *harmony* was more than a catchy slogan, it was in George Rapp's words "the very essence of the coming millennial kingdom" which can be attained only through the relentless pursuit of Christian perfection.[27] The fundamental mission of the Harmonists was to help to restore that harmony between human beings and the entire universe which was part of the original divine plan of creation. The Harmonists in their day were convinced that the spiritual success of their communal life had worldwide implications. This conviction might yet prove true if the ideal of global harmony should become a goal consciously and universally pursued by the world's spiritual and political leaders alike.

But millennialism does not always prove so friendly and benevolent. At various times it has inspired and encouraged violence and destructiveness. This story of millennial and apocalyptic violence is the subject of the following chapter.

– 9 –

A Story of Apocalyptic Violence

Since the beginning of the 1990s, a number of seemingly bizarre, very violent, and, in some fashion, religiously inspired tragedies have shaken our faith in religion as a benign and positive force. These destructive events have occurred both in the United States and abroad, and the mind-sets that have produced them continue to baffle and threaten us. No doubt, for Americans, the massacre in Waco, Texas, and the bombing of the government building in Oklahoma City stand out in our minds as the most shocking of these horrors. For Europeans and Asians respectively, on the other hand, the synchronized suicides of the Solar Temple members and the nerve gas attack on the Tokyo subway, allegedly perpetrated by millenarian sects (as indicated above in chap. 4), have produced an equally harrowing effect. Given the interrelatedness and the rapid communications of today's society, each of these events also has had a global impact, affecting all of us. It is all too obvious, for example, that a terrorist attack on a Tokyo subway could just as well occur in metropolitan New York, and the same kind of mentality that would engineer the destruction of a government building in Oklahoma City could equally perpetrate terrorist carnage in Paris.

Because the perpetrators of this wanton violence are known to be groups and individuals with strong millennial tendencies, their pernicious actions only inspire further dread and apprehension as we draw closer to that highly charged millennial landmark of the year 2000. Certainly the fears of the present moment are further reinforced when we reflect even casually on the persistent record of apocalyptic violence through the course of history.

Apocalyptic Violence in the Past

Apocalyptic millennialism throughout history has almost always taken the form of ecstatic enthusiasm, if not frenzy or mania. At times, however, this frenzy expresses itself in the form of violent behavior. A literal reading of the Book of Revelation could no doubt, by itself, easily encourage violent, revolutionary solutions to injustice and oppression. But if we further combine this orientation with a charismatic and pathological leadership, we have the perfect, lethal formula for religiously motivated violence. Unfortunately, there are too many historical instances of violent apocalyptic movements to include in this short survey, but the following should give a sufficient picture of millennialism's dark side.

Even in pre-Christian times, several Jewish millenarian groups were known to have turned to violence in their zeal to bring about the reign of God in the land of Israel. The daring and furious uprising of the Jewish Zealots against the Roman occupation between 66 and 70 C.E. was motivated and energized by just this belief in the imminence of God's reign. Even as they fought to the last man at Masada, these religious enthusiasts were convinced that their efforts would be well rewarded in the coming messianic kingdom. While the Christian Crusades, which began in 1095, were not initially a response to millennial preaching, the futility and devastation of these protracted wars soon put an apocalyptic pall over the whole endeavor. The holy city of Jerusalem increasingly took on the image of the ideal millennial city, and the wars to capture it for Christendom were regularly described through the symbols of Antichrists, Satanic beasts, and Armageddon.

The dawn of the fourteenth century saw the climax of a chiliastic movement called Flagellantism, which had its beginnings in the previous century in the form of bands of men marching in penitential procession throughout many Italian towns. Their zeal and enthusiasm for corporal penance had already reached a high point around 1260, which was Joachim of Fiore's prophetic date for the start of the third age. Self-flagellation had always been a characteristic practice of this penitential movement — hence their popular name of "Flagellants." The Flagellants gained many additional disciples with the devastation of the Black Death around the year 1348.

The movement spread rapidly, especially in Germany, where masses of people showed an intense longing for the coming of Christ's millennial kingdom. The German Flagellants, however, had strong anticlerical feelings and directly opposed the religious authority of Rome. They claimed to be taught directly by the Holy Spirit and found full absolution from their sins in their harsh penitential practices. Their most influential leader was Konrad Schmid, who proclaimed himself to be the Messiah and taught that self-flagellation was the most important preparation for the coming millennium. In the meantime they vented their spleen and fury on priests who dared contradict their views and organized large-scale massacres of Jews, who for uncertain reasons had also become the object of their odium. They were condemned by a papal decree in 1349, and shortly thereafter, the movement came to a violent end when the secular authorities, whom it also flouted, stepped in and brutally exterminated most of its disciples.[1]

A century later the condemnation and execution of the Czech religious reformer Jan Hus set off a powerful wave of religious-nationalist protest throughout Bohemia and Moravia. The resulting Hussite movement was primarily motivated by the desire to reproduce the style and values of the primitive church, as well as the related theological conviction that Holy Communion ought to be administered under both species — bread and wine — to laity and clergy alike (Utraquism). One branch of the movement, the Taborites, named after the biblical Mt. Tabor and composed mostly of peasants and poor workers, became more radical in its opposition to Catholic nonbiblical traditions and to any semblance of idolatrous practice having to do with statues, images, and elaborate liturgical practices. The Taborites, under the competent military leadership of their commander, John Zizka, handily defeated the armies of the German emperor Sigismund, who had functioned as the swordbearer of the Roman Church.[2]

Taborite priests and prophets had predicted the coming of Christ for February 1420, and the tenacity and savageness of the Taborite peasant armies were very much based on the conviction that this was the end-time battle against the demonic forces of the

Antichrist, that is, the pope. Once having saved Prague from the siege of their common enemy, the Taborites in their fanatical zeal for "pure Christianity" turned on their more moderate Hussite brethren and went on a rampage of destruction of monasteries, statues, and holy places throughout the city. Taborite apocalyptic teaching ultimately served as a justification for unbridled violence and wanton destruction.

It was the Protestant Reformation, however, with its insistence on the direct inspiration of the Holy Spirit, especially in reading the scriptures, which unwittingly opened the floodgates for bizarre millenarian ideas. Once again, some of these proved to be particularly violent in their manifestation. Such were the apocalyptic and righteous revolution of Thomas Müntzer's Anabaptist peasants, who ravaged the province of Thuringia in the Peasant Wars of 1524, as well as the anarchical "millennial kingdom," established at Münster by John of Leyden from 1532 to 1535. Both movements quickly turned to fanatic extremism and ultimately met their defeat in the bloody massacre of thousands of peasants and the cruel execution of their ecstatic leaders. Commentators are already comparing David Koresh with John of Leyden, both seemingly crazed prophets of violence.[3]

The English Civil War of 1642–48 also provides a striking example of a remorselessly militant millennialism in strange combination with the pursuit of such political goals as democracy, tolerance, and middle-class opportunity. Under the leadership of Oliver Cromwell, Puritans and independents alike had taken up arms against the Stuart king, Charles I, using apocalyptic imagery to depict him as the servant of the papal Antichrist. The beheading of the king and the establishment of the Republic in 1649 further convinced the more millenarian-minded revolutionaries of the imminence of Christ's kingdom on earth. The most radical of these were the "Men of the Fifth Monarchy" (imagery from the Book of Daniel), who, as they began to lose confidence in Cromwell and his rump parliament, sought to hasten Christ's Second Coming through the use of intimidation, violence, and insurrectional plots. After the execution of their leaders and the restoration of the Stuart monarchy, the movement fell apart, and many former members were absorbed into more peaceful millenarian groups, such as the Quakers.[4]

But if these historical examples seem somewhat remote for

the contemporary reader, we might do well to examine some of the more recent and widely publicized examples of millennialism gone awry. Under this category, we must be sure to include the tragedy of Jim Jones and the People's Temple, the violence at Ruby Ridge, and the holocaust of David Koresh and the Branch Davidians.

The Jonestown Tragedy

In previous chapters, we have seen how intimately the spirit of millennialism is tied to the American heritage. We have observed its power to inspire national purpose, the beauty of its dreams, and the disappointment of its delusions. While we have also explored millennialism's potential for supporting a pessimistic doomsday fatalism, we have yet to examine thoroughly its fanatic, destructive, and violent manifestations.

In this century, the story of violent millennialism begins in 1978 with the national shock waves produced by the murders and mass suicide of a whole religious community in Jonestown, Guyana, a location earmarked as a safe and utopian haven for the followers of James Jones and the People's Temple. Jim Jones and his disciples not only shared an apocalyptic faith in an imminent catastrophic end of the world, but also harbored a deep distrust and resentment of the government and established society, which they viewed in biblical terms as the Great Babylon of Revelation. From Jonestown down to Oklahoma City, this same theme of antigovernment sentiment will continue to haunt the variety of potentially violent millennial movements, whose course we will trace both here and in the subsequent chapters.

Jim Jones's Pursuit of a Harmonious Society

Jim Jones began his ministerial career as a very dedicated, peace-loving, God-fearing pastor. Though poorly trained for the ministry, he somehow managed to gain official status in the Church of the Disciples of Christ. Having himself some degree of Native American blood, Jones was particularly offended by the persistence of racism in American society, and especially in the Christian churches. By the early 1960s as the Cold War reached its most tense moments, Jones also became thoroughly convinced that a worldwide nuclear holocaust was inevitable. He felt that this nuclear conflagration was a necessary means to destroy the reigning unjust society that prevented the emergence of a truly just, color-blind, and harmonious new world. He had traveled to Brazil, to California, and eventually to Guyana in pursuit of a haven from the coming nuclear holocaust, as well as a location for building a new kind of human community which would serve as a harbinger and forerunner of the new humanity which would emerge with the destruction of the old, perverted order.

Jim Jones' People's Temple was very much a "rainbow" community, as was his own immediate family. He and his wife, Marcelline, had adopted seven children, of Asian, African, and Caucasian heritage, and his congregation reflected this same pattern of a cross-cultural America. Jones's vision of a harmonious, interracial society — reflecting the diversity of God's creation — was a powerful source of attraction to the many idealists among his followers. While the People's Temple primarily drew a clientele of the poor, minorities, the sick, and the elderly, it also had a place for educated professionals who were driven by the craving for a better world.[5] Given both their limited education and their sense of hopelessness, the majority of the members were easy to manipulate.

On the practical level, Jones soon began to see Communism as the path toward building his more just and loving society. For this reason it became clearer to him that the American government was the main obstacle to achieving a utopian society. In a sermon given at the Redwood Valley, California, temple in the early 1970s, Jim shook his fist at the American flag and spat on a copy of the Bible. What he called the "sky God" of most Christians had to be torn down in order to rid people of a false hope in "the sweet bye and bye."[6] By this time he had effectively abandoned a Christian worldview, so that his apocalyptic and millennial views took on a purely secular, indeed fanatic, cast. His abandonment of Christianity also paved the way for what can only be called his own self-deification.

Millennialism Gone Amiss

From the time of his arrival in Mendocino County, California, with his band of faithful followers in 1964, Jones had quickly established himself as a charismatic leader, with alleged powers to heal both spiritual and physical ailments. His healing demonstrations were carefully staged and usually based on deceit and delusion. His audience was regularly spellbound by his ability to diagnose and/or even predict illness, unaware that much of his knowledge derived from clandestine visits by his trusted staff to the medicine cabinets of temple members, or from the records of local officials or even on occasion of medical doctors. Combined with his natural sense for the dramatic, Jones's seemingly "supernatural" powers served to surround him in a cloak of mystery and to provide him with an extraordinary authority over his disciples. His proclivity to fraudulence aside, he was, otherwise, right in line with a long tradition of charismatic millennial leaders.

Like many of these charismatic figures before him, Jones began to exercise absolute authority over his followers. He frequently admonished his flock about their moral responsibilities, especially toward the sick, the aged, and poor minorities. On one occasion when he railed against his flock for "jumping into bed" only with good-looking parishioners, while disregarding the old and sickly members of the congregation, at least one attractive young female disciple offered to make love to "the most shriveled, old, toothless, dimwitted black man in the place."[7] Far worse, Jones even induced a good number of his followers to sign suicide pacts, in the eventuality that his utopian plans were to fall apart.

Jones's utopian expectations were clearly apocalyptic in nature. He had become absolutely driven at this point by the conviction that a global nuclear conflagration was imminent. This catastrophic war he believed would be the final battle with the forces of Satan and of the Antichrist, which he closely identified with the U.S. government. Accordingly, in 1977 Jones induced his parishioners to follow him to the jungles of Guyana, where they were to establish the community of Jonestown, as a refuge from the coming devastation of nuclear conflict and as the vanguard of a truly communistic and just society, under the spiritual and political guidance of the Reverend Jones. The urgency of this migration also resulted from a growing official scrutiny of the church in Redwood Valley, as an ever-increasing number of defectors began to make public some of the more questionable activities of the People's Temple.

Shortly after the Jonestown settlement had begun, a steady flow of reports from Guyana made it evident that Jones was keeping many of the commune members in the jungle compound against their will. As a result, a group of former members and relatives of present members of the People's Temple convinced Congressman Leo Ryan to begin an official investigation of Jones's activities through a delegation that would scrutinize conditions at the commune and work for the release of those members who wanted to leave. On November 14, 1978, Ryan arrived in Guyana with a group of aides, reporters, and photographers; they were also accompanied by thirteen very fearful relatives of members of the People's Temple. By November 18, Ryan had arranged to fly from Georgetown with a small delegation to the jungle compound at Jonestown. By the following day, news came back that Leo Ryan and two NBC reporters had been gunned down at the airstrip, that representatives of the temple in Georgetown had been systematically murdered, and that Jim Jones had induced the vast majority of his congregants into mass suicide by drinking cyanide-laced Fla-Vour-Aid. Jones had convinced most of them that this was the best path to a safe and better world.[8]

By the time the final tally was taken, the body count had reached 912, shocking the world and making Jonestown into a synonym for the horrors of twentieth-century perversions of religious zeal. While Jones had long abandoned Christian belief, the community he had established was truly apocalyptic and millennial in its own special way, and it was these very beliefs that had both guided its development and ultimately left it prey to its own tragic destruction.

From Ruby Ridge to Mt. Carmel

We might be tempted, of course, to dismiss Jonestown as a freak occurrence resulting from the rare mix of a megalomaniac leader with a vulnerable, naive following. On the other hand, even our brief survey of earlier millennial movements, such as those of Müntzer and John of Leyden, makes it clear that the saga of the People's Temple was but one in a long series of historical apocalyptic visions that were turned violent by madness, power, and excess. More recent cases of misguided millennialism are even more difficult to dismiss as idiosyncratic accidents, for they not only demonstrate very similar patterns of thought and action, but, even more frighteningly, reveal evident common historical patterns which are likely to repeat themselves as similar tragedies in the future. The starting point for this more recent wave of apocalyptic violence was, without doubt, the fatal encounter between the FBI and a family of religious radicals at Ruby Ridge, Idaho, in 1993.

While there is certainly a uniqueness about Randy and Vicky Weaver's politico-religious worldview and their ultimate confrontation with federal authorities, there are general patterns to their story that are quite characteristic of contemporary right-wing millennialism. The Weavers came out of a Bible quoting, evangelical Protestant cultural milieu, very much influenced by dispensationalist doctrine. Hal Lindsey was their favorite author. There is no doubt that their view of history was apocalyptic, in that they were convinced that the world is quickly running out of time and is headed for a divinely decreed catastrophe. As dispensationalists they were convinced that the end-time was near at hand, but unlike most Christian evangelicals, they did not believe they would be rescued by the rapture at Christ's return; in fact they viewed the rapture as a theological error. Accordingly, they would have to survive on their own during the final days of tribulation. They would have to learn to be self-sufficient, so as to defend themselves both economically and militarily against "the end-time government of the Antichrist."[9]

Obviously, the whole mentality of "survivalism" fit in perfectly with the Weavers' religious worldview, which was drawn primarily from a movement called Christian Identity. This small but influential religious movement mimics both the biblical literalism as well as the apocalyptic orientation of Christian evangelicalism. The hate-filled theology of this self-proclaimed "church" will be outlined in detail in the following chapter, which will describe its influence on the militia movement. Here it will suffice to say that from a political perspective, the Identity movement has from its origins been antigovernment, fostering both civil disobedience (e.g., in the form of refusing to pay taxes) and, when necessary, even armed confrontation with the state.[10]

Behind this seditionist mentality lies the belief in a worldwide demonic *conspiracy,* led by the Jews and supported by the United Nations. The U.S. government, having also been bought out and corrupted by this grand-scale conspiratorial force, functions as an evil agent of Satan. For this reason, the movement's believers regularly refer to the government as the Zionist Occupation Government, or ZOG, for short.

And so it was that when heavily armed federal marshals and an FBI hostage team surrounded Randy and Vicky Weaver's cabin on Ruby Ridge in the summer of 1992, this family of Identity believers was easily convinced that they were in the midst of an apocalyptic showdown, defending themselves against the onslaught of satanic forces. The gunning down of Vicky Weaver and of her young son, Samuel, during the siege only further convinced the radical religious right of the reality of this conspiracy. At his trial in 1993, Weaver would be acquitted of all but minor firearms charges. The FBI sharpshooter who killed Randy's wife and son is currently on trial for that incident. Ironically, the Weaver trial took place while the federal agencies involved, the Bureau of Alcohol, Tobacco, and Firearms (BATF) and the Federal Bureau of Investigation (FBI), were fully engaged in a tragic fifty-one-day armed standoff with another millennial group — the Branch Davidians in Waco, Texas.

Mt. Carmel, David Koresh, and the Fifth Seal

No doubt the event that has done most to place millennialism into disrepute, as well as to put fear and apprehension into the hearts of many Americans at the approach of the year 2000, is the fiery holocaust at Waco, Texas, in 1993. This tragedy came at the end of a long government siege of the radical apocalyptic community which called itself the Branch Davidians. From the flow of news reports during the siege it became clear that the Davidians were a breakaway group from the Seventh-Day Adventists. The Davidians had established themselves in a compound they dubbed Mt. Carmel and seemingly entertained very bizarre ideas about the Book of Revelation and the Second Coming of Jesus. The government law enforcement agents viewed them primarily as a militant cult, misguided and manipulated by a deranged leader who went by the name of David Koresh, and who forced the group members to serve his "lust for money, women and power."[11] The official charge was likelihood of firearms violations, while unsubstantiated accusations of "child abuse" were widely leaked to the news media.

David Koresh and his followers came by their millennialism

quite honestly, for while they represented a split from the Seventh-Day Adventist Church, they had for the most part been thoroughly weaned and nurtured in that tradition. In fact, the Koresh group traced its historical roots directly to a renegade Bulgarian Adventist reformer, Victor Houteff, who had moved to California in 1929. Houteff, while firmly convinced of the Adventist message, was totally disenchanted with what he perceived to be its compromise with modern worldly culture. He failed to receive approval of the main body of Seventh-Day Adventists, but was successful in gaining a significant following. In 1935 he and his followers moved to Texas, where they established a millennial community called Mt. Carmel. It was Houteff's dream and mission to convince 144,000 Adventists to truly reform themselves as a necessary preparation for the second Advent.[12] Firm belief in the coming millennium shaped all life and thinking at Mt. Carmel. As a clear reminder of the closeness of the final hour, Houteff had placed a clock with the time set at eleven o'clock on the floor of the main building.

After his removal from the roles of the Adventist church, Houteff and his followers officially took the name "Davidian Seventh-Day Adventists." The term "Davidian" was chosen to reflect the movement's distinctive belief in the imminent restoration of the ancient kingdom of David in Palestine.[13] As opposed to Christian Identity thought, Davidian theology encouraged close ties to the Jewish tradition, and the history of Mt. Carmel reveals an ongoing rapport and empathy with the State of Israel.

Houteff's death in 1955 was a great disillusionment to his followers, who believed it was his prophetic role to announce the new Davidic Messiah. His wife, Florence, momentarily preserved Davidian millennial enthusiasm by predicting that the messianic kingdom would begin to unfold on April 22, 1959. Approximately nine hundred believers gathered at Mt. Carmel to await the event. Many had sold their homes or businesses in order to make the trip. When this date passed uneventfully, most of the followers lost heart and abandoned the movement. About fifty followers remained faithful to Florence's leadership and moved to a new Mt. Carmel, situated about ten miles east of Waco — the site of the recent tragedy. After much bickering over land and finances, the Davidians splintered into different smaller groups.

The most notable of these was led by Ben Roden, whose family would lead the movement for the next generation. It was Roden who called his followers the Branch Davidians,[14] a term which reflected both continuity with Houteff's millennial message and Roden's unique claim to represent the historical embodiment of the anointed "Branch" predicted in Zech. 3:8 and 6:12. Roden visited Israel and proclaimed the settlement of five Seventh-Day Adventists there as a sure sign of the dawning of the final age. Upon Ben Roden's death, his wife, Lois, succeeded in the leadership role, and traveled widely in an attempt to spread the Davidian message, especially among influential statesmen. Her son, George, who expected to be the next in line as leader of the Davidians, became increasingly disgruntled and jealous as his mother showed more and more favoritism to an illegitimate high school drop-out named Vernon Howell, who had joined the Mt. Carmel community in 1981. George accused Howell of having an affair with the sixty-seven-year-old prophetess, which Howell would never deny.[15] An intense rivalry between the two men quickly set off a bizarre series of events that would tragically affect the future of the Waco community.

Howell, in the meantime, married the fourteen-year-old daughter of a long-time Branch Davidian, and took her with him on a trip to Israel, where in 1985 he claimed to have a special revelation from God, opening up for him the hidden meaning of the scriptures and making clear to him his chosen role in the imminent end-time scenario.

Upon his return, the rivalry with George Roden over control of Mt. Carmel reached a violent climax. In November 1987, Roden challenged Howell to a grotesque duel that was meant to settle their claims to prophetic leadership. Roden exhumed the body of a long-dead Davidian woman, claiming that the true prophet would be able to raise her from the dead. Howell's response was to sneak into the compound with several armed followers in order to photograph the corpse as evidence of the exhumation. In a gunfight which ensued Roden was slightly wounded, and Howell and his seven comrades were tried for attempted murder. The seven were acquitted, and Howell was released as the result of a hung jury. Shortly thereafter, Roden was charged with an ax-murder in an unrelated case. He was declared not guilty by reason of insanity and was sentenced to indefinite confinement in a state hospital. In the meantime, Howell and his followers returned triumphantly to Mt. Carmel, having paid off sixteen years of delinquent taxes, thereby gaining title to the property.[16]

In 1990, still inspired and directed by his 1985 "religious vision," Howell legally changed his name to David Koresh: "David" suggesting his commitment to a renewed Kingdom of Israel and "Koresh" (the Hebrew name for Cyrus) suggesting his role as God's chosen deliverer and avenger. Just as the ancient King Cyrus had delivered the Jews from the Babylonian captivity, so was the latter-day Koresh destined to protect true believers from the oppression and corruption of modern American society — the new Babylon.

Koresh's whole self-understanding and his sense of mission were inextricably tied to his "inspired" reading of the Bible, especially of its prophetic books. Finding the code to the Book of Revelation was, for him, the key to understanding the entire Bible. More specifically, he saw himself as the messianic prophet, chosen to open or explain the mystery of the seven seals and thereby reveal the fullness of God's plans for the Last Days. Koresh pictured himself as the last in a line of Adventist prophets, extending back to William Miller, the charismatic but failed forecaster of the Last Days. It had long been part of the Adventist tradition to tie the movement to the three angels of Rev. 14:6–12. William Miller was understood to have announced the good news of the first two angels by proclaiming the beginning of the end-times and with it the imminent fall of "Babylon." Ellen White, for her part, had faithfully proclaimed the message of the third angel by calling for return to the Saturday Sabbath as a rejection of "paganized," mainstream Christian customs.

Koresh continued this analogy with the angels of Revelation, identifying Victor Houteff, Ben Roden, and Lois Roden as the fourth, fifth, and sixth angels, while he cast himself as the long-awaited angel of the seventh trumpet in Revelation 10 and 12. As the angel of Revelation, Koresh assumed the twofold task of both opening the scroll through biblical interpretation and of ushering in the prophecies through his own life and that of the other Branch Davidians.[17] More specifically, he saw himself as the latter-day messenger who was to unfold the mystery of the seven seals. This was all consistent with the Adventist emphasis on prophetic understanding of "present truth." Although Koresh, like Houteff before him, had been removed from the Adventist Church rolls, it would be impossible to understand him or his followers outside the context of the Adventist tradition.

In the course of revealing the mystery of the seven seals, Koresh also began to identify himself with the Lamb of God in the Book of Revelation — the Lamb who alone is worthy to open up the scroll with the seven seals (Rev. 5:5). For this reason, Koresh was convinced of the inevitability of his own violent death, inasmuch as the worthiness of the Lamb depends on its having been slain (Rev. 5:9). Throughout the long siege at Waco, Koresh continuously sought time to expound the message of the seven seals and was in the process of writing such a commentary when the FBI launched its gas attack on April 19, 1993. Through the ingenuity of one of the Davidians who escaped the fiery holocaust on that day, this commentary was preserved on a disk and has thrown a great deal of light on the thinking of this very controversial end-time "prophet" and millennial leader.

On the basis of the Psalms, which he read in apocalyptic fashion, Koresh also taught the doctrine of two Messiahs. Jesus Christ was all that Christianity said of him — the Son of God, the Savior of the World, and the long-awaited Messiah. Contrary to many media reports, Koresh never claimed identity with Jesus. But there was to be a second Messiah — one for the Last Days — whom Koresh found prophetically described in Ps. 45:7–8 as the anointed one (Messiah) of God. This Messiah, he claimed, was not to be confused with Jesus Christ, for this second Messiah marries virgin daughters, and his children shall be made "princes through all the land" (Ps. 45:9–16).

Koresh makes it clear in his commentary on the seals that he, indeed, claimed to be this second Messiah — the prophet of the Last Days. On this basis, he also declared that it was his sacred trust to have sexual relations with a variety of women at Mt. Carmel, while imposing a law of celibacy on the rest of his followers. He considered the twelve children born of these diverse unions as being destined for "an exalted status in the coming kingdom of God that would be set up in Israel."[18] Specifically, he connected them with the elders of Revelation, who in God's coming kingdom would reign on the earth as kings and priests of God (Rev. 5:10). In all, then, Koresh had presented himself as final messenger (angel of the seventh trumpet), as the Lamb of

God, and as the end-time Messiah, but never did he claim to be either divine or a new manifestation of Jesus Christ.

The end-time Messiah, according to Koresh, would not come in meekness and humility, as Jesus, the first Messiah, had come. Koresh frequently compared the second Messiah with the conquering, victorious rider on the white horse of Rev. 6:2. As he read the scriptures, especially the prophetic books, the second coming of the Messiah was to be with power and majesty for the violent destruction of God's enemies. That enemy, in Koresh's understanding of "present truth," was the U.S. government, the leading player in a global, satanic conspiracy. Biblically speaking, this enemy was the new Babylon.

In light of this worldview that permeated the Davidian mind, it should come as no surprise that when the BATF launched its raid (called a "dynamic entry") on the Davidian compound on February 28, 1993, the action was seen by the Davidians as the beginning of the final apocalyptic struggle with the forces of Babylon. Koresh claimed to have regretted the loss of lives, of both ATF agents and of Davidians on the occasion, but felt that the community had no recourse but to fight back to defend itself against an unjust attack. When the ATF was subsequently replaced by an FBI "hostage rescue team," the continuous harassment of the Davidians through the pumping in of loud music, Tibetan chants, the sounds of rabbits being slaughtered, and so on, only confirmed their religious convictions that they were surrounded by hostile and evil forces and that the final Armageddon was beginning to unfold right in Waco. Communications between Koresh and the FBI were not very successful, for the government simply viewed him as a con man and dismissed his theological explanations as "bible babble."[19]

From the biblical context within which he always worked, Koresh began to interpret his predicament at Mt. Carmel as the unfolding of the fifth seal of Rev. 6:9–11. The message of this passage is that the martyrs who had gone before would have to wait a little longer "until the quota was filled of their fellow servants and brothers to be slain" (6:11). Koresh and his followers began to suspect the worst. On the other hand, they were buoyed by the conviction that this tragic situation would lead inevitably to the opening of the sixth seal, in which God would wreak his terrible vengeance upon those who had shed the blood of the martyrs

(Rev. 6:12–17). Their prophetic expectation of their own violent demise was indeed fulfilled on April 19, 1993, when the FBI sent heavy combat vehicles to pump the riot-control agent CS into the Davidian compound. By noon a fire broke out, and within minutes buildings of Mt. Carmel had turned into a deadly, flaming holocaust, killing seventy-four members of the Branch Davidians — fifty-three adults and twenty-one children. On the previous evening, Koresh had been diligently at work on his promised commentary on the seven seals.

This day soon became a symbol of infamy for many disgruntled and conspiracy-obsessed Americans, and together with the tragedy of Ruby Ridge helped to spawn the rapid growth of militant apocalyptic movements. If the fifth seal of the Book of Revelation proved to have chilling implications for the Branch Davidians, for a growing number of religious radicals, Waco has led to the opening of the sixth seal — the time of God's violent retribution for evil. For them the words of Revelation once again ring true: "The great day of their vengeance has come" (Rev. 6:17). The following chapter will deal with militias, patriot groups, and other such movements that have hunkered down after Waco, and who wait for, and perhaps help implement, the unfolding of the sixth seal.

– 10 –

God's Soldiers of the End-Time

Independent militias have been growing in the United States ever since the aftermath of the war in Vietnam and have their more remote origins in antigovernment and tax-resistance movements dating from the beginning of the century. Since the tragedies of Ruby Ridge and Waco, however, the militia movement has grown exponentially. Much of the spiritual force behind this upsurge lies in the millennial belief in a coming apocalypse — the great day of God's wrath and retribution, as described in chapter 6 of the Book of Revelation (Rev. 6:12–17). The history of millennialism should clearly alert us to the likelihood of militant, even violent apocalyptic activity during these final hours before the turn of the new millennium. While we cannot predict with certainty the source of such violence, we have good reasons to keep a close eye on the training camps of the burgeoning militia movement.

Immediately following the deaths of Vicky and Sam Weaver during the FBI siege of Ruby Ridge, leaders of the loosely knit organizations which go by the umbrella term of the patriot movement met in Estes Park, Colorado, in the fall of 1992. Convinced more than ever of the existence of a government conspiracy to control and oppress American citizens in the name of a "new world order," Reverend Pete Peters, a Christian Identity leader, summoned together a group of like-minded patriots of varied stripes in order to formulate a uniform strategy for resisting this perceived government-led "terrorism." The list of attendees was a veritable *Who's Who* of die-hard racists and radical religious militants. Apart from Peters, the meeting was dominated by several white supremacists, such as the charismatic leader of the Aryan Nations, Louis Beam.

Beam had established a substantial police record for violent acts committed in the name of true religion and "the American way of life." Among his dubious credits was a nearly successful campaign of intimidation to prevent Vietnamese immigrants from bringing their fishing boats into Galveston Bay in Texas. He had long held the view that the rule of the white race in the United States had already been ceded to a group of international, Jewish-led conspirators, who used the various minorities, including blacks, Hispanics, and Asians, to keep white citizens under control. He was likewise convinced that a nationwide race war was inevitable and that it was necessary to prepare for this coming Armageddon.[1] For his Estes Park audience he played down racist and supremacist ideas and appealed to the common fear of a government conspiracy to deny the basic rights of citizens in an attempt to enslave them to a one-world government. Ruby Ridge had made his task a lot easier. Passing on his racist philosophy could always come later.

From the "religious" patriot perspective, with Ruby Ridge, the first shots had been fired to inaugurate both the "Second American Revolution" and the beginning of the final disasters and divine retribution which mark the opening of the sixth seal. According to the Book of Revelation, this would be a time when the great and powerful of this earth would call upon the rocks of the mountains to fall upon them and hide them "from the face of him who is seated on the throne, and from the wrath of the Lamb" (Rev. 6:17). The aftermath of Ruby Ridge, with the meeting at Estes Park, marked the beginning of the revitalized militia movement that today presents a serious challenge to the security and viability of the American system of government. As mentioned in the previous chapter, the Randy Weaver trial was still in the headlines when the government agencies began their months-long siege of the Branch Davidian compound in Waco. When Waco ended in an even greater disaster, the fanatic conspiracy theories of the radical religious right were given greater credibility, and the already thriving militia movement was further reinforced and energized.

While most militias have officially disclaimed any connection or sympathy with the Oklahoma City bombing of 1995, at least some patriot and militia leaders have made statements suggesting that there was some kind of parity and divine retribution between the destruction of innocent lives in Oklahoma City and in Waco. During the recent highly publicized trial of Tim McVeigh, the convicted mastermind behind the Oklahoma City tragedy, at least some cogent evidence emerged to suggest that the bombing was a "retaliatory strike" for the destruction of the compound at Waco.[2] Some of this evidence will be examined further below.

The Militias and the Coming Armageddon

The militias are to a large extent a rural movement and tend to attract traditional-minded, independent-spirited Americans who are alienated from the political process and are fearful that the federal government is bent upon destroying their beliefs and taking away their rights.[3] Militia members are by no means all racists, anti-Semites, or white supremacists, yet leaders who virulently hold such views have risen to positions of authority in the militias. John Trochmann, for example, who together with his brother David founded the Militia of Montana (MOM) in 1994, and who officially denies any kind of white supremacist philosophy, has, nevertheless, been a regular speaker at the Aryan Nations compound in Hayden Lake, Idaho, and has very close ties to the Christian Identity movement. Trochmann was at the barricades, supporting his friend Randy Weaver, during the Ruby Ridge standoff. He regularly has appealed to patriotism, defense against tyranny, and other such typically American themes in his recruiting efforts for MOM. Resistance to gun control and resentment for what many perceive as unjust and heavy-handed tax laws are among the other issues Trochmann has used to appeal to a broader range of potential recruits.

The Theology of Christian Identity

For Trochmann himself, however, all these evils and injustices herald the beginning of the end-times, in which the enemies of God will feel the judgment of the divine wrath. Like many of the most radical patriot leaders, Trochmann's bizarre theological views are inspired by the teachings of the small but influential Christian Identity movement, mentioned in the previous chapter in connection with Ruby Ridge. On the surface, the movement maintains many of the external trappings of evangelical and fundamentalist Christian churches: church meetings, hymn singing, preaching, and a variety of worship services. It also shares fundamentalism's unswerving convictions about the imminence of the catastrophic end of human history. Identity members consider themselves biblical literalists, while drawing a very peculiar and revisionist reading from the "literal" text. Apart from these structural similarities, however, Christian Identity is world's apart from evangelical or fundamentalist Christianity, for its essential appeal to hatred and violence is directly contrary to the central message of the Christian Gospel.

The Christian Identity movement is not new. It has its roots in the hard economic times of the 1930s and is a direct descendant of the antigovernment, tax-resistance movements of that period. Today it draws its membership primarily from the economically disadvantaged white rural population, including bankrupt farmers and unemployed farmhands or laborers. Because of its external similarities to a Christian church and its persistent appeal to the Bible, it can be particularly seductive to less-sophisticated, Bible-reared Christians.

The main object of Christian Identity's hatred and venom is the Jews, with African Americans coming in a close second. Both these antagonisms are based on a common conviction in the superiority of the Anglo-Saxon and northern European races. The movement inherited this fundamental dogma from a rather eccentric nineteenth-century theory, called "British Israelism," which naively argued that the people of Britain and northern Europe were the actual linear descendants of the ten lost tribes of ancient Israel. This bizarre doctrine was particularly popular among British titled aristocrats and military officers right into the first half of the twentieth century. Adherents went so far as to claim that the whole British legal system with its parliamentary institutes had been imported to the British Isles by the ancient lost tribes from the Middle East. The doctrine was used to defend and champion the cause of the British Empire and, in general, served as a conservative force in support of the status quo.

Once British Israelism had come to the United States by way of Canada, the movement began to undergo some radical doctrinal changes under the influence of American political, social, and economic forces. The American successors to the movement quickly became more virulently racist and outspokenly anti-Semitic in their doctrinal teachings. Apart from their rejection of people of color (blacks, Native Americans, and Asians), which was consonant with widespread American white supremacist attitudes, the U.S. branches of the British-Israelite Federation managed to develop a unique, if far-fetched, doctrinal variation on Jewish origins as well. The British Israelism movement had already laid the foundations for this new doctrinal twist through its teaching that modern Jews were actually a corrupt hybrid (through unlawful interbreeding) with the heathen Edomites (children of Esau). The new American version, under the influence of a more rabid anti-Semitic leadership, intends in one swoop to corroborate the superiority of the white races over people of color and to identify the Jews as the literal offspring of Satan.[4] Unlike their Christian evangelical counterparts, Identity believers view race rather than grace as the key to salvation.

Christian Identity's doctrine on the inferiority of nonwhites is also rooted in a revived nineteenth-century theory which argued for a pre-Adamic creation which produced all the racially inferior nonwhites. Adam, for his part, was viewed as "the first of the Caucasian race,"[5] and as such was the father of the True Israelites. The Great Deluge, which was viewed as geographically localized, was understood as a specific punishment for the Adamites, who, apart from the family of Noah, had committed the cardinal sin of corrupting the race through racial crossbreeding with pre-Adamites (i.e., non-whites). This pre-Adamite theory also served as a foundation for the Identity doctrine of Jewish origins — according to its unique reading of Genesis, the movement claims that Jews trace their roots back to Cain.

The figure of Cain is crucial to Identity doctrine, for he is understood to be the offspring of the serpent's copulation with Eve. Cain, according to this version, quickly gained mastery over the inferior pre-Adamites and passed on his Satanic bloodline as well as his inherently evil character to his direct offspring. These, of course, were the Jews, who could now be demonized as the progeny of Satan and collaborators in his nefarious schemes.[6] In this way, they are put forward as lead players in the worldwide conspiracy to undermine the forces of freedom and democracy. This conspiracy finds expression in the one-world movement espoused by the United Nations and has successfully co-opted the cooperation of the U.S. government through corruption and deceit. This is the reason that Christian Identity considers the U.S.

government to be an agent of Satan and refers to it as the Zionist Occupation Government (ZOG). And with this we have the principal theological basis for the strong antigovernment sentiment so prominent among the militias.

The Final Conflict

Trochmann and other Christian Identity leaders typically prefer to use these theological arguments rather than neo-Nazi and Klan rhetoric to advance their racist ideology among militia members or new recruits. Their strategy is to appeal to the deep concerns and general gripes of a broad public, while regularly using a code language that furtively elicits racial apprehensions. Several of the current militia leaders with white supremacist convictions have learned this technique from the 1988 presidential campaign of David Duke, who was careful to avoid extremist and racist rhetoric, while, at the same time, railing against affirmative action, racial quotas, spiraling welfare, high minority crime rates, and the low wages of immigrant labor. When the militia recruiters add to this list the issues of unjust taxation, the restraints of gun control, and foreclosure of family farms, they have tapped into the discontents and complaints of mainstream conservative America. Their litany of grievances is hard to distinguish from those heard on conservative talk shows or in the Republican speeches of Pat Robertson's Christian Coalition.[7]

The strategy of Christian Identity and of the white supremacists was very much abetted by a number of public events such as the Los Angeles riots following the first Rodney King trial, as well as the race-dominated trial of O. J. Simpson, which resulted in his rapid acquittal by a predominantly black jury. These events further tended to undermine the confidence of middle-class white Americans in the reliability of the justice system and in the ability of the government to protect their lives and property. There can be little doubt that these events also contributed to the growth of the mainly white militias and, at the same time, fanned the flames of racism among some of the membership. Within this context, it was relatively easy for militia leaders, with their unflagging support of second amendment rights and their persistent message of mistrust of government, to garner a broader based sympathy and support from middle America, and even to gain support from some members of Congress.[8]

While the patriot or militia movement is made up of many loosely knit, autonomous organizations, these separate units share a very similar ideology and reinforce their beliefs through a highly developed information network. This is comprised of numerous newsletters, magazines, military manuals, and so on, as well as a highly sophisticated system of computer bulletin boards. Militia literature, Website addresses, and other such information sources are regularly exchanged or sold at gun shows throughout the country. Affiliated organizations do not necessarily use the name "militia" in their title, but include many kindred groups with names such as Posse Comitatus; the Aryan Nations; the Covenant; the Sword and Arm of the Lord; the Order; and the National Alliance. In recent years, antiabortion extremists, such as Operation Rescue and the Army of God, are increasingly joining forces with radical militia groups. Erich Rudolph, the North Carolina fugitive and prime suspect in the 1996 Olympic Park bombing as well as in the bombing of an Atlanta abortion clinic and a lesbian bar, has already been hailed as "a true warrior of God" by several prominent Patriot leaders.[9]

While many ideological differences separate these diverse organizations, they all share the common conviction that the federal government is not to be trusted, and might even be the greatest threat to the American way of life. The more radical — those indoctrinated with the theology of Christian Identity — are further convinced that this same government has sold out to a Jewish-led world conspiracy bent on creating a one-world government. (The popular symbol for this militant conspiracy is the nefarious "black helicopter" sightings which are regularly reported in militia and other sympathetic sources, such as *Soldier of Fortune* magazine.) This conspiracy is presented as the final historical manifestation of Satan's power which portends the final apocalyptic combat between God and the forces of evil. In preparation for this great and ultimate Armageddon, it is the militias who are called to serve as God's end-time soldiers.

Ideology and Strategies

The militias are fueled by a powerful "religious" ideology and supported by a well-organized strategy. In addition to shared feelings of deep resentment and a sense of betrayal on the part of the federal government, the many and varied organizations that comprise the militia movement are also bound together by the "theological thread" of Identity doctrine, which we have just described above. This set of fanatical and distorted religious beliefs, which has been circulating throughout the ranks of the racist movement for the last fifty years, has now achieved greater prominence in the militias through the influence of proselytizing Identity leaders such as Richard Butler, Louis Beam, Pete Peters, and John Trochmann.

There can be no doubt about the apocalyptic and millennial nature of this teaching: it seriously proposes the imminence of God's judgment and retribution upon those who support the "satanic global Zionist" conspiracy and anticipates the reestablishment of a white, Anglo-Saxon, Christian society in preparation for the coming kingdom. In the meantime, it is the duty of God's end-time warriors to prepare for the final cosmic confrontation while "hidden in the caves and among the rocks of the mountains," anxiously awaiting the day of God's wrath (Rev. 6:16–17). Those who oppose this hostile agenda are simply identified as Antichrists, who deserve to be dealt with accordingly. It is not without reason that the Christian Identity ideology has been described by human rights groups as the "single most dangerous element" influencing the militia movement.[10]

The destructive impact of Identity doctrine can be seen in a declaration made early in the 1990s by a particularly violent organization calling itself the White Patriot Party. An excerpt from the declaration will sufficiently make the point:

> All 5,000 White Patriots are now honor bound to pick up the sword and do battle against the forces of evil. Swear you'll not put down your sword until total victory is ours. Yahweh will fill your hearts with courage and strength and confidence.... Let the blood of our enemies flood the streets, rivers, and fields of the nation, in Holy vengeance and justice.... The Jews are our main and most formidable enemies. ...They are truly the children of Satan. Throw off the chains which bind us to the satanic, Jewish controlled and ruled federal government.[11]

This hate-filled bigotry of Identity doctrine has no serious internal relationship with the apocalyptic teachings of Christian dispensationalism, whose style and external trappings it tries to mimic. Only the most ignorant and confused of Bible-reared Christians can be guiled by the lure of Identity preaching. Even outsiders to the world of Christian discourse have no difficulty in detecting in Identity beliefs a complete parody and distortion of legitimate Christian apocalyptic. Antidefamation experts, such as Kenneth Stern of the American Jewish Committee, have not been fooled by the smokescreen of religious language used by Identity-influenced militias, and warn that these teachings have the potential to spawn a serious nationwide epidemic of virulent anti-Semitism.[12] Given this violent potential of the radical right in the last two decades, all Americans, regardless of race or creed, should maintain a serious vigilance regarding all those paramilitary organizations which are governed by a millenarian view of history. Chances are that their brand of millennialism will be less than peaceful in character.

But if religious ideology provides the internal engine of the militia movement, practical strategies in pamphlet or book form make the groups more effective and potentially more dangerous. Chief among these is a proposal put together by Louis Beam, the Aryan Nations leader, which explains and promotes the strategy he calls "leaderless resistance." A proposal with the same title is circulated through computer bulletins and incorporated into militia manuals. Beam's theory calls for a decentralization of tactical decisions among the militia organizations through the creation of the so-called "phantom cell" — a small local unit which is able to respond quickly to any emergency situation without the need of approval from a central command. The strategy assumes a consensus on general principles and goals among the affiliated militia organizations, while granting the small phantom cells the freedom to act spontaneously whenever the occasion demands. This loose organizational mechanism obviously has the additional advantage of making it difficult to trace an order to some central command figure in any of the organizations — a feature that had to appeal to Beam as a long-time Klan militant.

Another source of strategy and even inspiration for some of the radical militia organizations is a 1978 novel written by William Pierce, a former member of the American Nazi Party and founder of the fascist-oriented National Alliance. The book, called *The Turner Diaries*, contains a fictional account of the strategies and methods used by a group of white supremacists to carry on a revolutionary guerrilla war against the federal government. It includes such brutal accounts as the assassination of federal officials, Jews, and other minorities, as well as the destruction of synagogues and select public facilities. According to Pierce's narrative, the bloody revolution eventually brings about the "liberation of North America" from the power of ZOG in the year 1999, fulfilling the long-awaited dream of a white-ruled millennial America. The book is widely circulated in militia and survivalist circles, and certainly has at very least the potential of serving as a guide book for various forms of domestic terrorism.

At least one violent white supremacist organization, known as the Order, actually used *The Turner Diaries* as a blueprint for carrying out what they called a "white revolution." Their radical founder, Robert Matthews, used scenarios garnered from the *Diaries* to help perpetrate a series of armed robberies, including a $3.8 million armored car heist in 1983. The following year, the group murdered Jewish talk show host Alan Berg outside his home in Denver. Federal authorities have received some information to the effect that William Pierce had received some monetary rewards from the Order in appreciation for the guidance provided by *The Turner Diaries* — a charge which Pierce denies to this day. Matthews was eventually killed in a shootout with the FBI in December 1984.[13]

The guerrilla war described in the *Diaries* begins with a truck-bomb attack on a federal building, making use of a powerful fertilizer-based mechanism which creates a gaping hole in FBI national headquarters, destroying many innocent lives along with those described as the "guilty." Parallels between this fictional attack by Earl Turner and his commandos and the actual Oklahoma City bombing of 1995 are almost too uncanny to be coincidental. The Oklahoma City bombing in 1995 also used a fertilizer bomb (made from ammonium nitrate) to successfully blow away the whole front of the Alfred P. Murrah Federal Building, resulting in 169 fatalities, including many innocent children. In the novel, Earl Turner, the revolutionary leader, condoned the destruction of innocent life on the grounds that this was an unavoidable side effect of active military engagement. While militia leaders publicly condemned the terrorist bombing in Oklahoma City and expressed regrets for the wanton loss of life, privately (in militia meetings), many seemed more upset by what they interpreted as one-sided media reporting, with allegedly too much coverage given to the tragedy of Oklahoma City as compared to those of Ruby Ridge and Waco.

There is much that has been left unknown about the background and possible militia connections of Timothy McVeigh and Terry Nichols, the two convicted perpetrators in the case, but Morris Dees, author and attorney at the Southern Poverty Law Center, is not without justification when he describes the Oklahoma City bombing as "a page out of the Turner Diaries."[14]

Only a few fanatics in the movement were willing to describe the bombing as an act of "divine retribution" for government violence perpetrated at Ruby Ridge and at Waco. Even fewer would endorse Beam's and Trochmann's claim that the bombing was itself part of a government plot to try to discredit the growing militia movement. On the other hand, even while repudiating the bombing attack, many militia patriots clearly believe that Oklahoma City might well be just the "opening shot" in what might become a long series of reprisals for what they consider oppressive government acts.

The Opening Shots: Oklahoma City and Justus Township

It would be a major misrepresentation to depict all militia adherents as radicals bent on violent overthrow of the government. The most common militia philosophy is rather one of vigilance and readiness — the expression of an almost obsessive fear of a global conspiracy to create a world order that could take away the most sacred freedoms of the American people. This survivalist mind-set is defensive, watchful, and reactive rather than revolutionary, militant, and aggressive. But for those few who are, indeed, bent on violence, there can be little doubt that Beam's principle of "leaderless resistance" could easily serve as an organizational model and as a battle strategy. In fact, militia training manuals regularly employ the phantom-cell model as the theoretical foundation for their practical guidelines.[15] Comparing this basic strategy with some of the most distinctive features of the Oklahoma City bombing, several analysts have suggested the theory that the perpetrators, McVeigh and Nichols, might well have been members of one such "phantom cell," which decided on its own to bomb the federal building as a "retaliatory strike" for the fiery deaths of the Branch Davidians two years earlier to the day.[16]

McVeigh's refusal to give federal agents anything but his name, rank, and date of birth after his arrest is strikingly consistent with the guidelines proposed by Beam and widely diffused through the code of conduct outlined by the Michigan Militia for patriots "captured" by the federal government. McVeigh's dependence on the strategy of "leaderless resistance" obviously remains speculative, as there are no facts to conclusively support this claim. What we do know as a fact, however, is that McVeigh had both a detailed familiarity as well as a genuine obsession with *The Turner Diaries*. He was known to sell large quantities of the book at gun shows, and carried a copy of the book with him everywhere. One gun dealer goes so far as to claim that McVeigh would even sleep with the book under his pillow.[17]

McVeigh was also known to be very agitated about the government's conduct at Waco in 1993. It is a known fact that McVeigh had even made a "pilgrimage" to Waco to pay his respects at the site of the Branch Davidian compound, and there is strong evidence that he had some ties with the Michigan Militia, as well as with Elohim City, a Christian Identity commune in Oklahoma. Persistent denials of any such connections, both by McVeigh and by the militia, would also fit nicely with the strategy of leaderless resistance. Neither can it go unnoticed that the Oklahoma bombing took place exactly two years to the day (April 19, 1995) after the Waco tragedy. On the basis of these facts, it would not be at all far-fetched to view the Oklahoma bombing as a possible vengeance attack by an extremist militia phantom cell, which used the good services of McVeigh and Nichols to accomplish its bloody mission.

An even more clear-cut instance of an apocalyptic, millennial militant movement in direct confrontation with the government is the more recent standoff of the Montana Freemen in the spring of 1996. Fortunately, this event ended without the bloodshed of Ruby Ridge, Waco, or Oklahoma City. This peaceful outcome, however, was primarily due to the new policies of engagement drawn up by the FBI under the inducement of what has been

God's Soldiers of the End-Time

fittingly called "Weaver fever." Apart from the public pressure against another Ruby Ridge or Waco debacle, there can be little doubt that the patience and professionalism of the government agents involved also contributed greatly to the nonviolent resolution of the siege. On the other hand, the element of luck also played a big role in the peaceful solution, for the lethal combination of deadly weapons with the revolutionary ideology of the Freemen had created another tinder box ready to go up in flames.

The phenomenon of the Freemen was not something new to the American political and social scene, especially in the western states. It descends from a long line of tax protest and "sovereign citizen" movements, going back at least to the 1930s. More directly, it has closer historical links to the violent antigovernment movement of the 1960s called Posse Comitatus, which challenged the legitimacy of the IRS and the Federal Reserve System, while at the same time espousing the most virulent racist and anti-Semitic views. From the religious point of view, many of the Freemen had direct connections with the Christian Identity movement, which, we have already seen, holds militant apocalyptic and millennialist ideas. Both LeRoy Schweitzer and Rodney Skurdal, the two most influential Freemen leaders, had been thoroughly indoctrinated with the nefarious teachings of Christian Identity.

Schweitzer, who also had ties with the neo-Nazi group called the Order, had gained notoriety as a tax resister, and also routinely defied government regulations on business as well as government-mandated traffic laws. His partner, Rodney Skurdal, was a member of the "sovereign citizen" movement, which interpreted all government attempts to control the citizen, through Social Security cards, marriage and drivers' licenses, and the like, as "acts of tyranny."[18] The Freemen, as they called themselves, especially targeted the U.S. court system for its "illegitimacy" and for its role in serving the "new world order" conspiracy. When Schweitzer and Skurdal joined forces with other Freemen near Jordan, Montana, in the fall of 1995, the group named their four-ranch compound "Justus Township" in an attempt to set up a "common law" court in defiance of federal judicial authority. Federal agents, holding arrest warrants for many of the occupants, ranging from conspiracy to defraud to intimidation of U.S. justice officials, surrounded the compound in the spring of 1996 to begin what would turn out to be a highly publicized four-month standoff. While both the government and the media viewed the occupants of Justus Township as a motley group of tax frauds, con artists, and anarchists, the Freemen themselves interpreted the event as the start of a holy war which pitted defenders of God's laws against those who would prefer the laws of men. To miss this apocalyptic and millennial dimension would be to seriously misinterpret the Freemen phenomenon.

Responding to the Militias

Oklahoma City and the Montana Freemen should serve as a warning against those who would simply dismiss the militia movement as an eccentric expression of the delusional fringe. For this reason the appeals of Kenneth Stern of the American Jewish Committee and Morris Dees of the Southern Poverty Conference to crack down on the militias both through tougher legislation and more vigilant law enforcement measures should be taken very seriously. Clearly, enhanced legal and criminal justice improvements will help to contain the potential for violence and anarchic behavior on the part of the militias. On the other hand, such responses alone do not get to the roots of the unrest, frustration, and hostility that obviously spark the movement. In fact, given the assault mentality of most militia members, a one-sided stress on legal and enforcement measures may only serve to deepen the widespread sense of a government conspiracy, especially among those who already feel alienated and expendable within the rapid changes of our postindustrialized society.

The 1996 presidential election campaigns, as well as other political indicators, have made it very clear that a sense of resentment against overly intrusive government penetrates deeply into the ranks of the American mainstream and that a significant cross-section of the population shares in varying degrees some of the militia's anger and frustration with a perceived breakdown of the judicial system. Rightly or wrongly, many angry white males, in particular, both in industry and on the farm, have the overpowering sense of being marginalized and victimized by the broader society. It is important that their concerns, fears, and frustrations also be brought into the public dialogue and that this growing class of Americans be encouraged to find legitimate political and legal vehicles for addressing their grievances. Failure to do this runs the risk of driving this population into the ranks of the militant militias. Political correctness would serve us all badly if it were to exclude such concerns from open discussion in the public square.

– 11 –

On Reading the Signs of the Times

Attempts to understand the motivation and the mind-set of violent millennialists must not be interpreted as a sign of sympathy or approval of their destructive and antisocial actions. A better understanding, for example, of the apocalyptic mentality which drove Timothy McVeigh to carry out the callous bombing of the federal building in Oklahoma City might prove useful in helping to curtail the nurturing of future domestic terrorists, without thereby providing any justification or excuse for such a wanton crime. Certainly devout Christians of whatever type of millennialist persuasion would totally and unconditionally distance themselves from these hate-ridden perversions of biblical faith. Yet despite the vast chasm that separates the devout millennialist from the violent apocalypticist, both groups share a common interest in discovering the religious implications of current worldly events. For that matter, the Christian imperative to learn "to read the signs of the times" is not new, but goes back to admonitions of Jesus himself, at least according to a well-known saying reported in Luke's narrative:

> He said to the crowds: When you see a cloud rising in the west, you say immediately that rain is coming — and so it does. When the wind blows from the south, you say it is going to be hot — and so it is. You hypocrites! If you can interpret the portents of earth and sky, why can you not interpret the present time? (Luke 12:54–56)

This saying, which Luke has directed to the crowds which went out to hear Jesus preach, was quite likely addressed in its original context to those who opposed Jesus' mission. For this reason

Luke preserves the word "hypocrites" in verse 56 — a word Jesus would not likely have used in addressing the "crowds." This adaptation by Luke of the original saying shows that he felt that the message of Jesus contained therein continued to have applicability to his own audience, some fifty years after the death of Jesus. In Luke's context, in which he is preparing the Christian community for the internal divisions, conflicts, and sufferings to come, the signs or omens of which he speaks are understandably seen as portents of coming catastrophe and persecution. No doubt, this emphasis represents Luke's own concerns, based, as they were, on the experience of the persecuted community of new converts from paganism to whom he addressed his Gospel.

Announcing a Turning Point in History

In the context of Jesus' own preaching, however, his choice of meteorological signs as an analogy for understanding the signs of the coming kingdom suggests that the portents in question could be either of a menacing or of a promising type. After all, weather signs can serve to foretell both positive conditions, such as rain after a drought, or negative ones, such as the onset of a destructive storm. What really matters in Jesus' saying, however, is that just like the indicators of weather change, so also the signs of "the present time" herald a *turning point, a radical turn of events*. In addressing the synagogue at Nazareth (Luke 4), Jesus appeals to the prophet Isaiah to explain the messianic significance of his own ministry to the poor and outcasts, as well as his healing ministry to all who were sick of mind or body (Luke 4:14–21). In short, by the "signs of the times" Jesus understood his own preaching, healing, and related ministerial activities. These were the signs announcing the good news of the breakthrough of the eternal kingdom into the present. Jesus, then, was not a preacher of doomsday and judgment, but rather the herald of new joy and hope. His forecasts of judgment are simply the reverse side of his message of hope: the lot of those who of their own free will reject the invitation to the kingdom.[1]

Just as Luke did not hesitate to apply Jesus' directive to a whole different set of signs reflecting the realities of his own generation, so Christians through the centuries have felt free, if not obligated, to attempt to interpret in faith the signs of their own historical situation. In this they are perfectly justified, provided they do not change the message of hope into one of calamity or the good news of salvation into a "cryptic blueprint" for spying out the human future.[2] As human beings we are inclined "to try to peep behind the curtain of the future,"[3] but it was precisely against this type of vain curiosity that Jesus himself reminded the Pharisees that "you cannot tell by careful watching when the reign of God will come" (Luke 17:20). Instead of providing tools for prediction, the evangelists challenge their readers to bear witness to the reign of God that has already come in power: "The reign of God is already in your midst" (Luke 17:21).

Jesus' announcement of the kingdom was essentially a call to action — rather than an invitation to scrutinize the times and details of his coming reign. When Jesus proclaimed "the *time* of fulfillment," he was bypassing all apocalyptic fantasy with a call to present decision.[4] St. Paul captures the meaning of Jesus' message when he tells the Corinthians: "Behold, now is the acceptable *time;* behold, now is the day of salvation" (2 Cor. 6:2). In both instances, the Greek word for time in the original text is *kairos,* which means a *special* time of God's entry into human history, with its corresponding demand for repentance and moral decision in conformity with the ideals of the kingdom. In the New Testament, "to read the signs of the times" is to recognize in world events the imminence of a coming *kairos* — that is, a *turning point* in human history — and to discover the ethical demands of that special moment. Throughout church history attempts to interpret the signs have been frequently tied to expectations of the parousia and the coming of Christ's millennial kingdom. Contemporary Christian theologians, however, if they do not altogether disregard millennial belief, show little consensus as to its meaning. In the following pages of this chapter, I will describe some of the principal ways of understanding millennialism, and offer an assessment of their relative worth.

Varieties of Literal Interpretation

A literal interpretation of the coming millennial reign of Christ on this earth is very widely held, especially by those Christians who go by the name "evangelical." On a practical level, evangelical Christians claim that their beliefs and practices are more solidly based on Gospel or biblical teachings than are those of the Catholic and mainline Protestant churches. Overall, they stress the apocalyptic dimension of Christian faith, which puts very heavy emphasis on end-time doctrines, such as the rapture, the tribulation, the Second Coming, and, of course, the millennium. For them, to read the signs of the times means primarily to be on the lookout for ominous events and circumstances that might herald the beginning of the Last Days. The apocalyptic doctrines of the evangelicals defy easy categorization, for their end-time scenarios are highly nuanced, much-diversified, and ever in flux. But despite the great diversity and dynamism of their end-time convictions, they usually identify themselves as either *premillennialists* or *postmillennialists,* while continuing to argue intensely about the subvarieties of interpretations within these two general groupings (see chap. 4, above, and glossary at the end of the book).

In chapter 7, a good deal of attention was given to the dispensational premillennialism of Darby and Scofield, as well as to the "Armageddon theology" of Lindsey and Walvoord, to which the former gave birth. Despite the significant public impact of dispensationalism on both religious and secular thought in America, it is by no means the only theological system within the premillennialist camp. In fact, during the 1980s and 1990s, premillennialism has undergone a great deal of change, especially as a direct result of dialogue with its own critics. Among other significant developments, a growing movement of progressive premillennialism has already greatly modified the more rigid biblical literalism of the premillennial past.

Even the *Scofield Reference Bible* — the standard bastion of dispensationalist thought — has been undergoing a number of critical revisions, and premillennialists, as a whole, have become more cautious in their biblically based speculation on the millennium, the parousia, and the end-times in general. To a great extent they have also shifted the standard dispensationalist emphasis on the millennial role of the State of Israel to that of Israel's spiritual heirs. While millennialists, in general, continue to be divided on questions of the rapture, the tribulation, and other aspects of the millennial timetable, they have made substantial progress in smoothing over these differences by focusing on major themes of agreement, such as the certainty of Christ's glorious return and the promise of an era of peace and righteousness on earth. There is also agreement that this millennial kingdom, for its part, will enjoy a period of universal global peace and harmony both within the human family as well as among all of creation. After this will follow the general resurrection, the judgment, and the beginning of eternal life.[5] Despite these moderating adjustments of the premillennial hard line, the principal beliefs about the human future remain essentially very pessimistic. This is true primarily because of the premillennial emphasis on divine wrath, punishment, judgment, and tribulation. In this it still stands quite distinct from the more historic postmillennial interpretation of the end-times.

Postmillennialism, while overshadowed by premillennialism in recent years, is still very much alive and well in evangelical churches (as well as on the Internet). After all, postmillennialism was the dominant theological view of American evangelicals from the late eighteenth through the nineteenth century. Since the heyday of premillennialism under the aegis of Hal Lindsey, postmillennialism has revived in a number of forms. Prominent among these is "dominion theology," which places more emphasis on the political engagement of Christians than was typical of classic postmillennialism with its focus on personal conversion. Dominion theology, which ultimately aims at the establishment of a Christian republic,[6] has provided much of the structure and rhetoric for the recent vitality of the Christian Coalition movement in the United States. In general, all postmillennialism puts much more confidence in human effort and in the necessary role this plays in preparing for the arrival of the millennium. The millennium is a time in which the church reigns with Christ on earth. This reign, however, is the result of Christ's spiritual coming and serves as a preparation for his final physical return in glory. The optimism of the postmillennialist stance consists mainly in the belief that the spiritual presence of Christ in the church will be more than sufficient to provide the power to conquer the forces of evil, and so Christ can reign over the faithful right within history.[7]

The postmillennial view supposes a significant continuity between the present experience of the church and the future realities of the millennial reign. The key to the coming millennium, in which Christianity will prevail in an age of peace, is the successful preaching of the Gospel throughout the world. Reading the signs of the times for postmillennialism is a question of recognizing the presence of the Spirit in the universal preaching of the Gospel. For premillennialism, by way of contrast, it consists in identifying the evils, violence, and catastrophes that presage the tribulations of the end-time. Despite the many differences that separate pre- from postmillennialists, it must not be overlooked that evangelical millennialists — of either variety — share the common belief in a future kingdom of righteousness here on earth.[8]

Even amillennialism, which rejects all literal belief in an earthly interregnum between the present age and the final judgment, has found a place in the theology of some influential evangelical thinkers. Following Augustine, these more progressive evangelicals interpret the millennial kingdom of Revelation 20 as symbolic of the present reign of believers, already victorious on earth through their faith. As one author puts it: "Satan is in some sense already bound, and the saints are already reigning with Christ."[9] Although etymologically "amillennialism" would mean any teaching that negates millennial doctrine, evangelicals who embrace amillennialism staunchly affirm their belief in the inerrancy of scripture and in the importance of the text of Revelation 20, while at the same time giving the text a figurative rather than a literal reading. Evangelicals of this persuasion regret the use of the term "amillennial" to describe those who interpret the passage figuratively, for they feel that the designation tends to undermine the seriousness with which they take the millennial symbol.[10]

While most evangelicals have deep concerns about the chronology of the millennial timetable, amillennialists maintain the simplest chronology of end-time events. For them, there will be only one return of the Lord, and that will be at the time of the final judgment and the transformation of creation into a heavenly Jerusalem. The interim period — the age of the church — will be marked by a mixture of good and evil throughout. The Last Days, however, will be characterized by an intensification of the conflict with the forces of evil and fierce persecution of the church.[11] Within this simple chronology there has been little interest in speculation about the timetable of the end-times, and amillennialists are often criticized by other evangelicals for what is perceived as an indifference to "the signs of the times." The fact is that logically an amillennialist reading of the signs would have to do with detecting omens of the final tribulations (for which they have little enthusiasm) or with recognizing moments of temporary spiritual triumph in the midst of evil and suffering. The latter approach to reading the signs, which is decisive for Christians of the postmillennialist school, is totally foreign, if not anathema, to the apocalyptic concerns of the premillennialists.

The amillennialists, who are represented for the most part by evangelicals from the Calvinist or Reformed traditions, expect to see both signs of radical evil as well as evidence of the power of grace and goodness, for in their reading of the Gospels, Christ has already triumphed over Satan, though the victory will not be complete until the final consummation (the time of which is beyond human knowing). In this reading, amillennialists believe they represent a biblical realism, as opposed to the pessimism of the premillennialists or the optimism of the postmillennialists. For their part the millennialists (pre- and post-) suspect the amillennialists of removing the kingdom of God from human history and of holding up a wan image of the human future which lacks any real connection with the present world.[12]

In this brief overview, I have just touched the surface of the variety of millennial interpretations to be found in evangelical theology. Evangelical millennialists are further subdivided, for example, according to the chronology they hold for the rapture: before, during, or after the great tribulation of the Last Days. Thus we have pretribulation, midtribulation, and posttribulation premillennialists and other such nuanced categories. At times evangelicals themselves grow impatient with what appear to be subtle squabbles over eschatological fine points and are inclined to restrict these arguments to late-night rap sessions in seminary dormitories. Yet even behind the apparently petty disagreements of the various schools, some very important issues are at stake. Evangelical millennialism promotes a truly biblical corporate understanding of human destiny and a communal understanding of eschatological fulfillment. The millennial symbolism about which the various schools argue brings out clearly the here-and-now, historical significance of the kingdom of God. Finally, the enthusiasm for God's rule embodied in their millennial expectation far outstrips any excitement that has ever been generated by the personalistic eschatology of the mainline churches.

Within evangelicalism, amillennialism is something of an anomaly — albeit an important one. On the other hand, it remains the standard doctrine of the theology of the mainline Christian churches, for whom "reading the signs of the times" becomes a very different kind of operation. Whatever mainline theology has to say about the millennium, it will be sure to take as its starting point a figurative rather than a literal interpretation of the doctrine.

The Millennium as Symbol

It is not always easy to define what we mean by "mainline" (or "mainstream") Christian churches, but the term would certainly cover the Catholic, Orthodox, Lutheran, Calvinist, Anglican, and Episcopalian churches, as well as the majority of Methodists and even Baptists. Certainly there are many individual members of these churches whose beliefs correspond more closely to those of sectarian Christians, Adventists, Pentecostalists, and evangelicals. For the most part, however, the mainline follows the amillennialism of Augustine, taking the text of Revelation 20 in a figurative sense, as symbolic of the present reign of Christ within the church. This traditional Christian theology expects no other return of Christ than that of the Last Day and the final judgment. Protestant mainline theology is particularly adamant, if not rancorous, in its rejection of a literal millennialism. No doubt this combative stance is, to some extent, a reflection of the in-house conflict that often exists between millennial-minded congregants and the classical theology of the ministers and church leadership. Typical of the classical Protestant response to millennialism is that of the Lutheran theologians Hans Schwarz and Ted Peters. Schwarz dismisses millennialism as a "blind alley in eschatology" in direct contradiction to the teaching of Jesus, who preached "a kingdom that is neither of nor in this world."[13] Peters, for his part, while giving millennialism more serious attention than Schwarz, nevertheless describes its biblical interpretation as myopic — out of touch with "the wider context of biblical and other apocalyptic literature." He also sees it as providing an escape from Christian social responsibility.[14]

In addition to direct clashes of this sort, a good number of Christian theologians, Protestant and Catholic alike, simply ignore millennialism completely or dismiss it with a curt pronouncement. Oxford theologian John Macquarrie, for example, in his book on *Christian Hope,* totally disregards millennial doctrine, except for a brief remark to his readers that the whole idea of the "second coming of Christ has come more and more to be understood symbolically as the triumph of his cause rather than as his personal return."[15] In his influential work on the Christian doctrine of the afterlife, popular American theologian Morton Kelsey covers a wide range of Christian beliefs, including death, resurrection, survival after death, and the problem of hell. In the three pages he devotes to Christ's Second Coming, he argues that resurrection belief has no need of a literal doctrine of the millennium.[16] The renowned ecumenical theologian Hans Küng manages to put together 936 pages on the "essence, history, and future of Christianity," while equally avoiding any discussion of millennialism, except for a brief paragraph on "the expectation of an end-time." Küng seems to justify this millennial snub on the grounds that "Jesus constantly refused to put a precise date to the end of the world" or the coming of the kingdom.[17]

Among Catholic theologians, Monika Hellwig rightly insists that "the reign of God as the promised goal of Christian life and hope necessarily has a this-worldly, public dimension." Beyond this she feels no further need to discuss millennial belief.[18] Dermot Lane's otherwise comprehensive update on Christian eschatology also manages to ignore the whole millennial heritage quite completely,[19] and Karl Rahner, in his monumental volume *Foundations of Christian Faith,* makes no explicit mention of millennialism, though he probably has it in mind in his passing reflection on the dangers of inner-worldly utopias.[20]

Few then are the mainline contemporary theologians who seriously incorporate millennial symbolism into the heart of their eschatology. Those who do, for the most part, remain within the tradition of Augustine and Jerome by spiritualizing the whole Book of Revelation and identifying the image of the thousand-year reign with the age of the church. One way or another, these scholars still continue to voice the conviction of Jerome that "the saints will never have a terrestrial rule, but only a heavenly one." At the same time, however, they maintain that the symbol of the millennium is an important expression of the historical dimension of the reign of God and a powerful reminder of God's lordship over history.

For German theologian Alois Winklhofer, for example, the millennium symbolizes the presence of Christ in the church from the time of his death and resurrection to the present. During this time, the victory over Satan and sin has already been won ahead of time, but the final consummation of Christ's reign is deferred to the indefinite future. In the meantime, both evil and goodness will exist side by side until the final judgment and the inauguration of the heavenly kingdom.[21] A literal earthly paradise or millennial kingdom within history is dismissed as a naive, materialistic reading of the biblical text. The present age of the church is a time of growth and maturing under the power of the Spirit in preparation for the final consummation of history in the eternal kingdom of God.

The biblical image of the millennial kingdom of Christ is seen as a powerful symbol of hope and comfort in the face of the continued presence of evil and injustice. The rule of Christ and his saints shows that through Christ's hidden presence in the church the battle is already won in advance — what remains is a mopping-up operation. Properly understood through the cultural imagery it employs, the vision of the millennium is primarily a vision of the present age, providing a faith understanding of the present challenges and sufferings in view of God's future promise and guarantees. The last things — Armageddon, the rule of the beast, the murder of God's witnesses, the seals of divine vindication, the victory of the Lamb — are constantly occurring in the present. Evil, even in its most destructive and vicious forms, is turned to serve the Lord's purpose, becoming a negative sacrament of transformation and renewal.[22]

For all mainline eschatology, despite the ever-present threats of terror, injustice, and persecution for those who pursue the ideals of the kingdom, the hidden power of Christ periodically emerges in the form of unexpected victories over hatred, bigotry, violence, and envy. The final triumph occurs, however, only when time enters eternity and the great multitude of the Apocalypse ascends with Christ to the glory of heaven.[23] Basically this is the theology expressed in the classic formulations of the church creeds, which say nothing of a terrestrial rule of Christ and his saints within history.

As with the amillennialism of some evangelicals, so also with the mainstream theologians "reading the signs of the times" consists essentially in recognizing these temporary triumphs of the Spirit. At the same time, the so-called amillennialists of both traditions also recognize a certain future reference in the biblical apocalyptic symbols. They will not deny, for example, that Jesus, when asked, was willing to give precise signs of the time of his coming and the consummation of the world (Matt. 24:3).

Certainly the most prominent of these signs listed by Matthew is the beginning of the calamities or the tribulation, as described throughout chapter 24, an emphasis that is reflected in the Book of Revelation as well. Even the new *Catechism of the Catholic Church*, while completely ignoring any notion of a millennial kingdom, presents the tribulations of the end-time as a literal prediction.[24] Included among the tribulations are the confusion brought by false prophets, conflicts between nations, natural disasters such as pestilences and earthquakes, and a general "increase of evil" in the world (24:4-12). This period of sorrow will be followed by cosmic catastrophes: darkening of the moon, falling of the stars and the return of the Son of Man on the clouds of heaven (24:29-30).

Even a literal understanding of the Antichrist as an end-time historical figure is not altogether dismissed, though the literal reading is also combined with a symbolic interpretation which views the Antichrist as a perennial force of deception manifested again and again in various individuals throughout the stages of history. This latter view had already been formulated by Thomas Aquinas, who argued that "in all tyrants Antichrist lies hidden."[25] Both the conversion of Israel (Rom. 11:25) and the universal preaching of the Gospel (Matt. 24:14) are also recognized as real signs of the end. But because of the biblical conviction that Christ is already present in the church ("I am with you always, until the end of the world" [Matt. 28:20]), the parousia itself is seen as simply a new mode of his presence — a triumphal and glorious one at the consummation of history.[26]

This classical (Augustinian) approach to the "Last Things" is also quick to point out the ambiguity of signs, claiming that almost any period of history is prone to interpret its own evils and sufferings as the sure signs of the final tribulations.[27] It is also very firm in its insistence on the impossibility of predicting an end-time chronology, falling back on the admonition of Jesus that we know neither the day nor the hour (Mark 13:32). It is evident in the Gospels that Jesus' announcement of the kingdom and his injunction to read the signs of the times were not intended to assuage human inquisitiveness about the future. To read the signs is to accept the call for a decision, to respond to a call for action; it is not an invitation to "spy out" the future for the sake of human curiosity.[28]

The amillennialism of mainline Christianity serves as an important warning against the seduction of false prophets of the end-time. With the help of biblical research both mainstream and evangelical theologians have been able to show that the main import of Jesus' apocalyptic warnings is the call to constant *watchfulness* for the eruption of divine power into human history. The real apocalyptic challenge is to recognize and respond to the special responsibilities of the present moment on the basis of "an ethic of waiting for his return."[29] The signs of the times are reminders to be on guard and to be ready to take a decisive stand, especially in those special moments of history when the Master returns in power — that is, when the call for justice and ethical behavior becomes especially urgent and critical.

Breaking the Deadlock: The Age of the Spirit

At this point, one might justifiably conclude that Christian theology of the millennium is hopelessly divided by an impassable chasm separating literalist from symbolic interpretations. In recent years, however, a third option has appeared which represents something of a middle path, preserving some of the most worthwhile features of both literal and symbolic millennialism. This breakthrough results from new advances in biblical studies, from the recent revitalization of Christian eschatology, but more particularly from a revival of the apocalyptic theology of the twelfth-century Italian abbot, Joachim of Fiore.

In a way that reflects the current ecumenical tone of Christian theology, it is primarily the work of the leading German Protestant theologian, Jürgen Moltmann, which has been responsible for the new interest in the Catholic abbot's millennial theology. In particular, Moltmann is intrigued by Joachim's identification of the ancient notion of a Sabbath of world history with the idea

A page from an early edition of Joachim of Fiore's *Exposition of the Apocalypse,* one of the holy abbot's most influential works. Joachim was called by Dante "a man endowed with a prophet's spirit."

of the age of the Spirit. In this way Joachim had reestablished the biblical link between final destiny and new creation, and at the same time located the fulfillment of messianic or millennial hope right within history. The age of the Spirit provides for a period of justice, peace, and the vindication of the poor and the oppressed within the confines of historical time. Joachim's millennial kingdom, in a word, represents the completion rather than the end of history.[30]

Though a visionary genius and astute biblical scholar, Joachim was very much a man of his day. His naming of dates for the start of the Last Age, his identification of contemporary figures with the Antichrist, and even his unique method of scriptural analysis were all tied to a peculiarly medieval mind-set. Moltmann and other contemporary theologians sympathetic to Joachim's thought have attempted to disregard these time-conditioned ways of thinking, while still upholding the profound significance of Joachim's essential religious vision. Moltmann, in particular, applauds Joachim's doctrine on the age of the Spirit as serving to restore the messianic and prophetic dimension of Christian hope — a Gospel perspective that had been shoved more and more under the ecclesiastical carpet ever since Constantine's establishment of a "Christian Empire."[31]

Initially, then, Moltmann simply dismissed Joachim's idea of three successive world ages as part of the medieval baggage and interpreted the age of the Spirit as symbolic of those moments when God seems to be moving into his creation to reconcile enemies, overcome hatreds, and remove injustice and violence.[32] In this view, the age of the Spirit stands for the transforming power of the Spirit both in personal lives and in history. It calls for a break with the present pattern of the world; it announces the end of the "old order" and the dawn of a new creation. A firm belief in the ultimate establishment of this new creation (or, in Joachim's terms, this "new order" — *novus ordo*) on earth is the core content of millennial faith. The millennium is *God's future* coming to us in a series of "historical presents." At least for the early Moltmann, then, the millennium is not a future event about which to speculate, but rather an expectation for which we should be ever prepared. Nevertheless, as an event within history, its coming can be discerned through the eyes of faith by reading the signs of the times.

Moltmann's more recent work has taken a very different turn. Reflecting his commitment to theological renewal in light of the Holocaust, he now calls attention to the biblical notion of the special divine promise made to Israel, as expressed in the teachings of Paul: "I ask you, then, has God rejected his people? Of course not! ... No, God has not rejected his people whom he foreknew" (Rom. 11:1–2). From the beginning, he argues, the hope of the church has been inextricably tied to the destiny of Israel. But it is precisely this messianic hope for the coming kingdom that links the church with Israel. From Moltmann's perspective, the promise of the scriptures requires not the conversion of the Jews, but rather a parallel coexistence of two harmonious communities of hope — a future epoch within history when Israel will respond to its special call "alongside the Church."[33] Because of this emphasis on the messianic promise and its fulfillment, Moltmann has begun to envisage the millennium in a way closer to Joachim's successive stages of history. The prophetic coming together of Israel and the church is an expectation of such momentous proportion that it requires nothing less than a special age of the Spirit — a time of fulfillment at the completion of history.

Like Joachim before him, Moltmann appeals to the image of the angel of Rev. 14:6, "the herald of the everlasting Gospel,"[34] who is calling all humanity, Gentile and Jew, to the kingdom, but not to the church. Together they will constitute the new messianic people. This latest turn in Moltmann's thought has certainly brought him much closer to literal millennialism, which he now rejects only when it is treated as a separate object of faith, divorced from the broader context of the biblical message. In support of this more literal and material turn in his view of the millennium, Moltmann appeals to scriptural passages such as Mark 14:25, which cites Jesus' mysterious saying: "Truly, I say to you that I shall not drink henceforth of the fruit of the vine until the day when I drink it new in the kingdom of God." For Moltmann this passage makes it quite clear that Jesus was anticipating an earthly kingdom, complete with wine and human fellowship. It is certainly a difficult passage to dismiss as spiritual symbolism. What is beyond question is that Moltmann has powerfully reawakened Joachim's claim that Christian hope is not only directed to the world beyond; it also includes a real messianic fulfillment right here on earth.[35] No doubt, in this view, "reading the signs of the times" also requires a continual eye on the people of Israel.

The Millennium as Turning Point

In New Testament thinking, to proclaim a time of fulfillment (a *kairos*) is tantamount to proclaiming the imminent breakthrough of God's reign. Jesus himself announced the great *kairos* — the once-and-for-all ushering in of the divine kingdom; the New Testament authors also announce the *kairos* of the Lord's triumphant return — the consummation of the kingdom. In every case, announcing a *kairos* is making *a call to action*. The description of the millennial kingdom in Revelation 20 is itself a proclamation in picture form of God's breakthrough into history, and for this reason it also calls for a decisive moral response. At the same time, it clearly calls attention to certain important aspects of God's future reign which constitute standards for present action and behavior.

Moltmann's reappropriation of Abbot Joachim's apocalyptic of reform places particular importance on these ethical demands of the coming kingdom, while, at the same time, relating these demands to the concrete realities of the present historical situation. In this way, Moltmann has effectively made eschatology more relevant to history and has thereby helped to restore millennialism to its proper place at the heart of Christian eschatology. On the other hand, what he proposes as a middle path still remains too ambiguous on the whole issue of literal versus symbolic interpretation, leaving that important debate up in the air. Furthermore, it does not show clearly the relationship between the notion of the millennium and that central New Testament theme of a *kairos*— that is, a turning point in history under the impact of the Spirit.

In my judgment, a more complete resolution of these issues had been proposed by a theologian of a previous generation, Paul Tillich. Tillich, a refugee from Nazi Germany in 1933, took up his work in the United States, where he became one of the most influential Christian theologians of the twentieth century. Tillich was one of the very few mainline theologians to insist on the importance of the symbol of the millennium. In general, he lamented the neglect of millennialism in traditional theology, convinced that the image of the thousand-year reign was "decisive for the Christian interpretation of history." As a symbol, it provides an important counterpoint to the negativity of the catastrophic emphasis so common in many current apocalyptic theologies. From a positive perspective, it helps keep alive the biblical prophetic tradition which has perennially envisaged a time of fulfillment within history.[36] Like Moltmann, Tillich was convinced that the image of the thousand-year reign was also crucial in providing a counterbalance to the purely transcendent or other-worldly conception of Christian hope.

As seriously as Tillich took the biblical millennial imagery, he was equally convinced that millennial language, like all eschatological language, is struggling to express that which lies beyond our present experience. Theological language about the Last Things, in particular, is a language of hope and anticipation, based on trust in the divine promises rather than on pseudo-information about the human future. For this reason, Tillich is absolutely unambiguous about the nature of millennial talk. It is not literal but symbolic: there simply is *no thousand-year reign of*

Christ looming in the human future. If taken literally, millennialism falls fully into the realm of fantasy, becomes inconsistent in details, and takes on all the trappings of utopianism.[37]

The core of utopianism is the literal understanding of a time of absolute fulfillment in history prior to the final coming of God's transcendent kingdom. In Tillich's view, to expect such a time of complete victory over the demonic forces of evil within the confines of human history is always utopian. Utopianism runs counter to the fundamental biblical conviction that the complete victory over evil is never accomplished within time, but necessarily awaits the heavenly Jerusalem of God's eternal rule. The Marxist expectation of a coming perfect and classless society is a good example of recent utopianism finally gone awry.

Tillich argued that the true intent of the millennial passage of Revelation 20 is far from utopian. To the contrary, it was meant as an actual warning against utopianism. The fact that Satan is not chained permanently clearly suggests to Tillich that the millennial kingdom effects only a partial, fragmentary conquest of the demonic forces within history.[38] A literal meaning would not only tie Christian hope to a product of fantasy (a biblical version of Shangri-La); it would also inevitably miss the important insights contained in the symbolism. For this reason, I doubt that even Moltmann's highly nuanced version of a real messianic period at the end of history can escape Tillich's accusation of utopianism. Given the wealth of biblical apocalyptic images used in composing the picture of Revelation 20, a symbolic interpretation is both true to the genre of the text and faithful to the author's intent of encouraging his readers in their daily struggle against oppressive, sinful structures.

Armed with a persuasive biblical analysis, Tillich was also able to relate the millennial symbol to that central New Testament concept of the *kairos* — the time of fulfillment of the promises God has made "in endless ages past" (Titus 1:2–3). *Kairos* is the special time of prophetic thought and unlike ordinary time[39] is intimately tied to personal action and decision in critique of the status quo. For this reason the defining element of *kairos* is not timetable but moral urgency. Paul reminds the Romans of this urgency when he writes: "You know the time [*kairos*] in which we are living. It is now the hour for you to wake from sleep" (Rom. 13:11).

The real genius of Tillich's insight on the meaning of the millennium was his understanding of Rev. 20:1–10 as a rich, imaginative expression of the notion of *kairos* which is a major New Testament theme. In fact, throughout the course of history, Tillich tells us, whenever the prophetic spirit arose in the churches and people spoke of a "third stage," "the coming rule of Christ," or "the one thousand-year-period," they were actually describing the experience of a *kairos*.[40] Today, as in the past, a *kairos* occurs in the form of "partial victories" over the demonic powers in culture, politics, and society.[41] Proclaiming a *kairos* is always the valiant act of a prophetic spirit. It is a time of decision. It is "the right time, the time in which something can be done."[42] Moments of *kairos* do not occur frequently, but when they do they are opportunities not to be missed.

Every *kairos* is both a divine breakthrough and a special event in history. As a historical event, it is open to analysis and reflection; as a moment of divine breakthrough, a *kairos* must be grasped through the power of the Holy Spirit. In other words, *kairos* discernment is possible only through an act of faith, but a faith that is informed, at the same time, by critical analysis of the current situation. It is for this reason that *kairos* can be an important tool for reading the signs of the times.

From this perspective, then, to read the signs of the times is not to predict or describe a coming millennial age or to identify the catastrophes and tribulations which are to precede it. It is not to speculate about the times or the circumstances of the Lord's coming. It is rather to remain alert in faith to the possible dawn of a new time of fulfillment (*kairos*) and to be ready to respond to it with moral decisiveness. In a word, to read the signs of the times is to exercise the gift of spiritual discernment.

But this spiritual discernment will not attempt to bypass the concrete historical, political, or social factors which constitute the world-situation. True discernment requires a realism — albeit a belief-ful one — to examine and analyze the vicissitudes of history through the eyes of faith. Only such a belief-ful realism can provide the necessary grounds for a truly dynamic and vital millennialism — one that retains all the urgency and enthusiasm of the early church, without the pitfalls and naïveté of biblical literalism.

To believe in the imminent coming of the millennial kingdom

is, in fact, to proclaim a *kairos* — that is, to announce prophetically a turning point or crossroads in human history and to invite women and men of goodwill to meet with courage and conviction the moral challenge demanded by this moment. Surprisingly, however, not all of today's prophets are religious. In the following chapter we look at some secular readings of the signs of the times.

– 12 –

The World at the Crossroads

There is no dearth of secular scholars — historians, economists, sociologists, and political scientists — seriously engaged in the risky task of predicting the coming state of the world at the beginning of a new century and a new millennium. The presence of three zeroes in our calendar date seems to hold as deep a fascination for these "secular prophets" as it does for a wide variety of preachers, religious teachers, and ordinary believers. We have already referred to historian Paul Kennedy's work *Preparing for the Twenty-First Century* and Bill Gates's *The Road Ahead*, to which list we might also add Peter Drucker's *Post-capitalist Society*, as illustrations of this type of futurist investigation. In this chapter, however, I will focus primarily on the work of the historical sociologist Immanuel Wallerstein, comparing his analysis with the recent popular publication in economic history called *The Fourth Turning*, as well as with Drucker's more scholarly *Post-capitalist Society*.

Wallerstein's reflections have an additional fascination in that despite the strictly secular, areligious presuppositions of his analysis, he finds theologian Paul Tillich's notion of *kairos* to be a very helpful tool in discerning major changes in the "world-system." And following Tillich's example from an earlier date, Wallerstein today proclaims that we are about to enter a critical turning point in history — or, in Tillich's terms, we are at the threshold of a new *kairos*. In view of this unexpected meeting of minds, it might prove useful to begin with Wallerstein.

The End of the World-System?

Wallerstein made his mark as a historical sociologist through his "world-system" approach to understanding historical, economic,

Immanuel Wallerstein. A highly regarded historical sociologist, Wallerstein foresees a total collapse of our present economic world-system shortly after the year 2030.

and political change. His three major volumes (*The Modern World-System,* vols. 1, 2, and 3) trace the beginnings of the capitalist world-economy from its origins in the late fifteenth century through its "second great expansion" in the early nineteenth century. World-system analysis assumes that individual nation-states find their way to the core or are pushed to the periphery of the economic order by reason of the dynamics of the worldwide capitalist system; little significant social and economic change is caused directly by actions taken independently by individual states or their leaders.

Even those critics who are little persuaded by Wallerstein's historical rendering of the rise of capitalism admit that he offers a very convincing and accurate picture of the nature of social and economic change once this Western system had been globalized through the spread of British industrialism in the nineteenth century.[1] Since then, the key to the economic positioning of sovereign states within the global capitalist system has been their ability to establish a favorable division of labor and equitable balance of trade within this system. Nation-states that provide low-wage, low-profit goods and services to highly competitive, monopolized, high-wage, and high-profit countries will not manage to accumulate capital for their own industrial development. Locked into this unfair rate of exchange, they are inevitably pushed more and more to the periphery, where their activities essentially serve to enrich the countries of the core. Countries that share at least some core-like activities vis-à-vis peripheral nations are described as "semiperipheral." Fundamentally, the entire world-economy is ultimately based on the exploitation of the peripheral and semiperipheral nations by the capitalist core. Periodically, however, the very dynamics of the system bring about major crises that create a repositioning of nation-states in the world-system, as nations move in or out of the core position.[2]

How the World-System Works

Following the lead of French historian Fernand Braudel, Wallerstein attributes these normal periodic adjustments and changes in the world-system to the expanding and contracting rhythms of cyclical history. Wallerstein's recent work has drawn special attention to the so-called longwave — identified and elucidated by Russian economist Nikolai Kondratieff in the late 1920s — as being among the mechanisms that bring about this regular, predictable cyclical change. Kondratieff's longwave theory was developed at a time when the study of economics was very much infatuated with the notion of business cycles. It claims that a careful plotting of the history of "commodity prices, wages and other economic statistics"[3] will make it clear that major fluctuations of the economy tend to occur in cycles of fifty- to sixty-year periods.

The rising side of the longwave (called the A-Phase) is always marked by vitality and prosperity, whereas the declining side (the B-Phase) represents a time of economic stagnation. Kondratieff's longwave theory had won significant early recognition after he was able to use it successfully to predict both the coming of the Great Depression as well as the subsequent recovery almost "a decade in advance" of the events.[4] Using current developments in longwave theory, Wallerstein argues that the economy since 1974 finds itself in the midst of a downturn or B-Phase of a Kondratieff cycle, *which is likely to return to an A-Phase, however, around the year 2000.*

Wallerstein's appropriation of Kondratieff's theory provides him with another important tool for world-system analysis and serves to complement with economic specificity his earlier more general use of Braudel's cycles for understanding historical changes in the world-system. But if Braudel had first taught Wallerstein to view history in terms of rhythmic cycles (cyclical history), he also instructed him in the necessity of looking at history from the perspective of the long term — *la longue durée*. This latter historical angle, which Braudel called structural history, embraced a far greater time frame than cyclical history, examining the rise and fall of historical systems over spans of hundreds or even a thousand years.[5] In order to recognize either the birth or the demise of a historical system (e.g., an empire, a feudal system, etc.), however, Wallerstein found it necessary to add another historical category to Braudel's original distinction of temporalities. Oddly enough, Wallerstein found this category readily available in the work of Protestant theologian Paul Tillich. As we have seen, Tillich had early on appropriated and adapted the New Testament term *kairos* as a tool for interpreting the world-situation from a theological perspective. As a biblical term, *kairos* meant a historical moment of divine breakthrough into history. Wallerstein, for his part, became convinced that this idea of *kairos*, or fulfilled time, once shorn of any of its theological underpinnings, was very useful for his own sociological, historical analysis of global dynamics in the *longue durée*.[6] It gave him an additional *temporality* to be used in analyzing moments of structural crisis and major transition in the world-system — those epochal moments in which human decision can really change the course of history.[7]

Braudel's notions of cyclical and structural history, enriched by the Kondratieff longwave and Tillich's concept of *kairos*, together provided Wallerstein with the strategic apparatus he needed for discerning and forecasting major changes in the world-system.[8]

Projections of the Coming Global Economy

From B-Phase to A-Phase of the Kondratieff Wave. In his more recent work Wallerstein pays more and more attention to sociological and economic projection, while maintaining a firm foothold in history as a guide to the future. In attempting to identify likely economic global trends for the coming century, Wallerstein distinguishes three distinct time frames, each of which has to be addressed separately. These are: (1) the next few years, until around the year 2000; (2) the first twenty-five to thirty years of the new century; and (3) the period immediately following phase two.[9] Wallerstein courageously offers his prognosis for each of these periods.

The first time frame, according to this analysis, fully belongs to a normal swing in the longwave of the Kondratieff cycle. For this reason, while the present economic situation is far from chaotic, it does show a number of typical symptoms of a Kondratieff B-Phase cycle, which represents a regular downturn in the normal economic rhythm. A growing financial instability, frequent short-run market fluctuations, high rates of worldwide unemployment, increased social unrest, bankruptcies and downsizing, military paralysis of the great powers (here he cites Bosnia), and a general sense of political uncertainty are among the indicators cited by Wallerstein. He lists the years 1842–49, 1893–97, and 1932–39 as earlier examples of B-Phases in recent history. These periods, however brief, share the same pattern of negative indicators, and were all followed very shortly by a time of significant recovery.

For the second time frame, following the same fluctuation of the normal Kondratieff cycles, Wallerstein projects *the approach of a new A-Phase — around the year 2000*. The present B-Phase is now beginning to be played out, and the world market, now leaner and meaner, is set for a new period of prosperity. (This certainly seems true of the American economy as well as the financial market, at least since 1997.) The resulting new A-Phase, however, will differ quite markedly from the last A-Phase (i.e., the period from 1945 to 1973) in a number of significant ways, but, perhaps more than anything, by reason of the radical shift in world economic leadership. In a way that defies the popular view, Wallerstein sees this earlier period (even extended to 1990) as dominated by a U.S. economic hegemony, despite the tensions of the Cold War and the obvious rivalry between the two superpowers. Without underestimating the historical significance of the Soviet Empire and its affiliated "antisystemic" socialist states, Wallerstein points out that time shows in retrospect that the United States had, in fact, remained the dominant world power throughout the Cold War — the unrivaled leader of a worldwide capitalist system that would eventually prove too powerful for all its opponents. In fact, as Wallerstein sees it, the socialist states were "themselves institutional products of the capitalist world-economy," formed from its own contradictions and constrained by the operation of other capitalist institutions.[10] Their collapse was inevitable.

Whatever else might be its limitations, the situation of a single hegemonic power tends to create an environment of stability throughout the world-system — a stability which, in turn, tends to legitimize the social order which emerges from the global economic system. When periods of hegemony come to an end, however, and the former hegemonic power takes a more humble place within the newly constituted system, the immediate results are less stability, less legitimacy, and, consequently, less peace.[11] Wallerstein already points to disquieting signs of U.S. hegemonic decline, such as an increase of economic strength among allied nations, a decrease of U.S. clout in world financial markets (as decision making becomes more dispersed), loss of the stability created by the Cold War, and "a decline of popular willingness to invest lives in the maintenance of hegemonic power."[12]

All this, in Wallerstein's view, is normal enough in terms of the workings of the cyclical process, and, accordingly, what should now be expected is the rise of replacement structures through the process of repositioning in the world-system.[13] The major difference this time is that the resulting new A-phase will have to operate within the context of a major split in world hegemony. This split will help engender a situation of such intense competition and global power struggle, with a resulting political and social unrest, that it will be bound to neutralize much of the effect of the economic recovery. In a word, unlike the earlier A-Phase, the coming time frame will yield little in terms of order and predictability but much by way of chaos and uncertainty.

The most likely scenario in this new fight for the core, claims Wallerstein, will be a bipolar competitive system, pitting a pragmatic alliance of Japan and the United States, on one side, over against the European Community, on the other. China might well emerge as an important component of the Japanese/U.S. pole, while Russia will more likely be drawn into an alliance with the European Community. It is important to note, however, that maintaining China and Russia as loyal and viable partners will require heavy financial investments on the part of both sides of the equation, which may in the long run put a new kind of drain on the resources of the world-system.[14]

A Period of Increasing Chaos. The second of Wallerstein's time frames (2000–2030), then, will be an ambiguous mix of economic recovery and prosperity resulting from a normal cyclical change in the system, combined with the intense competitiveness and instability created by a growing bipolar hegemony. While for Wallerstein this central struggle for control of the world-system clearly seems to constitute the root cause of growing disorder and uncertainty, there are other contributing factors that further exacerbate the situation. Wallerstein bases his ultimately negative prognosis for the period 2000–2025 (or 2030) on the weight of these factors, only some of which directly result from an emerging bipolar world-economy.[15]

One factor that is a logical consequence of the new economic power struggle will be the pressure on the opposing powers to make substantial financial investments in the potential megamarkets of China and Russia. As Wallerstein sees it, this competitiveness will not be based on ideology, but on blatant material self-interest. As compared to the 1945–73 A-Phase, the approaching cycle will have even less available investment funds for the countries of the South, the consequence of which will be an even greater North-South gap than the already existing one.

Closely related to this first factor will be a "truly massive pressure for *migration* from South to North," exacerbated by the expanding economic gap between the two regions. This pressure will be brought to bear both by unskilled and educated classes of the nonindustrialized countries, as well as by the economic interests of core-nation employers, who will feel the pressure to employ migrants at a lower wage level. Major demographic changes, which will see continued decline in the population growth of wealthy regions and the projected population explosion among the poor nations, will run parallel with economic pressures for large-scale migration to North America, the European Community, and even Japan. The perceived economic and social threat of immigration gone out of control has already produced highly charged political reactions bent on limiting immigration as well as the social and legal rights of both legal and illegal immigrants. This will eventually create a situation as volatile as that created by the growing dispossessed class in Great Britain and France in the early nineteenth century.

A third factor that will tend to undermine any anticipated prosperity in the coming A-Phase, even in the industrialized countries, is the direct result of the successful distribution of economic wealth during the 1945–73 time frame. That A-Phase was responsible for the creation of many high-paying jobs that helped create the very extensive middle-strata population we have today. From an economic point of view, however, this expansion of the middle class added significantly to the cost of production, which ultimately resulted in the B-Phase trend of downsizing. The effect of the downsizing, however, has been to push countless workers out of the middle-class economic status to which they had become accustomed and which they had hoped to pass on to their posterity. Wallerstein does not deem it likely that the downsizing trend will change even with the cyclical upturn, nor does he expect this large segment of the population in economic decline to passively accept its fate. It might well be that this worsening situation is at least a contributing factor in the growing appeal of the patriot militias and the obvious increase in antigovernment sentiment nationwide.

Since 1945, it is not only the North that has experienced a striking growth in the middle-class strata. In the peripheral nations as well, the middle class and those who aspire to this status have more than doubled in numbers, and now that decolonization has been complete, their leaders can no longer distract this significant population with immediate promises of political victory. They must directly confront the economic situation, which for the reasons already cited does not look promising. The growing hiatus between economic expectation and the realities of the market can only serve to aggravate the situation. This threat to the erstwhile middle class and to what Wallerstein terms "the supplicants to middle class status" is another major difference between the past and the coming A-Phase.

Still a fourth factor listed by Wallerstein that will make a big difference in the coming A-Phase is the lack of room for further economic expansion of the world-economy. Capitalism has always depended upon its ability to expand into new geographical zones to maintain its favorable rate of profit and continued accumulation of capital. Wallerstein details the signs of "economic squeeze" that signal the end of economic expansion and its accompanying process of commodification.[16] This realization of the "limits of growth" combined with the spiraling costs of maintaining and renewing our ecological base, as well as the completion of the urbanization process worldwide, will put very serious constraints on the anticipated economic growth of the coming A-Phase. Furthermore, amid this uncertain and highly competitive economic situation, the "old liberal solution" (Wallerstein's term) of assuaging the discontent of marginalized classes through political power-sharing and distribution of welfare benefits is clearly reaching its own limits of credibility. The recent spate of "workfare" legislation in the United States proves his point.

National states, like those of the former Soviet Union and the former Yugoslavia, will continue to have great difficulty maintaining internal order; ethnic, religious, and linguistic groups will continue to grow in power; ethnic wars in the South and minority conflicts in the North will be on the rise; nuclear proliferation will be inevitable; and periodic North-South wars (like the Gulf War) will continue to exact an economic price from the hegemonic powers of the core nations. Add to this the economic and social stresses caused by AIDS (which Wallerstein compares to the medieval Black Death) and the coming time frame promises to be one of growing disorder, instability, and chaos.

Opportunity following Collapse. The time frame about which Wallerstein says least — quite understandably — is the third one, which begins somewhere around 2030. Ultimately, the chaos of the second time frame will reach such proportions as to cause a collapse of the economic world-system as we know it. This epochal event, cataclysmic beyond description, will nevertheless bring human civilization to a *crossroad* — a bifurcation in which genuine choices can be made independently of the cyclical rhythms of a historical system in demise. For Wallerstein this will occasion a rare opportunity to help create a new historical system (or systems) and to rebuild society "in ways that are humanly satisfying."[17] Obviously this historic moment will require a "fundamental moral choice" about the world's future. But, as he puts it, this future remains "both unknowable and up to us."[18]

Historical Turnings and Epochal Transition

William Strauss and Neil Howe are popular writers, with some limited claim to academic credentials, working out of the Washington, D.C., area. They have been very successful in recent years in bringing their cyclical understanding of history to the public imagination, especially by applying it to the task of forecasting the future of the American republic. Like Wallerstein, their analysis and predictions are heavily economic in thrust, but, at the same time, totally immersed in the political, social, and cultural context. What is unique to their method is their claim that a correct understanding of history enables us to prophesy about the future with a high degree of confidence. This is a view not widely accepted among historians, who, for the most part, view prediction with about the same enthusiasm as they would view a loathsome disease. Nevertheless, the authors make their case for the cyclical approach to history, and apply their method to making detailed predictions about the unfolding of America's future — especially over the next thirty years.

In their popular volume called *The Fourth Turning*, the authors immediately go on the offensive by attacking the conventional academic opposition to *prediction* on the part of historians. Their strategy is to impugn the validity of what they call "linearism": the view that time represents "a unique story, with an absolute beginning and an absolute end."[19] Linearism, so defined, is no doubt the dominant view of the historical academy. Strauss and Howe, nonetheless, deplore the "triumph" of linearism in the academy, convinced that this conception of time perpetuates the false assumption that the journey through history is forever new and never repeats itself. The ultimate effect of this linear belief is to create an attitude which sees history itself as irrelevant. The authors maintain that this attitude goes a long way to explain history's lack of popularity among American students.

As opposed to this "straight line" view of history, the authors propose the cyclical notion of time, which enables the historian to search for "history's patterns and rhythms," which, despite the particularity of new circumstances, are bound to repeat themselves at regular intervals. It is through understanding the cycles of history that we are able to predict the human future. In support of their position they like to quote Winston Churchill, who once wrote that "the farther backward you look, the further forward you are likely to see."[20]

In contrast to Kondratieff's economic cycles of fifty- to sixty-year periods, Strauss and Howe appeal to the ancient notion of the *saeculum* (meaning "an age") — a time span of eighty to one hundred years, reflecting the period of a long human life. Within this time unit, history reveals a regular rhythm of four cycles: growth, maturation, entropy, and destruction, each succeeding the other about every two decades. The authors, who call these cycles "Turnings," locate the First Turning of this current *saeculum* in the period immediately following World War II. This was a time of economic growth, exuberance, and confidence. The Second Turning began in the mid-1960s — a time of awakening and emergence of a counterculture highly critical of the institutions that had been so glorified in the previous Turning. The present period, which began in the mid-1980s, belongs to the Third Turning — a time of unraveling, in which individualism replaces institutional loyalties and the old civic order begins to collapse. This Turning, which is epitomized in the rampant culture wars of today, is likely to last to the middle of the next decade (which the authors rather jauntily dub the "Oh-Oh decade"). At that point we will enter the Fourth Turning — a historic moment of catastrophic crisis and upheaval which will mark the end of one epoch and the beginning of another.[21]

As part of their technique for predicting future scenarios based on the rhythms of historical cycles, the authors have also developed an elaborate typology of generational "archetypes," which, they claim, appear consistently within the unfolding of the historical cycles. They list these categories as the Prophet, the Nomad, the Hero, and the Artist, and by correlating these archetypal patterns with the actual generations of this *saeculum,* they claim to produce a more accurate picture of the "mood" that can be expected to carry the day during the unfolding of a particular Turning. The so-called millennial generation (born 1981–2000), for example, having been born during the Third Turning, will face the crisis of the Fourth Turning with the mind-set of the Hero: amid the threat of chaos, they will remain committed to the pursuit of order and harmony and will be willing to sacrifice even their lives in defense of the civic institutions.[22]

There is no doubt that Strauss and Howe's elaborate methodology leads to detailed and specific predictions that at times stretch the limits of credibility. Yet their analysis of history and of the current situation is sufficiently based in the realities of the economic, political, and social order as to demand our serious attention. Their projections give us at very least a realistic possible scenario for the early decades of the twenty-first century: we are currently in a time of unraveling (a Third Turning), which will quickly usher us into a period of political and economic crisis (a Fourth Turning) as early as the year 2005. This last Turning of the *saeculum* will achieve crisis proportions around the year 2025, requiring a radical concerted response in order to avoid national, if not global, disaster. The catalyst event to set off the crisis could range from antigovernment cyberterrorism (e.g., destroying IRS databases) to the spread of killer viruses or the outbreak of anarchy throughout the former Soviet republics.[23]

As indicators of the present unraveling, the authors cite a wide variety of signs or signals of rising chaos. These include the growth of public debt, shrinkage of the middle class, controversies over welfare, exacerbation of cultural and racial tensions, and the ongoing battle against crime and drugs. The "culture wars," including gender conflict, sex-preference issues, and controversy over multicultural education, are having the effect of "atomizing" an increasingly diversified population.

The study of historical Turnings through the course of American history convinces the authors of the imminence of a wrenching upheaval to be expected in a Fourth Turning. Previous Fourth Turnings in American history occurred at the time of the Civil War and at the time of the Great Depression/World War II. All were preceded by an unraveling analogous to the kind we are experiencing today.[24] So, once again, by the middle of the next decade the authors foresee a dramatic collapse — the beginning of an earth-jarring social, political, and economic chaos. While recognizing the uniqueness and particularity of historical events and of current experiences, the authors would have us believe that even the most random-looking events are carried by the inevitability of circular rhythms. The great crisis of the Fourth Turning will happen one way or another — its occurrence is inevitable.

At the core of this crisis, as in many previous ones, will be a great devaluation of the market, affecting both financial and property assets. This will result in public debt, poverty, and unemployment. Economic distress will be accompanied by social and cultural breakdown, fueled by racial, religious, and class conflict. New developments in technology will continue to produce destructive side effects in terms of personal stress, ecological damage, and highly destructive weaponry. Political despotism will be rampant, and the war against international terrorism will become increasingly difficult.[25]

But despite the pessimism of their prognosis, the authors claim that a Fourth Turning, with all its pain and destruction, is a necessary prelude to the rebirth or high of a new First Turning. Fourth Turnings are as inevitable as the coming of winter after autumn, but the nature and outcome of the wintry season are never foreordained. But Fourth Turnings provide us with an opportunity to break from the confines of cyclical time and to "steer our own destiny" for the future. The authors, on an optimistic note, express the confidence that Americans, by preparing themselves today, will be able to meet the "Great Crisis" of the coming decades, and turn the conflagration of societal collapse into a new rising from the ashes. But to do that they will have to "make personal and public choices akin to the harshest ever faced by ancestral generations."[26]

Although his chosen profession is hardly shy about speculation concerning the future, Peter F. Drucker, the noted Claremont economist, is far less confident in the art of prediction than the more popular writers, Strauss and Howe. His claim is that our focus ought to be not on analyzing the future (always a risky business at best), but rather on the present actualities. Even now we have more than enough evidence to conclude that our society has already moved into a new order. We have already crossed the "divide" that separates us from the capitalist society created by the Industrial Revolution, and we now find ourselves in the midst of a major global transition to a postcapitalist, knowledge-based society. The Industrial Revolution not only had created the capitalist system, but had also produced the class warfare so widely publicized by Karl Marx, and with it the antisystem called Communism. With the collapse of Communism in 1991, it was easy to discern the end of the antisystem, and with it, according to Drucker, the end of the nineteenth-century belief in "salvation by society."[27]

Peter F. Drucker. Drucker's assertion that we are moving into a post-capitalist, postindustrial world in which knowledge-workers will assume the pivotal position is a kind of secular millennialist vision which underscores the need for new levels of economic harmony.

But Drucker sees as equally ominous the transnational coalition brought together in early 1991 to decisively defeat the forces of Saddam Hussein and to reverse the Iraqi invasion of Kuwait. Contrary to the conventional wisdom, Drucker argues that the war was not fought for economic advantage, since Iraqi control of Kuwaiti (as well as Saudi) oil wells would actually have made for a more plentiful and therefore a cheaper supply of petroleum. It was rather a reaction of the world community against what was perceived as the serious threat of international terrorism that forged the unity of the alliance. The resulting so-called Gulf War marks the dramatic end of the political centrality of the nation-state, which has been tied inextricably from the outset to the inner workings of the capitalist global economy. When the interests of the nation-state are pushed aside in favor of global concerns, there is reason to question, as Drucker does, whether the capitalist system is still in tact.[28]

There is other evidence as well, according to Drucker, that we have entered a postcapitalist society. The lynchpins of the capitalist system have traditionally been labor, land, and money (or capital supply), but these have each become less central as "the main producers of wealth have become information and knowledge."[29] Information wizards, like Bill Gates, or builders of business information systems, like Ross Perot, have become for today the equivalent of the nineteenth-century steel barons. The Industrial Revolution, from 1750 until 1900, had effectively created a unique global society based on technological advance and capital investment. Until the end of World War II, the main focus of the revolution was industrial *productivity*. Following World War II, a revolution in management changed the face of industry by systematically applying knowledge (as opposed to skill) to industrial production. The GI Bill of Rights marked the beginning of the age of the knowledge-worker, which has evolved into our time of the Knowledge Revolution, in which knowledge is now applied even to the understanding of information, so that the decisive "factor of production" is now neither land, labor, nor capital, but knowledge.

The capitalists and proletarians of capitalist society are either gone or irrelevant to the present economy (hence the necessary demise of Marxism). The only significant class distinction in today's marketplace is that between *knowledge*-workers and *service*-workers. The knowledge-workers replace the capitalists in that they control both the means and the tools of production. They control the means through the ever-growing pension funds, which increasingly govern the supply and allocation of money throughout the developed world.[30] They control the tools because as knowledge-workers, they can take their knowledge with them wherever they travel throughout this fast-moving global society. Despite the appearances of capitalism — the market economy and the market institutions — we are in the midst of an economic and social revolution of historic proportions. We are in a period of radical transition to a postcapitalist society, in which wealth is produced by information and knowledge.

This change is neither anticapitalist nor noncapitalist, but coopts the capitalist system and the market for its own ends — which reflect a whole new set of priorities centered around the basic economic resource, called *knowledge*. Following the normal rhythms of history, Drucker expects this transition period to last until 2010–20. The challenges ahead require a high degree of harmony and cooperation between the knowledge-worker and the service-worker, between specialists and managers, between transnational and national interests, between free trade and protectionism, and, most important of all, between developed and developing countries. Failure to take responsibility for "Third World" development will ultimately produce a devastating inundation of immigrants from South to North, beyond the capacity of developed nations to absorb.[31]

What future society will look like beyond this period of transition — that we cannot know. Yet what is evident is that we are in a time of great flux — a time of opportunity *to actually make our future*. For Drucker the turn of the millennium turns out to be the time for a "call to action."[32]

At the Crossroads

Peter Drucker correctly notes that ever since the French Revolution there have appeared any number of secular transformations of millennial belief. We have already noted in an earlier chapter the particular case of Joachim of Fiore, whose prophetic vision had inspired any number of reformers — secular and religious alike — for many centuries after his death. The millennialism of these secular creeds, however "nonspiritual" in its concerns,[33] follows the basic patterns of religious apocalyptic belief by predicting the end of the present world order, followed by the hope for a new, just, and harmonious society. As in the case of their religious predecessors, these secularized versions of millennialism predict the profane equivalent of the kingdom of God on earth, but only after the *catastrophic* collapse of the present age or system. One wonders whether Drucker would recognize in his own prognosis, as well as in that of Wallerstein, Strauss, and Howe, other instances of secularized millennialism.

All three theories anticipate a growing stage of economic chaos and social calamity, culminating in a disastrous upheaval (a time of tribulation?), which may well serve as a necessary purifying preparation for the emergence of the secular, righteous kingdom. At first glance, it would seem that Wallerstein's prediction is the more sanguine, in that it anticipates the imminent end of a B-Phase, that is, an economic downturn. But then his A-Phase, or upturn, which follows around the year 2000, is ambiguous at best. As a cyclical period of prosperity, it will, nevertheless, be more than neutralized by a series of undermining factors. These lead in the long run to a period of ever-increasing chaos, which will deteriorate rapidly between the years 2005 and 2025. For Strauss and Howe, we are in the last years of a Third Turning — a time of social unraveling — and will enter the catastrophic Fourth Turning around the middle of the next decade, that is, 2005. Drucker seems somewhat less pessimistic in his claim that we are already in the midst of a major historical transition, which will last until 2010–20. But the challenge of overcoming powerful new tensions through cooperation and harmonization will be formidable. And, for Drucker too, when we complete the stage of transition, there are still no guarantees.

The task before us, according to each of our authors, is nothing less than that of creating order out of increasing chaos. Each following his own methodology, and, seemingly, uninfluenced by religious or faith considerations, independently forecasts a coming period of crisis, upheaval, or collapse, all within a very similar time frame, that is, the early decades of the new millennium. Except for Wallerstein, who specifically designates the year 2000 as the beginning of a new A-Phase, the authors all agree on the period of testing as occurring between 2005 and 2025. Wallerstein, looking even further down the time line, points to the middle of the next century as the likely time of apocalypse, that is, of *complete* economic collapse.

While each of the three analyses spells out in alarming detail the wide range of economic distress that will be created by the coming economic disintegration, they all clearly concur that the single *most fundamental and potentially dangerous effect will be the widening of the economic gap between North and South, and between rich and poor everywhere*. With that they foresee the danger of massive immigration — on a global scale — that can only end in political as well as social chaos. Again at the social level, this basic state of economic inequity is likely to further encourage the "balkanization" of society into ethnic, religious, and racial groups in conflict with each other's interests.

Despite the bleakness of these predictions, it is important to note that each of the authors studied recognizes that we are at the threshold of a historic moment of epochal proportions — a unique time of opportunity as well as of risk. We are at the end of one epoch and the beginning of another — we are approaching "the next Great Gate in History."[34] This is one of those rare occasions in history when we have the opportunity to decide our own destiny, to rebuild society on the ashes of a collapsed system. Each of our secular forecasters is convinced that the year 2000 is bringing us to a real *crossroads:* a radical turning point, calling for moral response and decision. Which path we take will determine the future prospects of our world. If the religious person decides to look at this coming time period as a moment of *kairos,* that is, a special time of fulfillment, when the divine power breaks into human history, such a faith conviction is not lacking empirical support from significant secular analyses.

We have seen in the previous chapter that the biblical mandate to "read the signs of the times" means to be alert for recognizing just such a moment. The biblical awareness of *kairos* also carries with it the demand for moral decision and action right here and now. God's entrance into history, even in the form of partial victories, inevitably requires repentance and moral resolve in conformity with the ideals of the kingdom. This vision of the kingdom, which stands at the very center of millennial faith, demands a level of moral conduct which consistently prefers reconciliation to conflict, community to individual self-interest, and *harmony* to chaos and disorder. Finally, no matter how fearsome and uncertain the future might appear, the symbol of the millennial kingdom must continue to function as an emblem of *hope*—and never be distorted into an image of fear and terror.

– Conclusion –

The Year 2000 and Beyond

In the previous chapter, we examined the work of some significant secular analysts who, independent of religious beliefs, are predicting a major turning point in human history for the beginning of the new century. If their projections are correct, the year 2000 and the years which follow shortly in its wake will witness major upheavals in our economic and social system, to be followed by a rare and precious opportunity to establish a more just and humanly fulfilling society. The religious term for such a historic moment is a *kairos*.

Apart from the arguments put forth in these scholarly analyses, there is no reason to believe that the year 2000 will have any special millennial significance. As was already pointed out in chapter 1, the scientist Stephen Jay Gould has ably made the case for the arbitrariness of calendrical milestone dates, such as 1000 and 2000, as well as for the imprecision of these dates for marking the anniversary of the birth of Christ. Gould, all the while recognizing the psychological force of "even years with three zeroes,"[1] nevertheless makes as strong a case as any for approaching the coming millennial anniversary with calm, nonchalance, or even indifference.

Those believers who might still be tempted to identify the year 2000 with the beginning of the end-times might profit much from reading Gould's account. On the other hand, those religious believers who attribute unique historical importance to Christ's first coming will hardly be persuaded to view the bimillennial anniversary as just another calendar date.

Once the symbol of the millennium is understood as a *kairos*, or moment of special divine intervention into history, Gould's critique of the imprecision of the calendrical milestone date loses its force. In this reading, the millennial date of itself need not have any intrinsic significance. What matters is the judgment — based on analysis as well as on faith — that we are on the brink of a turning point in history. Since such moments need have no clearly defined beginning or end, it really does not matter whether the *kairos* should take place in the year 2000, 2001, 2033, or 2050. At whatever point there begins to emerge on a global scale a new consciousness, bent on the transformation of the present order, that moment deserves to be proclaimed as the beginning of a new *kairos* — which is a historical embodiment of the biblical symbol of the millennial kingdom. Apart from this *kairos* consciousness, the exact millennial timetable remains as flexible as the vicissitudes of history.

Millennial Vibrations

There is little doubt that we will continue to have the cynics, who are convinced that the year 2000 shall be a year like any other year, without any consequential human import. If, on the other hand, there is any such thing as a millennial mind-set, and if, furthermore, the year 1000 is to serve as any kind of guide, even the most cynical interpreter is forced to recognize the similarity of current cultural happenings to those which took place shortly before the year 1000. Who can fail to see the parallels between late tenth-century Flagellants and other apocalyptic cultists and the recent spate of misdirected millenarianism, in the form of the Solar Temple, Aum Shinrikyo, Heaven's Gate, Ruby Ridge, Waco, or Oklahoma City? But the millennial mood preceding the year 1000 was not exclusively apocalyptic. It was marked primarily by massive religious pilgrimages and gatherings to honor the saints — all geared to foster and support the Peace of God.

It is remarkable that today — as removed as we are from the Middle Ages — we once again experience such mass gatherings of enthusiastic believers, joining in solidarity and prayer, in hope for a change of course in themselves and in society. Such striking events as the Million Man March on Washington in 1995, the Million Woman March on Philadelphia in 1997, and the "Stand in the Gap" religious gathering of Promise Keepers on the

Washington Mall, also in 1997, are reminiscent in many ways of the tenth-century religious revivals. Despite controversies over the public value of these events, there can be no question that these were all spiritual revivals, aimed at producing repentance, reconciliation, and a moral renewal in all of the participants. As such, they are also signs of a growing consciousness that we are on the brink of a momentous historical transition — that we are on the threshold of a new *kairos*.

Harold Bloom, author and literary critic, basing his argument on the study of millennial movements through the centuries, claims that the seemingly unrelated phenomena of "angelicism, prophetic dreams, 'near-death experiences,' millennial fears, and apocalyptic yearnings" are all unmistakable omens of the same emerging consciousness.[2] Certainly, if angel-awareness alone is an omen of millennial mindfulness, Bloom's case is easily supported by even a cursory look at the recent spate of angel-centered films and the plethora of new books about angels available in the local bookstores. (I recently counted sixty-two titles dealing with angels on display in the "religion" section of a local Barnes and Noble.)

Of course, such cultural phenomena alone would not prove Bloom's thesis, except in conjunction with the historical, sociological, economic, and cultural analyses referred to in the last chapter. It is these studies that provide the rational basis for viewing the new millennial threshold as an extraordinary historical opportunity for bringing about what the scholar Georg Feuerstein calls "the creation of personal and collective meaning, revisioning and growth."[3] At various points in this book we have seen the convergence of a number of momentous events, such as the information revolution, major breakthroughs in biotechnology, the collapse of Soviet Communism, the emergence of a postcapitalist economy, as well as the ongoing threats of environmental pollution, political instability, and global terrorism. Together they point sharply to the emergence of a historic millennial moment that may well mark the end of the old and the beginning of a new order. To further interpret such an epochal moment as a special time of grace and divine intervention requires an act of faith, without which it is impossible to proclaim a *kairos*. *Kairos* thinking is at the same time realistic and belief-ful: it has been called a *belief-ful realism*.[4]

New Beginning and New Creation

Hans Küng, the Swiss ecumenical theologian, predicts what he calls an "epoch-making overall constellation which is already coming into view — a new world epoch, to mark the end of the modern period."[5] He sees growing evidence for this coming breakthrough in such positive signs as the transition from a military to a peace-time economy, the advances of eco-technology, the development of nuclear fusion, and the invention of environmentally friendly materials — all signs of an emerging postindustrial society. At the same time, Küng cautions his readers that while the coming *kairos* provides a unique opportunity for global transformation, it is an opportunity that can also be lost — as it was in Europe in the wake of World War I.[6]

Michael Lerner, author and editor of the liberal Jewish journal *Tikkun,* has recently expressed a similar conviction, insisting that we are living in the midst of a real historic moment, and for this reason, urges a new sense of community and cooperation in order to be able to meet the challenges of this emerging epoch. He is convinced that there are many individuals who feel isolated and alone in their personal conviction that they are living on the brink of a great historical breakthrough. For this reason he is calling for a movement — a global one at that — to help spread the new consciousness and to ensure individuals that their efforts are part of a much larger scheme and that their role really counts in this big picture.[7] Lerner's appeal to global responsibility is in many ways reminiscent of George Rapp's message to his nineteenth-century followers at New Harmony, Indiana, who might otherwise have failed to see the global significance of their otherwise remote and isolated communal experiment on the American frontier.

Authors like Küng and Lerner are well aware that visions of the millennium ought not to become the objects of a purely passive hope. As we have already seen, in the Book of Revelation, the symbol of the millennium, like the message of Jesus itself, is rather to be taken as a "call to action" (see above, chap. 11). To respond to a *kairos* is to make a new beginning — to work toward the restoration of God's original creation.[8] To read the millennium symbol as *kairos* is to retrieve the best of early Christian thought, taking Revelation 20 with the seriousness and urgency it deserves — all the while avoiding the pitfalls of a literal interpretation. Feuerstein insists on this need for active engagement when he reminds us that any paradise we hope to encounter is "the paradise whose gardens and springs we ourselves have patiently cultivated."[9] The initiative of a *kairos* is from God, but it will not bear fruit without our enthusiastic response.

In chapter 11, I tried to make the case that any authentic Christian millennial expectation will be on continual guard against all unrealistic utopianism. There will be no expectation of a complete victory over evil within the boundaries of history — the devil is bound only for a time. A *kairos* is always a fragmentary breakthrough of the divine power into history: it may last only for a moment in time. At any point in history, we can only hope for a "partial victory," but all such victories are real anticipations of the coming reign of God at the end of history and bear important witness to its ethical demands. The arrival of a *kairos* brings with it a variety of such demands, as well as an overpowering sense of moral urgency. To responsibly declare a *kairos* at this important juncture in history is to apply to the present moment the admonition that Paul gave to the Romans close to two millennia ago: "You know the time [*kairos*] in which we are living. It is now the hour for you to wake from sleep" (Rom. 13:11).

The Demand for a Global Ethic

The recognition of a *kairos* with all the moral challenge that it entails interfaces closely with the growing cultural awareness of the need for a global ethic. In the early chapters of this book, we explored some of the principal challenges and threats to the survival of humankind along social, cultural, economic, political, and ecological lines. What immediately became evident was the need for certain clear-cut, universally accepted ethical norms so as to effectively meet these challenges. Only ethical standards can provide reasons to avoid the dangers of corruption, greed, selfishness, racial and ethnic hatred, brutality, manipulation, intolerance, and lack of compassion, all of which can certainly undercut efforts to resolve the potentially catastrophic problems facing the human future. Unlike the past, the world we live in is so interconnected and interdependent that individual and separate ethical norms will not meet the need. As Hans Küng has aptly

The joy that Mother Theresa and the Dalai Lama show in each other's presence reveals that, at least for some religious leaders, crossing boundaries need not produce fear.

put it: "If ethics is to function for the well being of all, it must be indivisible. The undivided world increasingly needs an undivided ethic."[10] In short, the world-situation today demands nothing less than a *global ethic*.

In view of his analysis of the moral shortcomings that prevail in our modern technological society, Küng argues that at the most basic level such a global ethic will of necessity be an ethic of responsibility — as opposed to an "ethic of success."[11] So important is this need, according to Küng, that he sees no chance of the world's survival without the establishment of an effective and universally recognized global ethic. On the other hand, Küng also makes it clear that it is naive to try to establish a persuasive global code of morals without the full approval and confirmation of the world's religions. Historically, it is religion that has functioned as the principal teacher and purveyor of moral norms. Even today, Küng is convinced that only religion can provide the solid anchor and grounds that are necessary to support a genuinely global ethic.[12] On the basis of these convictions, Küng has formulated a slogan that has become a standard focus for dis-

Thoughtful dialogue across religious traditions helps foster mutual understanding and respect. Here Maryknoll Brother John Beeching converses with young Thai Buddhist monks.

cussion in cooperative dialogue among the representatives of the world's religions: "No survival without a world ethic. No world peace without peace between the religions. No peace between the religions without dialogue between the religions."[13]

The practical problem, of course, is to find sufficient agreement among the world's religious leaders as to what a universally acceptable moral code might be. To date, it has proven possible to find consensus only on very general moral principles, such as the conviction that true religion must be of service to humanity and that all peoples must be bound by the golden rule. The problem arises when dealing with specific criteria, for here the cultural and historical differences separating the religions make it difficult to find common ground. Nowhere is this seen more clearly than in the tension that exists between the demand for universal human rights and the persistence of specific historical and cultural moral norms embedded in the different religious traditions of the world.

In the effort to secure universal human rights, for example, great care must be taken not to try to impose certain moral standards that are peculiar to the historical and cultural context of western

European and North American societies. Universally acceptable models for human rights can be achieved only through dialogue and consensus.[14] The lifestyle and expectations of American women, for example, cannot be the determinative criteria in evaluating the violation of human rights among Muslim women. The Tibetan community (in exile) might be the best judge of whether the human rights of Tibetan boys are being violated when they are encouraged to enter the monastery at a very tender age. The Vatican and the Islamic community will inevitably cross swords with liberal humanism both in the area of the abortion controversy and on the issue of contraception, especially in view of liberal accusations that the religious laws of these communities violate human rights and perhaps even endanger the survival of the planet.

Constructive dialogue with other religions not only is essential for world peace and global stability, but can also serve as a helpful cross-check for a communal examination of conscience on matters of human rights. Finally, given the fact that a significant number of nonbelievers also share the planet with women and men of faith, Küng also proposes that nonbelievers join their voices to the growing coalition of world religions in search for a common global ethic.

The Idea of Global Harmony

Millennialism at its best, from biblical times to the present, reveals a consistent longing and pursuit of global harmony as the goal of its perennial vision. We have already seen how the New Testament and the Book of Revelation, in particular, carry over into their own context the ancient Isaian vision of universal harmony. As the second-century theologian Irenaeus so cogently argued, the millennium entails the restoration of the original harmony of the first creation. We have seen this vision of harmony revived again in the communal experiments of Joachim of Fiore and of the Rappites of New Harmony.

Harmony, furthermore, is an ideal that is also very well recognized and respected in the other great religious traditions of the world. Buddhism from its inception has fostered the ideal of harmony with nature, with our true mind, and with our fellow human beings.[15] Recently, with an eye on the millennium, the Dalai Lama has delivered lectures on the pursuit of universal harmony. Sociologist Robert N. Bellah tells us that "Japanese religion is fundamentally concerned with harmony — harmony among persons and harmony with nature."[16]

The Chinese religious and philosophical traditions of Confucianism and Taoism, while opposed to each other in so many respects, are each in their own way deeply rooted in the principles of wisdom and of harmony.[17] According to the Hindu spiritual master Sri Chinmoy, harmony is the primordial creative force, the very "life of existence" — the byproduct of sympathy and appreciation.[18] All authentic spiritual life is meant to foster the growth of individual and global harmony. In Islam the principle of harmony finds obvious expression in the beauty of its unique forms of art, architecture, and calligraphy, and at an even deeper level, the best of Muslim theology has always encouraged a balance and integration of the inner spiritual and moral life with the external discipline and social requirements of the shari'a.[19]

In his efforts to establish the grounds of a global ethic, Hans Küng appeals to the universal recognition of human rights and human dignity across the religious traditions. Küng is correct in that both the religions and the more secular humanists of today can embrace the ideal of "serving humanity" as their central ethical focal point. The problem is that when it comes to spelling out the specifics, the cultural and historical conditioning of each tradition often gives a different picture of what, in fact, tends to serve and to build up humanity.

While, at first glance, *the ideal of harmony* might appear to be an even vaguer norm, in practice, it has shown the potential to serve as a common, practical ethical standard, less subject to diverse philosophical and cultural interpretations. It is far easier to debate, for example, whether certain economic arrangements are productive of harmony among nations and with the earth's environment than to argue about which socioeconomic system best serves to produce a humanly fulfilling society. Similarly, there are very objective grounds to determine whether actions taken by Hindus or Muslims in northern India, or by Protestants and Catholics in Northern Ireland, are truly productive of a harmonious society. Since the *notion of harmony* is endowed with a positive symbolic significance across the world's religious divides, it has the power to serve as the *foundational principle for the construction of a truly global ethic.*

We have already seen that in the history of millennialism, those movements which were guided by the ideal of harmony proved to be the most constructive and successful and, at the same time, the most faithful to their biblical roots. The early medieval revival of millennialism took a very positive direction under the inspiring leadership of the prophetic-minded Calabrian abbot Joachim of Fiore. The type of new order he envisioned and tried to bring about took its lead from the ideal of harmony embedded in the apocalyptic symbol of the heavenly Jerusalem. The communities he founded were meant to incorporate these ideals and witness to them until the Lord's return. Their success would introduce new reforms into both church and society (see above, chap. 6).

The biblical notion of harmony found a later embodiment in the work of the Harmony Society of New Harmony, Indiana, and the historic community it established there between 1814 and 1824 in preparation for the return of the Lord (see above, chap. 8). We have seen earlier that their very effective work of community building (material and spiritual), their admirable work ethic, and their sense of spiritual connection with the larger goal of global harmony are ideals very much needed in today's world. The writings of Joachim and the experiment at New Harmony both illustrate the very constructive potential that is inherent in millennial belief. At the same time they illustrate the effective use of "harmony" as a social guide and an ethical norm.

As I mentioned earlier in this chapter, the Jewish writer Michael Lerner makes a strong case that individuals committed to a serious moral transformation of society at this epoch in history must begin to feel themselves part of a larger movement. But beyond this, argues Lerner, individuals must see themselves and their movement as directed toward some higher purpose and meaning. What Lerner is proposing is nothing less than a "politics of meaning," by which he means a concerted effort to empower individuals to base their lives on their "highest ideals and to fight for their realization."[20]

By definition, a politics of meaning invites us to get beyond individualism, selfishness, and the laws of the marketplace in order to foster the creation of a genuine world community. At the approach of a new millennium, it also means rejecting the rampant cynicism that would scoff at the possibility of introducing such idealistic aims into the political arena. It requires us to go beyond the pragmatism and economic self-interest of a market-driven society, in the interest of producing what Pope John Paul II has called "a civilization of solidarity and love."[21] For Lerner it is not all a question of political and social change, for these are only effective, he claims, to the degree that they are based on the foundation of a genuinely ethical and spiritual connection between people.

Such a connection will inevitably encourage a very different kind of economic reality.[22] A politics of meaning is a call to human *community* based on ethics and caring. In today's interconnected world, community must be no less than global, at least in terms of awareness, and must strive to get beyond all differences emerging from race, religion, gender, ethnicity, and economic status. Lerner's notion of a politics of meaning has rich possibilities for planning our voyage into the new millennium.

His vision and strategy are clearly suggestive of a harmony-centered global ethic. At the same time, the down-to-earth quality of his politics of meaning also throws practical light on what it might mean to be guided by such an ethic. For one thing, he puts us on guard against the dangers of *false harmony*, the special deceptive attraction of what he terms "repressive communities," such as the People's Temple, the Moonies, the Branch Davidians, the Solar Temple, Aum Shinrikyo, and Heaven's Gate. Such authoritarian societies know well how to play to the deep unhappiness that so often results from the delusory expectations created by our consumer society. Their offer of harmony and community, however, comes at too high a price, precisely because it demands the sacrifice of individual rights and freedom. Second, despite his optimism about society's future, Lerner warns that even if we should achieve a "meaning-oriented and loving society," this will not be the end of history. We would still have to be prepared for the emergence of "formidable new struggles, tensions and problems."[23] To put it in religious terms, a *kairos* is never more than a partial victory.

The Path to Global Harmony

As Lerner also makes clear, it is one thing to identify the principles and the goal of social and individual transformation; it is quite another thing to know "how we get there."[24] For this reason, if the vision of harmony is to be more than a utopian dream or a pious platitude, it is important to describe the path which can lead to its implementation. Keeping in mind the current tensions challenging our global future and guided by the lessons of history, I would propose the following three ingredients of a spiritual recipe for the creation of a more harmonious planet earth.

Applying the Racial Test

In today's world, especially in the United States, any judgment about the achievement of harmony must be measured against the standard of racial healing. All too easily racial tensions are brushed under the carpet and polite conversation continues while ignoring the deep wounds, resentment, and suspicions that go unaddressed. A number of recent events, including the beating of Rodney King, the Los Angeles riots of 1992, charges of police brutality against innocent, black immigrants in New York, and the senseless hate murder of James Byrd Jr. by white supremacists in Texas, all go to remind us that the cancer of racism is far from being eradicated in the United States. More than any other single event, however, it was the highly charged O. J. Simpson criminal trial which exposed the enormous racial gap that continues to divide our society.

In a wonderfully fair-minded and frankly insightful analysis of the racial issue, entitled *Racial Healing*, Harlon L. Dalton, an African American professor of law at Yale, courageously offers some realistic and practical suggestions for building a more racially harmonious society. The healing begins, according to Dalton, with the honest recognition that racism remains as "a deep and abiding wound" at the heart of American society.[25] He also argues the importance of unmasking the unconscious racism which underwrites the unspoken rules of social advantage and which is even more destructive than the glaring hatred of out and out bigotry. Finally, Dalton excuses no one from responsibility for racial disharmony and argues that blacks and whites must begin to share "a joint ownership" of the racial problem. Like the Harmonists of Indiana, Dalton recognizes the crucial role that small communities, like his own (racially mixed) Salt and Pepper Gospel Choir in New Haven, can play in leading the way in the day-by-day steps needed for racial healing. More than any other strategy, however, he calls for an open, honest, and full-scale dialogue, which is the opposite of "pretend conversation."[26] President Clinton's much-maligned "initiative on race" has brought the discussion to the national level and was, for that reason, at least a step in the right direction. In the religious situation of the present, the struggle for racial healing is the key litmus test determining the genuineness of our pursuit of God's kingdom on earth. Real conversation will go a long way toward helping us to pass the test.

Observing the Rules of Conversation

While confronting racism in its various forms provides a useful paradigm crucial for bringing harmony to ourselves and to our world, the need for genuine dialogue extends far beyond racial issues alone. We have seen the crucial need for dialogue between management and labor, economists and ecologists, rich nations and poor, religion and religion, multinational industry and local government, pro-life and pro-choice, feminism and the male establishment, and in so many other areas of local and global tension.

But if dialogue is so urgent for harmony, then it is worth reviewing the rules that govern good dialogue, or, to use a more popular term, good "conversation." The term "conversation," when looked at philosophically, means, above all, *questioning*, that is, following a question as far as it may go — in a spirit of cooperation, sharing, and searching for the truth. David Tracy, a theologian at the University of Chicago, has provided a careful and in-depth analysis of the necessary ground rules for a responsible, effective, and fruitful conversation. Among them he includes the following: (1) "say only what you mean"; (2) "say it as accurately as you can"; (3) "listen to and respect what the other says, however different or other"; (4) "be willing to correct or defend your opinions if challenged by the conversation partner"; (5) "be willing to argue if necessary, to confront if demanded, to endure necessary conflict"; and (6) "be ready to change your mind if the evidence suggests it."[27]

Of all these rules the most fundamental is *listening* — without which the others will fall apart. Adhering faithfully to the rules of responsible conversation is a necessary strategy for talking across barriers of ignorance, distrust, and hatred. It is an indispensable step on the road to local, national, and global harmony, especially in an age that is marked by suspicion and cross-cultural tension.

As I suggested earlier in the book, it is the individual religious traditions that stand in greatest need of internal dialogue in order to offset the bitterness and destructiveness of factional differences within their own ranks (see above, chap. 3). The need for observing the rules of respectful discourse was the main incentive behind Cardinal Joseph Bernardin's 1996 declaration *Common Ground*, which appealed to American Catholics to help prepare the church for its mission in the new millennium by approaching their differences with a "renewed spirit of civility, dialogue, generosity, and broad and serious consultation." Dialogue is basically another word for conversation, and Bernardin was deeply concerned that real conversation in the church was rapidly being undermined by a "polarization that inhibits discussion and cripples leadership." The Chicago cardinal dedicated the last pain-filled years of his life to the promotion of his "common ground initiative," aimed specifically at fostering "the basic principles of respectful dialogue."[28]

In support of his project, Bernardin appealed to the authority of Vatican Council II, which had encouraged Catholics "to create in the church itself mutual esteem, reverence and *harmony*, and to acknowledge all legitimate diversity" (italics mine).[29] While Bernardin's invitation to dialogue and internal harmony was directed to factions within the Catholic Church, it is clearly relevant to the current situation of other religious communities as well.

Oddly enough, respectful conversation and authentic dialogue seem to have made far better strides in initiatives across religious boundaries. Since the late 1960s, a number of small, but very effective, interfaith organizations have been formed with the goal of encouraging the religions of the world to take a joint responsibility for fostering world peace and for improving the conditions of life on the planet. Nongovernmental organizations such as the Temple of Understanding, the Global Forum, the Project on Religion and Human Rights, and the World Conference on Religions for Peace (WCRP) have been gathering together religious leaders from all the major traditions for intensive international discussions and joint reflection on the principal challenges that face human beings worldwide.

The World Day of Prayer for Peace convened in Assisi at the

invitation of the pope in 1986 was a dramatic public demonstration, which both symbolized and encouraged mutual respect and harmony among the world's religions. The Global Forum has sponsored international meetings in Oxford and in Moscow, encouraging dialogue between religious and diplomatic leaders, and the WCRP has been actively engaging religious leaders in cooperative programs to help ease tensions in Bosnia-Herzegovina, to deal with political and social turmoil in Sierra Leone, to address issues of human rights worldwide, and to work for the restoration of "ecological harmony."[30] Despite these significant successes, it is obvious that still more effective interreligious dialogue is badly needed if the world's religions are to overcome their historic reputation of encouraging violence, hatred, and warfare.

The Call to Spiritual Community

If listening is the foundation of all fruitful conversation, it is of crucial importance that human society in the third millennium find a place for the stillness and silence that listening requires. Technology has done wonders in advancing our means of communication, but these provide no guarantee of *genuine* human communication, which is by definition "a spiritual event that cannot be measured quantitatively."[31] The need for this deeper level of communication with ourselves, with the world, and with God has found expression in the closing decades of the twentieth century in an extraordinary rise of interest in spirituality.

Until these recent developments, spirituality — the inner search for meaning and ultimate purpose in one's life — was very much restricted to the discipline of the monastery or to the practices of sectarian holiness communities. Today it has become the vital concern of a broad spectrum of the general population both within and without the churches. No doubt this enthusiasm for the spiritual life is a form of reaction against the shallowness, impersonalness, and inhumanity of the consumerist, competitive, technological society that has dominated the last half of the century. It is, in short, the sign of "a search for a new wholeness,"[32] in resistance to the disconnections, loneliness, and meaninglessness of contemporary culture.

Michael Lerner, who, as a modern millenarian, is convinced that we are on the brink of a new epoch, also recognizes the vital necessity of a return to spirituality in preparation for this new beginning. To this end, he proposes that all of us draw up a program that would include "daily prayer, meditation, aesthetic enterprise, or spiritual orientation."[33] Isolated from the rest of life, even such spiritual practices can easily become narcissistic and can be co-opted by a "spiritual consumerism," but when linked with an active movement aimed at changing society, they can become the soul, the energy, and the underlying strength of that very transformative activity.

In support of Lerner's thesis, the Benedictine monk Laurence Freeman assures us that the silence of meditation "is by no means a negative state of absence but a creative power of extraordinary but non-violent force." In short, the practice of spirituality is not "a wholesale withdrawal from the world of work, family, local politics or television," but will require our full-scale engagement in the struggle for peace and social justice both locally and worldwide.[34]

In the Christian tradition, a genuinely spiritual life is one which is lived in the Holy Spirit — the Spirit of the Risen Christ poured out on his church until the end of time. We recall that for the twelfth-century reforming abbot Joachim of Fiore, the millennium meant the coming age of the Spirit — the final stage of the unfolding of divine life within human history. It was an age which would require the work and dedication of truly spiritual persons (*homines spiritales*). We have already referred to the growing intensity of the expectation of the coming of the Spirit among Christians across denominational lines. It is noteworthy in this regard that Pope John Paul II chose the Feast of Pentecost 1996 to solemnly open the preparations in Rome for the millennial Jubilee Celebration 2000. (It is on Pentecost that the church commemorates the sending of the Holy Spirit upon the apostles.) This growing sensitivity for the Spirit and spirituality both within and without the churches makes relevant once again Joachim of Fiore's call to *spiritual community*. An authentic spirituality cannot exist without community, for as theologian Frederick Parrella has recently remarked, "spirituality invites us to move out of ourselves and to stand in relation to others."[35]

Such a community today might be composed of small gatherings of friends, prayer groups, parish groups, academic and professional societies, cultural circles, social or political clubs, campus groups, or whatever other organizations share a commitment to the pursuit of harmony on a personal, communal, or global level. In recent years, I have been happily surprised to discover the bonds of true spiritual community with fellow members of a scholarly society (not a very common experience in academia). At my own university, by way of the annual observance of Harmony Week since 1991, I have watched with admiration the gradual cementing of genuine solidarity among a broad spectrum of students of every imaginable racial, cultural, and religious background. Regular university events throughout the year reinforce and keep alive the ideals and commitments expressed during Harmony Week.

Where and at what moment the "gift of community" will appear for each of us are impossible to predict, for "like the wind the Spirit blows where it wills."[36] What is important is that as individuals dedicated to universal harmony, we realize that we are not alone, but are part of a vast spiritual community guided by the power of the Divine Spirit at the outset of the new millennium.

Millennial Celebration

At the time of this writing the turn of the millennium is less than a year away. However inaccurate the calendrical anniversary, the symbolic power of the year 2000 makes it perfectly fitting that we seize this occasion to reexamine the meaning of the doctrine of Christ's return and the imminent coming of his millennial kingdom. On these grounds alone, this book differs with those critics, secular or religious, who would dismiss millennial belief as a delusional religious fantasy. At the same time, it also parts company with those who would predict the imminent arrival of a literal, material, thousand-year reign of Christ on earth. In rejecting literalism, it also stands opposed to the apocalyptic doomsday message that usually accompanies this brand of millennial belief. In its place, it offers a message of hope and a challenge to action — both more consistent with the good news of the Gospel. On the other hand, my disagreement with biblical literalism is itself part of a "conversation" and is not intended to diminish in any way the debt all Christians owe to fundamentalist and sectarian communities for having kept alive the spirit and fervor of millennialism within the Christian church.

What I am proposing, as a middle path, is the understanding of the millennium as a *kairos* — an epochal moment when the divine Spirit breaks into human history with power and promise, but also with a call to moral decision. Even as we presently find ourselves beset with wars or rumors of wars, with terrorism or the threat of terrorism, and with all the other momentous problems outlined earlier in the book, I am also proposing that, despite the odds, the coming millennium marks the beginning of a historical period of grace. Pope John Paul II has already proclaimed the new millennium to be "a time of great crisis" as well as "a time of great grace."[37] There is no doubt that a *kairos* is disruptive and makes imposing moral demands, but it also provides a unique opportunity to radically transform the world into a much better place.

At the time of the first millennial turning around the year 1000, many devout people embraced the religious and moral cause of the Peace of God movement. In the present *kairos,* the challenge to transform the world and society imposes the responsibility of overcoming the racial, ethnic, and other social conflicts that so deeply threaten the human future. Given the nature of this challenge, the path to peace at the turn to the third millennium requires a concerted effort to pursue the ideal of *harmony.* Harmony, like the notion of *kairos,* is biblically based and offers a concrete ethical check on our human decisions, both personal and political. It provides an uncomplicated and solid basis for a globally acceptable ethic.

Like the persecuted Christian communities in Asia Minor to whom John of Patmos presented the original disclosures of Revelation, so also we today stand in need of his message of assurance that, despite all surrounding threats, God is with us and still in charge — that he remains the Lord of History. Periodically we catch glimpses of the powerful workings of God's hand in such special world events as the collapse of apartheid in South Africa or the signing of the peace accord between Israel and the Palestinians. We see the same in thousands of less dramatic, everyday acts of forgiveness, reconciliation, and generosity. Such moments might be of short duration, but they have the power to inspire us with hope and move us to celebration.

There can be little doubt that it was sentiments of this sort that moved Pope John Paul II to proclaim the year 2000 as a jubilee celebration. Of course, the cynic may well ask whether it is fitting to celebrate before the victory is won. But here we can look at the example of Jesus, whose whole ministry was interspersed with banquets and celebrations with friends, with outcasts, and even with enemies. Jesus' dining with outcasts like Zacchaeus, with the tax-collector, and with women of ill-repute — with enemies of God's law — was meant as an act of reconciliation and therefore as an occasion of "celebrative joy." Yet among Jesus' critics, his feasting rather than fasting and his sitting down with publicans and sinners provoked as much resentment and sense of scandal in his day as did former president Jimmy Carter when in recent years he sat down with political pariahs such as General Cedras of Haiti or Presidents Mobutu Sese Seko of Zaire and Mengistu of Ethiopia in search of peaceful reconciliation.[38]

But still, why celebrate when such formidable tasks still lie ahead? Some biblical scholars have proposed that Jesus' own strategy was meant to celebrate God's presence in the messianic banquet, "prior to the destruction of evil," precisely so that "evil would be transformed by the celebration itself."[39]

At the turn of the third millennium, then, we do have reason to celebrate even before the apocalyptic battle is over. We celebrate the power of the Spirit in history, the birth of new spiritual communities, the beginning of a new thing, and the struggle for the restoration of the original harmony of creation. History has known other visions of global harmony, such as those of Isaiah, John's Revelation, St. Irenaeus, the Peace of God, Joachim of Fiore, and the Rappites of New Harmony, and more recently of Martin Luther King. Such visions have in different ways changed the course of history and have helped make this world reflect a little bit more the ideal of harmony that belongs to the promise of God's millennial kingdom. It is in the spirit of this new vision of global harmony that we have the opportunity to join together in solidarity to celebrate the arrival of the year 2000 and to await in joyful hope the coming of God's saving presence into our world.

Notes

1. Crossing the Millennial Divide

1. Peter F. Drucker, *Post-capitalist Society* (New York: HarperCollins, 1993), 1.
2. Stephen Jay Gould, *Questioning the Millennium* (New York: Harmony Books, 1997).
3. Lance Morrow, "There Is a Balm in Chiliad," *Time* (January 27, 1997): 82.
4. Phyllis Zagano, "The Media and the Millennium," *Catholic World* (January/February 1996): 19.
5. John Updike, *Toward the End of Time* (New York: Knopf, 1997).
6. William Grimes, "Hot Spots for the New Millennium," *New York Times*, December 29, 1996, 10.
7. Laura Bly, "2000 Party Plans All Over the Map," *U.S.A. Today*, April 7, 1997, 1.
8. Jill Smolowe, "Tonight We're Gonna Party Like It's 1999," *Time* (fall 1992 special issue: *Beyond the Year 2000*): 11.
9. Francis X. Clines, "The President Looks Forward to Millennium, and Vacation," *New York Times*, August 8, 1997, 8.
10. Alison Rea, "Does Your Computer Need Millennium Coverage?" *Business Week* (March 10, 1997): 98.
11. Wendy Murray Zoba, "The Class of '00," *Christianity Today* (February 3, 1997): 20–24.
12. Mihir Desai, "The End of Everything," *New York Times*, August 24, 1996, 1, 23.
13. Richard Landes, "Apocalyptic Expectations around the Year 1000" (Center for Millennial Studies, Boston University, March 5, 1998), 1; available at http://www.mille.org/1000–br.html.
14. Henri Focillon, *The Year 1000*, trans. Fred D. Wieck (New York: Frederick Ungar, 1969).
15. Ibid., 50.
16. Guy Bois, *The Transformation of the Year One Thousand: The Village of Lournand from Antiquity to Feudalism* (Manchester, England: St. Martin's Press, 1992), 147.
17. Richard Landes, *Relics, Apocalypse and Deceits* (Cambridge, Mass.: Harvard University Press, 1995), 26.
18. Ibid., 28.
19. Umberto Eco, "Waiting for the Millennium," *FMR Mensile Culturale* 2 (July 1981): 70–73.

20. Russell Chandler, *Doomsday: The End of the World* (Ann Arbor, Mich.: Servant, 1993), 47–48.
21. Focillon, *Year 1000,* 73.
22. Richard Landes, "Between Aristocracy and Heresy: Popular Participation in the Limousin Peace of God, 994–1013," in *The Peace of God: Social Violence and Religious Response around the Year 1000,* ed. Thomas Head and Richard Landes (Ithaca, N.Y.: Cornell University Press, 1992), 203; see also Landes, *Relics,* 40.
23. Frederick S. Paxton, "History, Historians, and the Peace of God," in *Peace of God,* ed. Head and Landes, 28.
24. Landes, "Apocalyptic Expectations," 1–2.
25. Paxton, "History," 40.
26. Landes, *Relics,* 36–37.
27. Paxton, "History," 27.
28. Landes, "Between Aristocracy and Heresy," 200.

2. Food Scarcity and Technical Abundance

1. Lester R. Brown, "Facing the Prospect of Food Scarcity," in *State of the World 1997: A Worldwatch Institute Report on Progress toward a Sustainable Society,* ed. Lester R. Brown and Linda Starke (New York: W. W. Norton, 1997), 23. See also Paul Kennedy, *Preparing for the Twenty First Century* (New York: Random House, 1993), 23–25.
2. Christopher Flavin, "The Legacy of Rio," in *State of the World 1997,* ed. Brown and Starke, 17.
3. Kennedy, *Preparing,* 23.
4. Ibid., 66.
5. Brown, "Facing the Prospect," 33.
6. Ibid., 23.
7. Russell Chandler, *Racing toward 1001* (Grand Rapids, Mich.: Zondervan, 1992), 47.
8. Bill Gates, *The Road Ahead* (New York: Viking, 1995), 89.
9. Ibid., 103.
10. Chandler, *Racing,* 46.
11. Ibid., 48.
12. Gates, *Road Ahead,* 256.
13. Chandler, *Racing,* 52.
14. Kennedy, *Preparing,* 87.
15. Ibid., 90.
16. Ibid., 94.
17. Chandler, *Racing,* 54.
18. See Jeffrey Kluger, "Will We Follow the Sheep?" *Time* 149 (March 10, 1997): 68–72.
19. Robert Wright, "Can Souls Be Xeroxed?" *Time* 149 (March 10, 1997): 73.
20. Kennedy, *Preparing,* 70.
21. Larry L. Rasmussen, *Earth Community, Earth Ethics* (Maryknoll, N.Y.: Orbis Books, 1996), 68.

3. Disharmony with Nature and Neighbor

1. Paul Kennedy, *Preparing for the Twenty-First Century* (New York: Random House, 1993), 71.
2. Ibid., 48.
3. Ibid., 63.
4. Russell Chandler, *Racing toward 2001* (Grand Rapids, Mich.: Zondervan, 1992), 132.
5. *USA Today,* October 24–26, 1997, A1, B1; and *New York Times,* October 26, 1997, A1; see Kennedy, *Preparing,* 57.
6. Kennedy, *Preparing,* 56.
7. Lester R. Brown, Christopher Flavin, and Hilary French, foreword to *State of the World 1997: A Worldwatch Institute Report on Progress toward a Sustainable Society,* ed. Lester R. Brown and Linda Starke (New York: W. W. Norton, 1997), xv.
8. Kennedy, *Preparing,* 31.
9. Christopher Flavin, "The Legacy of Rio," in *State of the World 1997,* ed. Brown and Starke, 13.
10. Kennedy, *Preparing,* 108.
11. "Earth Summit+5," *United Nations: Special Session of the General Assembly to Review and Appraise the Implementation of Agenda 21* (New York: United Nations, June 23–27, 1997), 2.
12. "Environmental Diplomacy: Analysis of the Kyoto Global Climate Conference" (February 6, 1998), 4–5; available at http://www.pbs.org/newshour/forum/december97/protocoll.html.
13. U.S. Department of Justice (FBI), *Report on Crime in the U.S. 1995* (Washington, D.C., October 10, 1996), 2; available at http://www.fbi.gov/ucr/95prs.htm.
14. "Crime Clock Chart 2.1," in *Crime in the United States* (Unified Crime Report, 1997), 4.
15. See U.S. Department of Justice, *Report of Bureau of Justice Statistics* (Washington, D.C., 1994), 4.
16. *New York Times,* August 10, 1997, 1A.
17. *National Drug Policy: A Review of the Status of the Drug War,* Report 104–486, House of Representatives, 104th Congress, 2d sess., March 1996, 4, 13; available at http://www.house.gov/reform/drug.htm.
18. Gideon Doron, "Israel and the Rabin Assassination," *Current History* 95 (January 1996): 8.
19. U.S. Department of Health and Human Services, *Addressing Emerging Infectious Disease Threats: A Prevention Strategy for the United States* (Atlanta: Centers for Disease Control and Prevention, 1994), 1–2.
20. Cited in ibid., 2.
21. Ibid., 1
22. Kennedy, *Preparing,* 27–28.
23. Ibid., 28.
24. *New York Times,* October 9, 1997, A1, 14; see also Russell Chandler, *Doomsday: The End of the World* (Ann Arbor, Mich.: Servant, 1993), 158–59.
25. *New York Times,* October 9, 1997, A14.
26. Chandler, *Doomsday,* 160.

4. The Millennial Religious Response

1. Massimo Introvigne, "Ordeal by Fire: The Tragedy of the Solar Temple," *Religion* 25 (1995): 271.
2. Ibid., 278.
3. Kurimoto Shin'ichiro and Serizawa Shunsuke, "The Pathology of the Peculiar Sect," *Japan Echo* 91 (Autumn 1995): 58.
4. Ibid., 60.
5. Evan Thomas, et al., "The Next Level," *Newsweek* (April 7, 1997): 32.
6. Ted Peters, *UFOs: God's Chariots?* (Atlanta: John Knox Press, 1977), 131–32.
7. Thomas, "Next Level," 35.
8. Hal Lindsey, *The Late Great Planet Earth* (Grand Rapids, Mich.: Zondervan, 1970).
9. Hal Lindsey, *Planet Earth — 2000 A.D.* (Palos Verdes, Calif.: Western Front, 1996), 12, 22.
10. The newsletter of Jack Van Impe Ministries International (November 10, 1997).
11. Lindsey, *Planet Earth — 2000*, 26.
12. Grant R. Jeffrey, *Apocalypse: The Coming Judgment of the Nations* (New York: Bantam Books, 1992), 143. See also John Wheeler Jr., *Earth's Two-Minute Warning* (North Canton, Ohio: The Leader Co., 1996), 164.
13. Wheeler, *Earth's Two-Minute Warning*, 160.
14. Lindsey, *Planet Earth — 2000*, 212–13. See also K. Hamilton et al., "Melody the Red Heifer," *Newsweek* (May 19, 1997): 16.
15. Jack Van Impe, *2001: On the Edge of Eternity* (Dallas: Word Publishing, 1996), 198–99. The Van Impes also have produced a video with the same title.
16. Wheeler, *Earth's Two-Minute Warning*, 134.
17. The newsletter of Jack Van Impe Ministries International (November 24, 1997) announces a new video with the title *Front Row Seats*.
18. The video *Left Behind* is advertised in the Van Impe magazine, *Perhaps Today* (May/June 1996).
19. Jeffrey, *Apocalypse*, 99.
20. Lindsey, *Planet Earth — 2000*, 71–72.
21. Advertised in *Perhaps Today* (May/June 1997).
22. Randall Balmer, *Mine Eyes Have Seen the Glory* (New York: Oxford University Press, 1993), 9.
23. The audiotape of the series is entitled *Jesus Christ Is Coming Back Again (A Study of End Time Events)*.
24. *Catechism of the Catholic Church* (New York: Doubleday, 1995), pars. 677, 680.
25. Ted and Maureen Flynn, *The Thunder of Justice* (Sterling, Va.: MaxKol Communications, 1993), 8.
26. Ibid., 201.
27. Ibid., 105.
28. Martin Marty, "Making Plans," *Christian Century* (January 3–10, 1996): 31.
29. Charles Austin, "A Time for Unity" (November 7, 1997), 1; available at http://www.thelutheran.org/9611/oagre8.htm.

30. See Geoffrey Wainwright, *The Ecumenical Moment: Crisis and Opportunity for the Church* (Grand Rapids, Mich.: Eerdmans, 1993).
31. Catherine Keller, *Apocalypse Now and Then* (Boston: Beacon, 1996), 11.
32. Ibid., 288.
33. Brian Daley, "Judgment Day or Jubilee? Approaching the Millennium," *America* 176 (May 31, 1997): 9–10.
34. Ibid., 18–21.
35. Anthony Pilla, "Virtues for the Journey to the Year 2000," *Origins: CNS Documentary Service* 26 (October 24, 1996): 296.
36. Avery Dulles, "John Paul II and the Advent of the New Millennium," *America* 173 (December 9, 1995): 10.
37. *Osservatore Romano* (May 29, 1996): 1.

5. On Reading the Book of Revelation

1. D. S. Russell, *Prophecy and the Apocalyptic Dream* (Peabody, Mass.: Hendrickson, 1994), 34.
2. Billy Graham, *Approaching Hoofbeats: The Four Horsemen of the Apocalypse* (New York: Avon, 1983), 4, 8.
3. Daniel J. Harrington, S.J., "A Catholic Reading of the Book of Revelation," *Warren Lecture Series in Catholic Studies* 24 (University of Tulsa, February 21, 1993): 5.
4. John J. Collins, *The Apocalyptic Imagination* (New York: Crossroad, 1992), 210.
5. Harrington, "Catholic Reading," 7.
6. D. S. Russell, *Divine Disclosure: An Introduction to Jewish Apocalyptic* (Minneapolis: Fortress, 1992), 135.
7. Leonard L. Thompson, "Social Location of Early Christian Apocalyptic," in *Rise and Decline of the Roman World*, ed. Wolfgang Haase and Hildegard Temporini, vol. 26.3 (New York: Walter De Gruyter, 1996), 2635.
8. Ibid.
9. Jean-Pierre Prévost, *How to Read the Apocalypse* (New York: Crossroad, 1993), 15.
10. Russell, *Divine Disclosure*, 133.
11. Bart D. Ehrman, *The New Testament: An Historical Introduction to the Early Christian Writings* (New York: Oxford University Press, 1997), 403.
12. Rudolf Schnackenburg, *Christ Present and Coming* (Philadelphia: Fortress, 1978), 34.
13. Prévost, *How to Read the Apocalypse*, 32–35.
14. John P. M. Sweet, *Revelation* (Philadelphia: Westminster, 1979), 10.
15. *Anchor Bible Dictionary* (1992), s.v. "Millennialism."
16. Prévost, *How to Read the Apocalypse*, 61.

6. The Reign of a Thousand Years

1. John P. M. Sweet, *Revelation* (Philadelphia: Westminster, 1979), 288.
2. *Anchor Bible Dictionary* (1992), s.v. "Millennium."
3. Richard Bauckham, *The Theology of the Book of Revelation* (New York: Cambridge University Press, 1993), 108.

4. Adela Yarbro Collins, *The Apocalypse* (Wilmington, Del.: Michael Glazier, 1979), 140.

5. Robert Jewett, *Jesus against the Rapture* (Philadelphia: Westminster, 1979), 122.

6. Bart D. Ehrman, *The New Testament: An Historical Introduction to the Early Christian Writings* (New York: Oxford University Press, 1997), 262.

7. Ernest Best, *A Commentary on the First and Second Epistles to the Thessalonians* (New York: Harper and Row, 1972), 199.

8. Beda Rigaux, *St. Paul: Les Épîtres aux Thessalonians* (Paris: J. Gabalda, 1956), 545.

9. Arthur W. Wainwright, *Mysterious Apocalypse* (Nashville: Abingdon, 1993), 22.

10. *Oxford Dictionary of the Bible* (1987), s.v. "Millennialism," 833.

11. Brian Daley, *The Hope of the Early Church: A Handbook of Patristic Eschatology* (Cambridge: Cambridge University Press, 1991), 31.

12. Cited in Richard K. Emmerson and Bernard McGinn, "The Medieval Return of the Thousand-Year Sabbath," in *The Apocalypse in the Middle Ages,* ed. Robert E. Lerner (Ithaca, N.Y.: Cornell University Press, 1992), 51.

13. E. Randolph Daniel, "Joachim of Fiore: Patterns of History in the Apocalypse in the Middle Ages," in *Apocalypse in the Middle Ages,* ed. Lerner, 83–88.

14. Wainwright, *Mysterious Apocalypse,* 50.

15. See Leone Tondelli, Marjorie Reeves, and Beatrice Hirsch-Reich, eds., *Il Libro delle Figure dell'Abate Gioacchino da Fiore,* vol. 2 (Turin, 1953).

16. Delno C. West, "A Millenarian Earthly Paradise: Renewal and the Age of the Spirit," in *Atti del II Congresso Internazionale di Studi Gioachimiti* (San Giovanni in Fiore: Centro Internazionale di Studi Gioachimiti, 1986), 269.

17. Ibid., 267.

7. America's Millennial Vision

1. Paul Boyer, *When Time Shall Be No More: Prophecy Belief in Modern Culture* (Cambridge, Mass.: Harvard University Press, 1992).

2. *Encyclopedia of American Religious Experience* (1945), s.v. "Millennialism and Adventism," by Charles H. Lippy, 832.

3. See Michael J. St. Clair, *Millenarian Movements in Historical Context* (New York: Garland, 1992), 274.

4. Lippy, "Millennialism and Adventism," 833.

5. Grant Underwood, *The Millenarian World of Early Mormonism* (Urbana: University of Illinois Press, 1993), 24. See also St. Clair, *Millenarian Movements,* 282.

6. Cited in Underwood, *Millenarian World,* 26.

7. Ibid.

8. Charles B. Strozier, *Apocalypse: On the Psychology of Fundamentalism in America* (Boston: Beacon, 1994), 173.

9. Ibid., 175.

10. See Strozier, *Apocalypse,* 179.

11. Ibid., 181–83.

12. Ira V. Brown, "Watchers for the Second Coming: The Millenarian Tradition in America," *Mississippi Valley Historical Review* 39 (1952): 451.

13. Lippy, "Millennialism and Adventism," 834.

14. Cited in Brown, "Watchers," 834.

15. Arthur M. Schlesinger Jr., *The Cycles of American History* (Boston: Houghton Mifflin, 1986), 128.

16. Raymond F. Bulman, "Myth of Origin: Civil Religion and Presidential Politics," *Journal of Church and State* 33 (summer 1991): 529.

17. Boyer, *When Time Shall Be No More*, 98.

18. Ibid., 108.

19. Strozier, *Apocalypse*, 189.

20. Boyer, *When Time Shall Be No More*, 120–21.

21. Ibid., 132–33.

22. John F. Walvoord, *Armageddon, Oil and the Middle East Crisis* (Grand Rapids, Mich.: Zondervan, 1990), 16, 228.

23. Hal Lindsey, *The Late Great Planet Earth* (Grand Rapids, Mich.: Zondervan, 1970), 149–50.

24. Boyer, *When Time Shall Be No More*, 141.

25. Ibid., 143.

26. Ibid., 149.

8. A Story of Hope and Shattered Dreams

1. Donald E. Pitzer and Josephine Elliott, *New Harmony's First Utopians 1814–1824*, special issue of *Indiana Magazine of History* 75 (September 1979): 233.

2. Karl J. Arndt, ed., *A Documentary History of the Indiana Decade of the Harmony Society*, 2 vols. (Indianapolis: Indiana State Archives, 1978), 2:xvii.

3. Pitzer and Elliott, *New Harmony's First Utopians*, 234–35.

4. Arndt, *Documentary History*, xviii.

5. Ibid., xvi.

6. John Archibald Bole, *The Harmony Society: A Chapter in German American Culture History* (Philadelphia: Americana Germanica Press, 1904), 4.

7. Arndt, *Documentary History*, xvii.

8. William E. Wilson, *The Angel and the Serpent: The Story of New Harmony* (Bloomington: Indiana University Press, 1964), 49.

9. Hilda A. Kring, *The Harmonists: A Folk Cultural Approach* (Metuchen, N.J.: Scarecrow, 1973), 45–46. In 1997 a new labyrinth, modeled on the cathedral labyrinth of Chartres, France, was completed at the historic village of New Harmony under the auspices of Purdue University and the Robert Lee Blaffer Trust. The new cathedral labyrinth fittingly lies adjacent to the Harmonist cemetery.

10. Michael J. St. Clair, *Millenarian Movements in Historical Context* (New York: Garland, 1992), 306.

11. Ibid., 311.

12. Ibid., 314.

13. Ibid., 318–19.

14. Ibid., 319.

15. Martin E. Marty, *Pilgrims in Their Own Land: 500 Years of Religion in America* (Boston: Little, Brown, 1984), 322.
16. Ibid., 323.
17. *Encyclopedia of American Religious Experience*, s.v. "Millennialism and Adventism," by Charles H. Lippy, 837.
18. St. Clair, *Millenarian Movements*, 322–23.
19. Ibid., 323; see also Lippy, "Millennialism and Adventism," 837.
20. Lippy, "Millennialism and Adventism," 837.
21. Ibid.
22. Ibid., 838.
23. Marty, *Pilgrims*, 366.
24. Arthur W. Wainwright, *Mysterious Apocalypse* (Nashville: Abingdon, 1993), 101.
25. Marty, *Pilgrims*, 367.
26. Russell Chandler, *Doomsday: The End of the World* (Ann Arbor, Mich.: Servant, 1993), 99.
27. Bole, *Harmony Society*, 46.

9. A Story of Apocalyptic Violence

1. William W. Meissner, *Thy Kingdom Come: Psychoanalytic Perspectives on the Messiah and the Millennium* (Kansas City: Sheed and Ward, 1995), 201.
2. Michael St. Clair, *Millenarian Movements in Historical Perspective* (New York: Garland, 1992), 134.
3. Arthur W. Wainwright, *Mysterious Apocalypse* (Nashville: Abingdon, 1993), 91–92, 102.
4. Ibid. See also St. Clair, *Millenarian Movements*, 191–217.
5. Thomas F. MacMillan, "Miracle, Mystery and Authority: Recalling Jonestown," *Christian Century* 105, no. 33 (November 9, 1988): 1014.
6. Bonnie Thielmann, with Dean Merrill, *The Broken God* (Chicago: David C. Cook, 1979), 53.
7. Ibid., 83.
8. Ibid., 145.
9. Michael Barkun, "Militias, Christian Identity and the Radical Right," *Christian Century* (August 2–9, 1995): 739.
10. Ibid.
11. Dean M. Kelley, "Waco: A Massacre and Its Aftermath," *First Things* 53 (May 1995): 27.
12. William L. Pitts, "The Davidian Tradition," *Council of Societies for the Study of Religion* 22, no. 4 (November 1993): 99.
13. James D. Tabor and Eugene Gallagher, *Why Waco? Cults and the Battle for Religious Freedom in America* (Berkeley: University of California Press, 1995), 35.
14. Pitts, "Davidian Tradition," 100.
15. Tabor and Gallagher, *Why Waco?* 41.
16. Kelley, "Waco," 22.
17. Tabor and Gallagher, *Why Waco?* 49–50.
18. Ibid., 68.
19. Kelley, "Waco," 25.

10. God's Soldiers of the End-Time

1. Morris Dees, *Gathering Storm: America's Militia Threat* (New York: HarperCollins, 1996), 34.
2. Tom Burghardt, "Leaderless Resistance and the Oklahoma City Bombing" (Bay Area Coalition for Our Reproductive Rights, April 23, 1996), 3; available at http://paul.spu.edu/sinnfein/beam.html. See also Dees, *Gathering Storm*, 174–76.
3. Dees, *Gathering Storm*, 15.
4. Jeffrey Kaplan, "The Politics of Rage: Militias and the Future of the Far Right," *Christian Century* (June 19–26, 1996): 657.
5. Michael Barkun, *Religion and the Racist Right: The Origins of the Christian Identity Movement* (Chapel Hill: University of North Carolina Press, 1994), 156.
6. Ibid., 170–71.
7. Dees, *Gathering Storm*, 116.
8. Ibid., 126–27.
9. Frederick Clarkson, "Anti-abortion Extremists, 'Patriots' and Racists Converge," *Intelligence Report of the Southern Poverty Law Center* (summer 1998): 14; see also the editorial on p. 2 of the same volume.
10. Ibid., 103.
11. Ibid., 98–99.
12. Kenneth S. Stern, "Militia Mania: A Growing Danger," *USA Today*, January 16, 1996, 6.
13. Dees, *Gathering Storm*, 143–44.
14. Ibid., 162.
15. Burghardt, "Leaderless Resistance," 3.
16. Ibid.
17. Dees, *Gathering Storm*, 156.
18. Mark Pitcavage, "Every Man a King: The Rise and Fall of the Montana Freemen" (Militia Watchdog Website, May 6, 1996), 4; available at http://www.greyware.com/authors/pitman/freemen.htm.

11. On Reading the Signs of the Times

1. Rudolf Schnackenburg, *Present and Future: Modern Aspects of New Testament Theology* (Notre Dame, Ind.: Notre Dame University Press, 1966), 16.
2. David Tiede, *Jesus and the Future* (New York: Cambridge University Press, 1990), 52.
3. Schnackenburg, *Present and Future*, 36.
4. Ibid.
5. Stanley J. Grenz, *The Millennial Maze: Sorting Out Evangelical Options* (Downers Grove, Ill.: InterVarsity, 1992), 129.
6. Ibid., 67.
7. Ibid., 76.
8. Ibid., 70.
9. Ibid., 151.
10. Ibid., 150.
11. Ibid., 152.
12. Ibid., 172.

13. Hans Schwarz, *On the Way to the Future* (Minneapolis: Augsburg, 1979), 190.

14. Ted Peters, *Futures Human and Divine* (Atlanta: John Knox, 1978), 28.

15. John Macquarrie, *Christian Hope* (New York: Seabury, 1978), 83.

16. Morton Kelsey, *Afterlife: The Other Side of Dying* (New York: Paulist, 1979), 150–52.

17. Hans Küng, *Christianity: Essence, History, and Future* (New York: Continuum, 1995), 69.

18. Monika K. Hellwig, "Eschatology," in *Systematic Theology: Roman Catholic Perspectives*, 2 vols., ed. Francis Schüssler Fiorenza and John P. Galvin (Minneapolis: Fortress, 1991), 2:362.

19. Dermot A. Lane, *Keeping Hope Alive: Stirrings in Christian Theology* (Mahwah, N.J.: Paulist, 1996).

20. Karl Rahner, *Foundations of Christian Faith*, trans. William V. Dych (New York: Seabury, 1978).

21. See Alois Winklhofer, *The Coming of His Kingdom: A Theology of the Last Days* (New York: Herder and Herder, 1963), 156. Other mainline authors addressing the millennial question in this way are Edmund J. Fortman, *Everlasting Life after Death* (New York: Alba House, 1976), and John A. T. Robinson, *In the End, God* (New York: Harper and Row, 1968).

22. Ibid., 154.

23. Ibid., 184.

24. *Catechism of the Catholic Church* (New York: Doubleday, 1994), nos. 676–77.

25. Thomas Aquinas, *Summa Theologica* 3, q. 8, art. 8; cited by Winklhofer, *Coming of His Kingdom*, 180–81.

26. Winklhofer, *Coming of His Kingdom*, 167.

27. Ibid., 182.

28. Schnackenburg, *Present and Future*, 22, 35, 38.

29. A. J. Conyers, *The End: What Jesus Really Said about the Last Things* (Downers Grove, Ill.: InterVarsity, 1995), 49.

30. Raymond F. Bulman, "The Topicality of Joachim of Fiore in Contemporary Systematic Theology," *Explorations: Journal for Adventurous Thought* 14 (winter 1995): 33.

31. Jürgen Moltmann, *History and the Triune God*, trans. John Bowden (New York: Crossroad, 1992), 109.

32. Jürgen Moltmann, *The Trinity and the Kingdom*, trans. Margaret Kohl (San Francisco: Harper and Row, 1981), 134.

33. Moltmann, *History*, 108–9.

34. Jürgen Moltmann, *The Coming of God: Christian Eschatology* (Minneapolis: Fortress, 1966), 198.

35. Ibid., 193.

36. Paul Tillich, *Systematic Theology*, 3 vols. (New York: Harper and Row, 1963), 2:163.

37. Paul Tillich, *Political Expectations* (New York: Harper and Row, 1971), 138.

38. Tillich, *Systematic Theology*, 2:163.

39. John A. T. Robinson, *Jesus and His Coming* (Philadelphia: Westminster, 1979), 61.

40. Tillich, *Systematic Theology,* 3:370.

41. Paul Tillich, "The Kingdom of God and History," in *Theology of Peace: Paul Tillich,* ed. Ronald H. Stone (Louisville: Westminster/John Knox, 1990), 43–44.

42. Tillich, *Systematic Theology,* 3:369.

12. The World at the Crossroads

1. Daniel Chirot, *Social Change in the Modern Era* (New York: Harcourt Brace Jovanovich College Publishers, 1986), 193.

2. Raymond F. Bulman, "Discerning Major Shifts in the World-System — Some Help from Theology?" *Review* 19, no. 4 (fall 1996): 6–7.

3. "The Longwave — an Introduction" (Longwave and Social Cycles Resource Centre, January 1997), 1; available at http://we.idirect.com/longwave/lwintro.html.

4. Ibid.

5. Immanuel Wallerstein, *Unthinking Social Science: The Limits of Nineteenth Century Paradigms* (Cambridge: Polity Press, 1991), 135–48.

6. Immanuel Wallerstein, *The Capitalist World-Economy* (New York: Cambridge University Press, 1979), 271.

7. Bulman, "Discerning Major Shifts," 391.

8. Raymond F. Bulman, "Wallerstein's Millenarian Vision of the Coming Global Economy" (paper delivered at the Historical Forum, Duquesne University, October 1996), 5.

9. Immanuel Wallerstein, *After Liberalism* (New York: New Press, 1995), 29.

10. Ibid., 27.

11. Ibid., 25.

12. Ibid., 28.

13. Ibid.

14. Ibid., 31–32.

15. Ibid. The author discusses these differentiating factors on pp. 32–40.

16. Wallerstein, *Unthinking Social Science,* 23–27.

17. Ibid., 148.

18. Wallerstein, *After Liberalism,* 45.

19. William Strauss and Neil Howe, *The Fourth Turning: An American Prophecy* (New York: Broadway Books, 1997), 9.

20. Ibid., 20.

21. Ibid., 6.

22. Ibid., 294–95.

23. Ibid., 272–73.

24. Ibid., 207–12.

25. Ibid., 277.

26. Ibid., 22.

27. Peter F. Drucker, *Post-capitalist Society* (New York: HarperCollins, 1993), 13.

28. Ibid., 11.

29. Ibid., 183.
30. Ibid., 8.
31. Ibid., 14.
32. Ibid., 7–16.
33. Ibid., 12.
34. Strauss and Howe, *Fourth Turning*, 22.

Conclusion

1. Stephen J. Gould, *Questioning the Millennium* (New York: Harmony, 1997), 80.
2. Harold Bloom, *Omens of Millennium* (New York: Riverhead, 1996), 138.
3. Georg Feuerstein, "The Millennium Effect," *Parabola* 23 (February 1998): 75.
4. "Belief-ful realism" is a term used frequently by theologian Paul Tillich, especially in his early work. For details see my *A Blueprint for Humanity: Paul Tillich's Theology of Culture* (Lewisburg, Pa.: Bucknell University Press, 1981), esp. 103–10.
5. Hans Küng, *Global Responsibility: In Search of a New World Ethic* (New York: Continuum, 1993), 3.
6. Ibid., 2–3.
7. Michael Lerner, *The Politics of Meaning* (Reading, Mass.: Addison-Wesley, 1996), 165.
8. See Norman Cohn, *The Pursuit of the Millennium* (New York: Oxford University Press, 1957), 27. Cohn cites St. Irenaeus, the second-century theologian and bishop of Lyon, in support of the early Christian doctrine of universal restoration.
9. Feuerstein, "Millennium Effect," 79.
10. Küng, *Global Responsibility*, 35.
11. Ibid., 29.
12. Ibid., 53.
13. Ibid., xv.
14. John Kelsay and Sumner B. Twiss, eds., *Religion and Human Rights* (New York: Project on Religion and Human Rights, 1994), 36.
15. *The Teaching of the Buddha* (Tokyo: Buddhist Promoting Foundation, 1978), 71.
16. Robert N. Bellah, "Religion and the Technological Revolution in Japan and the United States" (Eighth Annual University Lecture in Religion at Arizona State University, February 19, 1987) (Phoenix: Arizona State University Press, 1987), 10.
17. Küng, *Global Responsibility*, 128.
18. Sri Shinmoy, *Yoga and the Spiritual Life* (New York: Aum Publications, 1974), 130.
19. Fazlur Rahman, *Islam* (Garden City, N.Y.: Doubleday, 1966), 315.
20. Lerner, *Politics of Meaning*, 59.
21. In George Weigel, ed., *A New Worldly Order: A "Centesimus Annus" Reader* (Washington, D.C.: Ethics and Public Policy Center, 1992), 23.
22. Lerner, *Politics of Meaning*, 13.

23. Ibid., 306.
24. Ibid., 285.
25. Harlon L. Dalton, *Racial Healing: Confronting the Fear between Blacks and Whites* (New York: Doubleday, 1995), 3.
26. Ibid., 165.
27. David Tracy, *Plurality and Ambiguity* (San Francisco: Harper and Row, 1987), 19.
28. See Philip J. Murnion, introduction to *Catholic Common Ground Initiative* (New York: Crossroad, 1997), 8, 19.
29. Ibid., 15, citing *Gaudium et Spes* 92.
30. *Multireligious Cooperation for the Social Reconstruction of Bosnia-Herzegovina* (New York: WCRP, July 1997); *Religion and Nation-Building in Sierra Leone — a Narrative Report* (New York: WCRP, April 1997); "The Riva del Garda Declaration," *Religion for Peace Newsletter* (February 1995): 7.
31. Laurence Freeman, "Silence" (John Todd Memorial Lecture, Bristol, U.K., 1997), 3.
32. Frederick J. Parrella, "Spirituality for the New Millennium" (lecture given at Woodside Priory, Santa Clara, Calif., November 12, 1997), 7.
33. Lerner, *Politics of Meaning*, 301.
34. Freeman, "Silence," 2, 7; see also Parrella, "Spirituality," 14.
35. Parrella, "Spirituality," 13.
36. Paul Tillich, *The Eternal Now* (New York: Charles Scribner's Sons, 1962), 87.
37. See Aquilina (pseudonym), "Why the Coming Millennium Is the Pope's Touchstone," *Our Sunday Visitor* (March 2, 1997): 10–11.
38. Jimmy Carter, *Living Faith* (New York: Random House, 1996), 140–53.
39. Robert Jewett, *Jesus against the Rapture* (Philadelphia: Westminster, 1979), 128, 133.

Glossary of Special Terms

Amillennialism. A term commonly used to describe the belief that there is no literal millennial kingdom. The passage in Revelation (20:1–10) is rather a symbol of the present reign of believers, already victorious on earth through their faith.

Apocalypse (from the Greek *apokalypsis*, meaning "revelation"). Another name for the Book of Revelation, the last book of the New Testament, which begins with the words, "The Revelation of Jesus Christ." The author of the book, written about 96 C.E., is a Christian called John who had been exiled for his faith to the island of Patmos. Tradition has it that the author is John the Apostle, but that is unlikely.

Apocalyptic. A religious worldview, believed to be revealed by God, which foresees a violent end to the present world order, to be followed by divine judgment in the form of catastrophes, trials, and tribulations which will precede the final days of history.

Apocalyptic Literature. A type of literature common in the Jewish world between 250 B.C.E. and 100 C.E., featuring heavenly journeys or angelic visitations in which the coming divine retributions are revealed to a prophet or visionary. This whole literary style derives its name from the Apocalypse (Book of Revelation), with which it shares many common features.

Armageddon. According to Rev. 16:16, the location of the disastrous battle in which "kings of the whole world," gathered by demonic spirits, are finally and completely routed by the power of almighty God. In dispensationalist circles, "Armageddon theology" has come to mean the biblically based belief in the inevitability of total human annihilation, usually by way of nuclear holocaust.

Chiliasm. In essence a synonym for millennialism, deriving from the Greek word *chilioi*, meaning a thousand. This was the term commonly used in the Eastern church, as well as in some traditions of Western theology.

Dispensationalism. A branch of evangelical theology which holds that God presents the human race with different times of testing or "dispensations" in the course of world history. The common interpretation is that we are now on the threshold of the seventh and final dispensation — the return of Christ and his millennial kingdom on earth. Dispensationalists are invariably premillennialists as well.

Eschatology (from the Greek *eschata*, "last things," and *logos*, "study of"). That branch of theology which studies the final end or destiny of humanity, both individual and communal. Traditionally, it includes such topics as death, judgment, heaven, hell (purgatory), the Second Coming of Christ, the millennium, and eternal life.

Evangelical (from Greek *euaggelion,* "gospel"). A name used by some Protestant churches to emphasize their conviction that their beliefs and practices are uniquely based on biblical teaching. These churches put great stress on personal conversion, rebirth in the Spirit, and expectation of the imminent return of Christ.

Fundamentalist. A term given to evangelical Christians who from the early decades of the twentieth century have firmly resisted all attempts to liberalize and modernize Protestant belief, in particular to undermine the inerrancy of the Bible. The name itself derives from a series of tracts, called *The Fundamentals* (published between 1912 and 1914), which attempted to identify and defend what the tracts' authors judged to be the essential, nonchanging beliefs of Christianity.

Kairos. A Greek word for "time" that carries the connotation of the right season, the right time for action, the critical moment. In the New Testament, it refers specifically to God's special interventions at turning points in history, for example, "The *time* is fulfilled and the kingdom of God is at hand" (Mark 1:15).

Liberal Protestantism. A movement in the Protestant churches beginning in the late nineteenth century, reaching its high point in the United States in the years between the two world wars. It is characterized by openness to secular thought, and especially to the modern critical methods of studying the Bible.

Mainline Churches. A term used to designate the established Protestant churches, such as Episcopal, Presbyterian, Methodist, Lutheran, and Congregationalist, which have, in general, been receptive to the influences of modern liberal Protestant thought and are generally opposed to the biblical literalism of the evangelicals.

Millenarianism. A wide range of beliefs emphasizing the imminent end of the present order and the hope for a peaceful, harmonious, and just new world. These beliefs can be tied to either a secular or a religious worldview.

Millennialism. The belief in the reality and imminence of the thousand-year reign of Christ on earth before the consummation of all things. It applies to any Christian religious movement influenced and guided by this belief and expectation. According to their end-time timetable, millennialists are either pre- or postmillennialists (see below).

Millennium. Literally means a period of one thousand years. The word derives from the Latin words *mille* (one thousand) and *annus* (year) and has been used from the first Christian centuries to denote the thousand-year reign of Christ with his saints depicted in Rev. 20:1–10.

Parousia. Originally a Greek word found in the New Testament which means both "coming" and "presence." It has become the technical term to designate the Second Coming of Christ in the Last Days.

Postmillennialism. The branch of millennialism which holds that Christ will return only after the time of the millennium, which is viewed as a kind of golden age of the church on earth. The millennial kingdom is spread throughout the world through the teaching and preaching of the Gospel.

Premillennialism. The branch of millennialism which holds that Christ will return *before* the inauguration of his thousand-year reign. It also maintains that shortly before Christ's return the world will be afflicted with terrible tribulation and evil. The millennium is brought about by God's power alone.

Prophecy. In the Old Testament, a concept that refers primarily to speaking out in the name of God's righteousness against injustices and immorality on both a personal and social level. The biblical prophet was concerned primarily with the contemporary situation of the day, whereas Christian fundamentalists today tend to interpret biblical prophecy as a matter of predicting future events.

Rapture. A pivotal apocalyptic doctrine of the dispensationalist school of premillennialism, which holds that true believers will be "caught up" to meet the Lord in the air just before the beginning of the great tribulation. The belief is based on a literal reading of 1 Thess. 4:13–18.

Revelation. Any act whereby God discloses or reveals his inner mysteries to the human race, so as to make known his will and purposes. It is also the name given to the last book of the New Testament (see Apocalypse, above).

Index

abortion, 41
Adso, 8
Adventism, 119–22, 139–40. *See also* Seventh-Day Adventists
Africa, 20, 43–44
African Americans, 38, 41, 146, 147
age of the Spirit, the, 94–95, 170–72
agriculture, 21–22, 27, 31
AIDS, 12, 42–43, 52, 185
American dream, the, 104–11
amillennialism, 163–64, 165, 168, 169; defined, 228
Anabaptists, 130
angels, 197
Antichrist, the: the Adventists on, 122; the beast of Revelation and, 79; current evangelical preachers on, 54; mainline churches on, 168; persons identified with, 79, 107; view of, around the year 1000, 8, 11
Antichrist (Adso), 8
Apocalypse Now and Then (Keller), 63–64
apocalypticism: of evangelical preachers, 51–57; recent fanatical, 47–51; around the year 1000, 11–13
apocalyptic literature, 68–69, 77; defined, 229
Applewhite, Marshall Herff, 50
Arafat, Yasir, 39, 59
Armageddon: American politics and, 108–11; defined, 229; Jehovah's Witnesses on, 123, 124; the militia movement and, 145–49; Revelation's depiction of, 79–80; the Van Impes on, 53
Armageddon (movie), 4
Army of God, the, 149
artificial intelligence, 27, 28, 29

Aryan Nations, 145, 149
Asahara, Shoko, 49
Asia, 34, 43
Augustine, 64, 93–94, 163, 165, 166
Aukerman, Dale, 110
"Auld Lang Syne," 5
Aum Shinrikyo, 49–50
automation, 26–29
AZT, 43–44

Babylon, 80
Bach, Johann Sebastian, 67
Bakker, Jim, 51
Balmer, Randall, 57–58
Beam, Louis, 143–44, 150, 151, 153, 154
beast, the (in Revelation), 70–71, 79
Bellah, Robert N., 203
Berg, Alan, 152
Bernardin, Cardinal Joseph, 208
Bible, the, 52–57. *See also* Revelation, Book of
biological weapons, 40
biotechnology, 29–31
Bloom, Harold, 197
Bois, Guy, 7, 9
Book of Mormon, 100–101
Boone, Pat, 110
Branch Davidians, 136–42, 154
Braudel, Fernand, 179, 180
Breyer, Jacques, 48
British Israelism, 146
British-Israelite Federation, 147
Buddhism, 202
Butler, Richard, 150
Byrd, James, Jr., 206

calendars, 2
Calvary Chapel movement, 58
Capet, Hugh, 10

capitalism, 178–85, 189–92
Carolingian Empire, 8, 9
Carter, Jimmy, 213
castellans, the, 10
Catholic Church: Jubilee 2000 and, 64–66; Marian visions and, 59–61; and millennial movements prior to the year 1000, 8–9; on the tribulations of the end-times, 168
celebration of New Year's Eve 1999, 3–7
Celebration 2000 (New York City), 5–6
census, U.S., 6
Cerinthus, 93
Chandler, Russell, 11, 125
chemical weapons, 40
chiliasm, 92–94; defined, 228. See also millennialism; thousand-year reign of Christ
China, 19, 21, 53
Chinmoy, Sri, 203
Christian Coalition, the, 148, 162
Christian Identity movement: the Freemen and, 155; the militias and, 149–51; Ruby Ridge incident and, 135, 136; theology of, 145–49
Churchill, Winston, 187
Church of Jesus Christ of Latter-Day Saints. See Mormons
civic millennialism, 104–5
Civil War, the, 102–4
Clinton, Bill, 6, 30, 207
cloning, 29–31
Cluny, Abbey of, 9, 13
Common Ground, 208
Communism, 189
community: Acts of the Apostles on the ideal, 88; Joachim of Fiore's vision of, 95–96; Jubilee 2000 and, 65; spirituality and, 209–11. See also Harmonists
computers, 6, 23–26
Confucianism, 203
Congregationalists, 98, 99
conspiracy theories, 54, 61, 135
conversation, 207–9
Coppola, Francis, 68

Covenant, the, 149
Coy, Bob, 58–59
crime, 37–39
Cromwell, Oliver, 130
culture wars, 187, 188

Dalai Lama, the, 202–3
Daley, Brian, 64
Dalton, Harlon L., 206
Darby, John Nelson, 106, 107
Darbyism, 107
Darwinism, 107
Dees, Morris, 153, 156
deforestation, 36
Dennis the Little, 2
Desai, Mihir, 7
disease, 42–43
dispensationalism: American politics and, 109–10; defined, 228; fundamentalism and, 108; history of, 106–7; on nuclear war, 108–9; on the rapture, 88
Dispositio Novi Ordinis (Joachim of Fiore), 95
DNA, 29–30
dominion theology, 162
downsizing, 184
Drucker, Peter, 177, 189–92, 193
drugs, 38–39
Duby, Georges, 7
Duke, David, 147
Dulles, Avery, 65
Dulles, John Foster, 105
Dürer, Albrecht, 67

Eco, Umberto, 11, 68
ecology, 32–37, 63, 64
ecumenism, 62–63
Edson, Hiram, 119, 120
Edwards, Jonathan, 98, 102
Eisenhower, Dwight D., 105
Elohim City, 154
Engels, Friedrich, 113
environment. See ecology
ergotism, 12, 14
ethics, 199–205
European Community, the, 182, 183
European Union, the, 54

evangelicalism: doomsday preachers and, 51–57; grassroots millennialism among, 57–59; literal interpretation of the millennium by, 160–65
Extraterrestrials: Global Invasion Approaching (video), 57

Falwell, Jerry, 51, 110
fascism, 107
feminism, 63, 64
Feuerstein, Georg, 197, 199
fiber optics, 23
first millennial divide. *See* year 1000
Flagellantism, 11, 128–29, 196
Focillon, Henri, xii, 7, 11
food scarcity, 19–22
Fourth Turning, The (Strauss and Howe), 186–87
Freeman, Laurence, 210
Freemen, the, 154–56
fundamentalism, 107–8; defined, 229
Fundamentals, The, 107

Gallagher, Christina, 61
gangs, 38
Gates, Bill, 24, 25, 177, 191
Glaber, Rodulfus, 8, 11
Global Forum, 208, 209
globalization, 34
global warming, 36
gnosticism, 93
Gould, Stephen Jay, 2, 195, 196
Graham, Billy, 69–70, 110
Graham, Sylvester, 120–21
Great Awakening, the, 98
Great Disappointment, the, 119, 120, 122
greenhouse effect, 36–37
Gulf War, the, 190

Hale-Bopp Comet, 50, 51
Halley's Comet, 12
Harmon, Ellen G., 120
Harmonists, the: and attempts at global harmony, 213; as an example of communal experimentation, 202; harmony as a guiding principle of, 204; overview of, 112–17; positive legacy of, 125–26; restoration of the labyrinth of, 221n.9
harmony: examples of visionaries of, 213; a global ethic based on, 202–5; the Harmonists' view of, 114–15, 125–26; *kairos* and, 212; Revelation on the millennial kingdom and, 85–88; steps toward establishing global, 205–13
Harmony Society, 113, 204. *See also* Harmonists
health care, 19–20
Heaven's Gate cult, 50–51
Hellwig, Monika, 166
Himes, Joshua, 119
Hinduism, 203
historical-critical scholarship, 107
Holy Spirit. *See* age of the Spirit
Hopkins, Mark, 104
Houteff, Florence, 137
Houteff, Victor, 137, 138, 139
Howe, Neil, 186–89, 192, 193
Howell, Vernon. *See* Koresh, David
human rights, 201–2
hunger. *See* food scarcity
Hus, Jan, 129
Hussein, King, 39
Hussein, Saddam, 190
Hussite movement, 129, 130

Identity movement. *See* Christian Identity movement
immigration, 33, 183–84, 193
Impact (movie), 4
Industrial Revolution, the, 27
information age, 191
information superhighway, 23–26
information technology, 23–26
International Bible Students Association. *See* Jehovah's Witnesses
International Global Climate Conference (Kyoto), 36–37
Internet, the, 24–25, 162. *See also* information superhighway
interreligious dialogue, 201–2, 208–9

Irenaeus, 93, 202, 213, 226n.8
Islam, 203
Israel: the age of the Spirit and, 171; current evangelical preachers on, 54–55; the Davidians and, 137; fundamentalism and, 108; premillennialists on, 161; religious violence and, 39. *See also* Jews

Japan, 27, 182, 183
Jeffrey, Grant R., 52, 54, 56
Jehovah's Witnesses, 122–25
Jerome, 93, 166
Jews: the Christian Identity movement on, 135, 146–47; evangelical preachers on, 54–55; the Flagellants and, 129; fundamentalism and, 108; the Mormons and, 101. *See also* Israel
Joachim of Fiore: communal experiments of, 94–96, 202; and current, balanced approaches to the millennium, 169–72; date for the start of the third age, 128; global harmony and, 213; harmony as a guiding principle of, 204; Moltmann and, 173; as offering positive visions of the future, 112; spiritual community and, 210
John of Leyden, 130, 134
John Paul II, Pope, xiii, 64, 205, 210, 212–13
Jones, Jim, 131–34
Jonestown Tragedy, 131–34
Jubilee 2000, 64–66, 210
Jubilee Year, 64
Justin Martyr, 92–93
Justus Township, 155–56

kairos: current views of ways to respond to, 198–99; defined, 229; as demanding moral decision and action, 194; harmony and, 212; Jesus and, 172; and millennial timetables, 196; reading the signs of the times and, 160; Tillich on, 174–76, 177, 180
Kaufman, Gordon, 110

Keller, Catherine, 63–64
Kellogg, John Harvey, 121
Kelsey, Morton, 166
Kennedy, Paul, 35, 43, 177
King, Martin Luther, Jr., 75, 213
King, Rodney, 148, 206
kingdom of God, 85–88, 160
Knights Templar, the, 48
Knowledge Revolution, the, 191
Kondratieff, Nikolai, 179, 180, 181, 187
Koop, C. Everett, 110
Koresh, David, 59, 130, 136–42
Küng, Hans, 166, 198, 199–201, 202, 203
Kyoto conference on global climate, 36–37

Lamb of God, the, 81, 140–41
Landes, Richard, 7, 13
Lane, Dermot, 166
Last Judgment (Michelangelo), 67
Late Great Planet Earth, The (Lindsey), 52, 109
leaderless resistance, 151, 153–54
League of Nations, 105
Lederberg, Dr. Joshua, 42
Left Behind (video), 56
Lerner, Michael, 198, 204, 205, 209–10
liberal Protestantism, 62–64; defined, 229
Liber Figurarum (Joachim of Fiore), 95
Limoges, Council of, 14–15
Lincoln, Abraham, 102–3
Lindsey, Hal, 52, 54, 55, 57, 58, 109, 110, 135, 162
linearism, 186
Los Angeles riots, 206
Luima, Abner, 41
Luther, Martin, 67

Macquarrie, John, 166
mainline churches, 62–64, 165–69; defined, 229
Manifest Destiny, 104
Martin, Marty, 62

Marx, Karl, 189
Marxism, 174, 191
Mary (Jesus' mother), 59–61
Mather, Cotton, 98
Matthews, Robert, 152
McVeigh, Tim, 145, 153, 154
Meacham, Joseph, 99
media, the, 4
meditation, 210
Medjugorje, 60
Melody (the red heifer), 54–55
Michelangelo, 67
Michigan Militia, 154
Middle Ages, the, 7–15
migration, 183–84. *See also* immigration
militia movement: on Armageddon, 145–49; ideology and strategies of, 149–53; the Montana Freemen and, 154–56; the Oklahoma City bombing and, 153–54; overview of, 143–45; responses to, 156–57
Militia of Montana, 145
millenarianism, 108, 123, 196; defined, 229
millennialism: the American Civil War and, 102–4; the American dream and, 104–11; background of, in the United States, 97–99; a balanced approach to, 169–76; comparison of tenth- and twentieth-century, 16; defined, xi, 229; in the early church, 92–94; of evangelical preachers, 51–57; of the fanatical religious fringe, 47–51; grassroots evangelical, 57–59; harmony as the basis of a constructive, 202–5; historical examples of apocalyptic violence of, 128–31; mainline churches' criticism of, 63–64, 165–69; in the Middle Ages, 94–96; Mormon, 99–102; Vatican, 64–66; around the year 2000, 7–15. *See also* thousand-year reign of Christ; *and specific movements and groups*
millennial kingdom. *See* thousand-year reign of Christ

millennium, the. *See* thousand-year reign of Christ
Millennium Dome (Greenwich, England), 5
Millennium Society, 4–5
Miller, William, 117–20, 139
Millerite movement, 117–20
Million Man March, 196
Million Woman March, 196
missionary movement, 103–4
Moltmann, Jürgen, 169–72, 173
Montana Freemen. *See* Freemen, the
Montanus of Ardabau, 93
Moomau, Don, 110
Mormons, 99–102
Morse, Reverend Jedidiah, 103
multinational corporations, 28–29, 33, 34–35
Müntzer, Thomas, 130, 134
Mussolini, Benito, 107

National Alliance, the, 149, 151
Nepos of Arsinoe, 93
Nettles, Bonnie Trusdale, 50
New Age religions, 59
New Israelites, 100
New Lebanon congregation, 99
New Light communities, 99
Newton, Sir Isaac, 55
New Year's Eve 1999, 3–7
New York City, 5–6, 41
Nichols, Terry, 153, 154
Nostradamus, 55
nuclear weapons, 40, 108–11
numerology, 77–79

Oilar, F. L., 107
Oklahoma City bombing: as domestic terrorism, 40; the militia movement and, 152–54; patriot and militia leaders' comments on, 144–45; *The Turner Diaries* and, 152
1000. *See* year 1000, the
Operation Rescue, 149
Order, the, 149, 152, 155

Palestine, 39
Papias, 92

parousia. See Second Coming, the
Parrella, Frederick, 210
Passion of Christ, 12, 16
patriot movement. *See* militia movement
Peace Councils, 13, 14–15, 16
Peace Movement, 13–15, 17
Peace of God, 13, 14, 15, 17, 196, 213
People for the American Way, 110
People's Temple, the, 131–34
Peres, Shimon, 39
Perot, Ross, 191
Peters, Pete, 143, 150
Peters, Ted, 50, 110, 165
photonics, 23
Pierce, William, 151
plagues, 12, 14
Planet Earth — 2000 A.D. (Lindsey), 52
political correctness, 157
population growth, 19–20
Posse Comitatus, 149, 155
postmillennialism, 102, 103, 162–63; defined, 230
poverty, 33, 43–44
preachers, contemporary doomsday, 51–57
predictions: consequences of end-time, 125–26; examples of failed end-time, 112–26; Paul's warnings regarding, 92; by secular scholars, 177–94. *See also* prophecy; timetables
premillennialism: American politics and, 108–11; conservative Judaism and, 54–55; defined, 230; elements of, 161–62; fundamentalism and, 107–8; history of American, 105–7; the rapture and, 56; on reading the signs of the times, 163; recent changes in, 161
Project on Religion and Human Rights, 208
Promise Keepers, 196–97
prophecy: the Book of Revelation and, 74–76; and contemporary preachers' timetables, 55; defined, 230; of evangelical preachers, 51–57; around the year 1000, 11. *See also* predictions; timetables
Protestant liberalism. *See* liberal Protestantism
Puritans, the, 97–98

Quakers, the, 130

Rabin, Yitzhak, 39
Racial Healing (Dalton), 206
racism, 41, 146, 147, 148, 206–7
Rahner, Karl, 166
rain forests, 36
Rapp, Frederick, 116
Rapp, George, 113, 114, 116–17, 125, 198
Rappites, the, 112–17, 213
rapture, the: biblical texts and, 88–92; defined, 230; grassroots evangelicals on, 59; premillennialism and, 107; prophecy evangelists on, 56; varieties of evangelical beliefs regarding, 164
Ratzinger, Cardinal Joseph, 60
Rauschenbusch, Walter, 105
Reagan, Ronald, 97, 105, 109–10
relics of saints, 13–14
religion: fanatical, and the response to the millennium, 47–51; a global ethics and, 200–201; violence and, 39–40. *See also* interreligious dialogue; *and specific religions and dominations*
Revelation, Book of: artistic style of, 68–70; the core message of, 70–72; current evangelical preachers on, 54; David Koresh and, 139–40, 141, 142; Heaven's Gate cult and, 50–51; history of the interpretation of, 67–68; key picture images in, 79–81; on the kingdom of God, 85–88; and the meaning of the millennium, 83–85; meaning of violence in, 72–74; numerology and, 77–79; prophecy and, 74–76; text of, describing the millennium, 82–83; Tillich on, 174–75

Index

Revolutionary War, the, 98–99
Rigdon, Sidney, 101
Rio Earth Summit, 36
Rio+5, 36
Robertson, Pat, 51, 110, 148
Robinson, Charles S., 103
robotology, 26–29
Roden, Ben, 137–38, 139
Roden, George, 138
Roden, Lois, 138, 139
Roman Empire, the, 73, 80
Roslin Institute, 29–30
Ruby Ridge, Idaho, 135–36, 143, 144
Rudolph, Erich, 149
Russell, Charles Taze, 122–23
Russell, D. S., 75
Russia, 34, 53, 182, 183
Rutherford, Judge, 124, 125
Ryan, Leo, 134

Sabbatarianism, 120
saints, devotion to the, 13–14
Satan, 83, 84, 85
Schlesinger, Arthur, Jr., 104
Schmid, Konrad, 129
Schwarz, Hans, 165
Schweitzer, LeRoy, 155
Scofield, Cyrus I., 106–7
Scofield Reference Bible, 106–7, 161
Second Coming, the: the Adventists on, 121; grassroots evangelicals and, 58–59; mainline churches on, 62, 166; the Millerites and, 119; Paul on, 89–92; the Puritans' belief in, 98; Revelation's depiction of, 80. *See also* thousand-year reign of Christ
Second Great Awakening, 117
Seventh-Day Adventists, 120–22, 136, 137, 138
Shakers, 99
signs of the times, the: current doomsday prophecy on, 53–54; evangelicals' reading of, 58–59, 160–65; Jesus on reading, 158–60; *kairos* and reading, 175; mainline churches' readings of, 165–69; Marian visions and, 60; prophecy evangelists on, 56–57
Simpson, O. J., 41, 148, 206
six-day theory, 55, 83
666, 78–79
Skurdal, Rodney, 155
slavery, 9–10, 102
Smith, Joseph, Jr., 100–101
Social Gospel movement, 105, 107
Solar Temple, the, 48–49
sovereign citizen movements, 155
Soviet Union, 110, 111
spirituality, 209–11
Stern, Kenneth, 151, 156
Stiles, Ezra, 98, 99
stock markets, 34
Strauss, William, 186–89, 192, 193
survivalism, 135
Swaggart, Jimmy, 51
Sword and Arm of the Lord, 149

Taborites, the, 129–30
Taoism, 203
technology, 22–31
televangelists. *See* evangelicalism
Temple, the Jerusalem, 54
Temple of Understanding, 208
terrorism, 40. *See also names of specific terrorist groups*
Tertio millennio adveniente (apostolic letter), 64, 65
Thomas Aquinas, 168
thousand-year reign of Christ: the early church's expectation regarding, 92–93; harmony as a sign of, 85–88; Jehovah's Witnesses on, 124; Joachim of Fiore on, 94–96; literal interpretations of, 160–65; mainline churches' interpretation of, 165–69; meaning of, 83–85; the rapture and end-time predictions regarding, 88–92; Revelation's description of, 82–83; Tillich's balanced approach to, 173–74
Tillich, Paul, 173–76, 177, 180

Times Square, 3
timetables, 55. *See also* predictions; prophecy
Tracy, David, 207
tribulation, the: amillennialism and, 164; the Book of Matthew on, 164; the Catholic version of, 60; evangelical preachers on, 55, 56, 59; literal interpretations and, 161, 162; Revelation's depiction of, 79, 80–81; the *Scofield Reference Bible* on, 106
Trochmann, David, 145
Trochmann, John, 145, 148, 150
Turner, Joseph, 119
Turner Diaries, The (Pierce), 151–52, 153, 154
Tyconius, 93

UFOs, 16, 50, 56–57
United Nations, 124, 147
United Society of Believers in Christ's Second Appearing, 99
Updike, John, 4
Ussher, Bishop, 118
utopianism, 174

Van Impe, Jack, 52, 53, 55, 56, 58, 111
Van Impe, Rexella, 53, 56
Vatican II, 65, 208
violence: apocalyptic, in the past, 128; crime and, 37–39; examples of recent apocalyptic, 131–42; religiously inspired, 39–40. *See also* militia movement

Wainwright, Geoffrey, 92
Wallerstein, Immanuel, 177–85, 192, 193
Walvoord, John F., 52, 109
Watch Tower, The, 122–23
Watt, James, 110
Weaver, Randy, 135–36, 143, 144, 145
Weaver, Samuel, 136
Weaver, Vicky, 135–36, 143
Weinberger, Caspar, 110
White, Ellen, 120, 121, 122, 139
White, James, 120
White Patriot Party, 150
white supremacists, 146, 147, 151–52. *See also* militia movement
Wilson, Woodrow, 105
Winklhofer, Alois, 167
Winthrop, John, 97
World Conference on Religions for Peace, 208, 209
World Day of Prayer for Peace, 208–9
World Health Organization, 43
Worldwatch Institute, 19, 22

year 1000, the: compared with the year 2000, 2; lessons to be drawn from, 15–17; millennial movements around, 7–15
Young, Brigham, 101
Y2K problem, 6, 25, 45

Zagano, Phyllis, 3
Zealots, the, 128
Zhirinovsky, Vladimir, 111
Zizka, John, 129
Zwingli, Ulrich, 67

Of Related Interest

Apocalypse
A People's Commentary on the Book of Revelation
Pablo Richard
ISBN 1-57075-043-2

Shows that the most powerful readings of the Book of Revelation are through the eyes of the oppressed, living out their Christian faith in the context of the modern empire.

Please support your local bookstore, or call 1-800-258-5838

For a free catalog, please write us at
Orbis Books, Box 308
Maryknoll, NY 10545-0308
or visit our website at www.orbisbooks.com

Thank you for reading *The Lure of the Millennium*.
We hope you enjoyed it.